JOSHUA
—and—
JUDGES

Text copyright © Steven D. Mathewson 2003

The author asserts the moral right to be
identified as the author of this work

Published by
The Bible Reading Fellowship
First Floor, Elsfield Hall
15–17 Elsfield Way, Oxford OX2 8FG
ISBN 1 84101 095 2

First edition 2003
10 9 8 7 6 5 4 3 2 1 0

Acknowledgments
Unless otherwise stated, scripture quotations are taken from
The New Revised Standard Version of the Bible published by
HarperCollins Publishers, copyright 1989 by the Division of
Christian Education of the National Council of the Churches of
Christ in the USA, and are used by permission. All rights reserved.

A catalogue record for this book is
available from the British Library

Printed and bound in Great Britain
by Bookmarque, Croydon

JOSHUA
—and—
JUDGES

THE PEOPLE'S
BIBLE COMMENTA

STEVEN D
MATHEWSO

A BIBLE COMMENTARY FOR

INTRODUCING THE
PEOPLE'S BIBLE COMMENTARY
SERIES

Congratulations! You are embarking on a voyage of discovery—or rediscovery. You may feel you know the Bible very well; you may never have turned its pages before. You may be looking for a fresh way of approaching daily Bible study; you may be searching for useful insights to share in a study group or from a pulpit.

The People's Bible Commentary (PBC) series is designed for all those who want to study the scriptures in a way that will warm the heart as well as instructing the mind. To help you, the series distils the best of scholarly insights into the straightforward language and devotional emphasis of Bible reading notes. Explanation of background material, and discussion of the original Greek and Hebrew, will always aim to be brief.

- If you have never really studied the Bible before, the series offers a serious yet accessible way in.

- If you help to lead a church study group, or are otherwise involved in regular preaching and teaching, you can find invaluable 'snapshots' of a Bible passage through the PBC approach.

- If you are a church worker or minister, burned out on the Bible, this series could help you recover the wonder of scripture.

Using a People's Bible Commentary

The series is designed for use alongside any version of the Bible. You may have your own favourite translation, but you might like to consider trying a different one in order to gain fresh perspectives on familiar passages.

Many Bible translations come in a range of editions, including study and reference editions that have concordances, various kinds of special index, maps and marginal notes. These can all prove helpful in studying the relevant passage. The Notes section at the back of each PBC volume provides space for you to write personal reflections, points to follow up, questions and comments.

Each People's Bible Commentary can be used on a daily basis, instead of Bible reading notes. Alternatively, it can be read straight through, or used as a resource book for insight into particular verses of the biblical book.

If you have enjoyed using this commentary and would like to progress further in Bible study, you will find details of other volumes in the series listed at the back, together with information about a special offer from BRF.

While it is important to deepen understanding of a given passage, this series always aims to engage both heart and mind in the study of the Bible. The scriptures point to our Lord himself and our task is to use them to build our relationship with him. When we read, let us do so prayerfully, slowly, reverently, expecting him to speak to our hearts.

PREFACE

Preparing this commentary on Joshua and Judges has been a terrific adventure, a tremendous joy, and a significant burden. The more I studied the books of Joshua and Judges, the more they studied me. They exposed problems in my relationship with God, and they inspired me to walk before him more faithfully. These books have also enlarged and enriched my knowledge of God. I wrote much of the material during my father's struggle with cancer, so I had to apply the scripture to my own life at every turn.

Because a commentary like this is really the product of a community of believers, I have several people to thank. First, I thank Naomi Starkey of BRF for all her help and for her patience when I asked to extend deadlines. Next, I thank my brothers and sisters in Christ at Dry Creek Bible Church, Belgrade, Montana, USA. Before I ever started writing, I preached through both Joshua and Judges. Like the believers in ancient Thessalonica, the believers at Dry Creek Bible Church received these sermons as the word of God which works in believers (see 1 Thessalonians 2:13). I also taught sections of these books in smaller class settings. In these classes, I learned more from people's questions and insights than they will ever realize. This experience reinforced the value of studying scripture together in a community of believers.

Another group of people at Dry Creek Bible Church deserve special mention. These people agreed to serve as prayer partners: Drake and Rhonda Albertson, Lonny and Keri Anderson, Lani Chaney, Chip and Nancy Drusch, Neil and Laura Lee Harvey, Jerry Hespen, Judi Johnson, Denise McCord, Becky McCotter, Shirley Molendyk, Jillian Pierson, Wini Pierson, Joe Skinner, Marge Skinner, Carolyn Steele, and Dennis and Judy Van Abbema. These prayer partners made the commitment to pray for the successful completion of this commentary, and I thank God for each of them.

I am also grateful for the teachers God has given to the church (see Ephesians 4:11–12). Several of them have sharpened my understanding of the texts of Joshua and Judges. I want to make it clear that I started the study process by working through the text—in Hebrew and in English—on my own. In each book, I wrestled with how the narrator shaped his material to convey his ideas. But then, I interacted with a number of commentaries that either confirmed or challenged my conclusions. With the current concerns in the USA about writers plagiarizing material, I am a bit nervous about presenting my material in a format that does not allow for footnotes or endnotes. I have learned from and borrowed ideas from dozens of works—commentaries, articles, grammars, reference tools, atlases, dictionaries, and books on archaeology. The bibliography at the end of this volume lists some of the major resources I have utilized. As far as commentaries are concerned, I have relied most heavily on Daniel I. Block's superb commentary on Judges, and on the fine commentaries by Richard Hess and David Howard on Joshua. For example, the line-drawing image in my comments on Joshua 15:1–12 comes from Howard's commentary. Also, I borrowed and adapted the comparison of Joshua and Judges to different stretches of the same river from Albert Baylis, *From Creation to the Cross*.

Finally, I thank my wife, Priscilla, for her encouragement and her efforts to guard my time to write. She is a remarkable woman who has modelled Joshua 1:7–9 in our home. I am grateful for the decision of my wife's parents, Jim and Shirley Perkins, and my parents, Maynard and Ruth Mathewson, to serve God faithfully all of their days. By making this choice, they stand with Joshua and the ranks of Israel in Joshua 24. They have left their children and grandchildren an incredible legacy and example.

Contents

PBC JOSHUA & JUDGES:
INTRODUCTION

When read together, the books of Joshua and Judges resemble different stretches of the same river. The Joshua stretch flows clear and strong. The people of Israel face challenges and experience solutions and victories. But downriver, the Judges stretch turns sluggish and murky, as sewage and industrial contaminants seep into the flow. The people of Israel create troubles for themselves as they allow the evil of their surrounding culture to pollute their morals. God is at work, though, in both stretches of river.

Former prophets

The key to understanding the books of Joshua and Judges is their location in the canon. English Bibles place them in a collection of 'historical books'. The history these books relate serves a larger purpose, however. In the Hebrew scriptures, Joshua and Judges join the books of Samuel and Kings as 'former prophets'. As prophetic books, they aim to challenge, indict and inspire God's people. The authors who composed them speak as prophets or preachers who are attempting to draw people closer to God and to his standards. Essentially, these prophets drew from events of the past to challenge a later generation of God's people about the way to live before God.

Reading narrative literature

A basic difference between the former prophets and the latter prophets is literary strategy. The latter prophets, like Isaiah and Jeremiah, employed poetry as the predominant vehicle for conveying their sermons. The former prophets, however, including Joshua and Judges, issue their challenges by telling stories. They select narratives from the continuous story of the events in Israel's history. This means that while the writers of Joshua and Judges do more than tell stories, they do not do less than that.

Therefore, understanding Joshua and Judges requires readers to read them as stories. The prophets who composed these books were first-rate storytellers. They were literary artists who skilfully used literary conventions to communicate theology. Unfortunately, reading the narratives of Joshua and Judges resembles playing the trumpet. It is easy to do poorly. This commentary will help you to read the narratives of Joshua and Judges in a way that achieves understanding.

Here is a brief overview of what readers must pay attention to when reading an Old Testament narrative. The first feature is the *plot*—the action or sequence of events. After an 'exposition' providing the information needed to set up the story, the action moves into a 'crisis' or complication. Tension rises until the plot reaches its 'resolution'. This may be a happy or a sad ending. Some stories contain a separate 'conclusion' or denouement which ties up loose ends. Second, readers should observe the *characters*—what role they play in the story, what they say, how they act, and how the storyteller or other characters describe them. A third feature is the *setting* of a story. When and where does it occur? How does a particular story function in the flow of the entire book? That is, how does it contribute to the overall message of the book? A final feature is the story's *point of view*. At what points does the narrator offer 'inside information' which the characters do not know? Where does irony (discrepancy) occur?

Let me briefly explain the terminology I use in this commentary. To begin with, I will refer to the prophet who composed each book as the 'narrator'. This term highlights the prophet's role as a storyteller. Our narrator writes his material as a prophet, a historian, a storyteller, an author, and an editor. Furthermore, I will refer to a story within a larger story as an 'episode'. For example, the Samson story consists of several episodes. Each episode is a self-contained story with its own plot. Finally, I will use the term 'scene' to refer to a particular segment of an episode or story. A scene does not stand by itself with a complete plot.

Take and read

This commentary, though brief, will help you to understand the text of Joshua and Judges, so take and read the biblical text before turning to my comments. This commentary is based on the New Revised Standard Version (NRSV), but you can use it profitably with any other English version.

The books of Joshua and Judges both contain numerous references to unfamiliar cities, rivers, mountains and other sites. The maps at the beginning of this commentary will help you to locate these features. You might also keep a Bible atlas open as you read. *The Macmillan*

Bible Atlas actually includes maps of every major event in the Bible, including the journeys and battles in Joshua and Judges.

The Hebrew Name 'Yahweh'

Throughout the commentary, I refer to the Hebrew name 'Yahweh'. This is the Hebrew name for God which most English Bibles, including the NRSV, render as 'LORD' or 'GOD' in all capital letters. Let me explain the significance of this name.

While the name 'Yahweh' was known and used in the book of Genesis, the meaning and significance of the name are not revealed until Exodus 3 (see also Exodus 6:2–3). Exodus 3 narrates Moses' encounter with God at the burning bush. In this story, God identifies himself to Moses by saying, 'I am the God of your father, the God of Abraham, the God of Isaac, and the God of Jacob' (Exodus 3:6). After God announces his intention for Moses to lead the people of Israel out of Egypt, a revealing dialogue takes place between Moses and God. When Moses asks God how to respond if the Israelites ask about God's name (Exodus 3:13), God replies: 'I AM WHO I AM... Thus you shall say to the Israelites, "I AM has sent me to you"' (Exodus 3:14).

The name 'Yahweh' appears to be related to the same Hebrew verb used in the expression 'I am'. In fact, the name 'Yahweh' is close in spelling to the Hebrew expression, 'He is'. God says, 'I am', while his people respond by saying, 'He is.' In Exodus 3:15, God indicates that this name 'Yahweh' (translated as 'LORD' in the NRSV) will serve as his 'title for all generations'. The term translated 'title' by the NRSV actually means 'remembrance'. Thus, the name 'Yahweh' will serve as a memorial name—the name by which God's people remember him. But what does the name memorialize? Obviously, it says something about God's existence. But there's even more! When God revealed the name 'Yahweh' to Moses, the people of Israel had been in bondage for about 400 years (see Genesis 15:13). The meeting with Moses at the burning bush resulted from God's decision to respond to the cries and groaning of his people, as well as his commitment to the covenant he had made with Abraham (see Exodus 2:23–25). Thus, the name 'Yahweh' memorializes God's ongoing care for his people. Every time later generations spoke the name 'Yahweh', they were to remember his willingness to act on their behalf when they faced suffering.

Why, then, do English translations like the NRSV translate the Hebrew name 'Yahweh' as 'LORD' or 'GOD' in all capital letters? The answer is complex, but let me try to simplify it. Originally, Hebrew texts contained only consonants, not vowels. The vowel sounds were part of the language, but people did not bother to write them in the text. The name 'Yawheh' was composed of four consonants— YHWH. However, Jewish people treated God's memorial name with such reverence that they did not pronounce it. Instead, they spoke the Hebrew word *Adonai*. This word is a title meaning 'lord, master'. The choice made sense because the title *Adonai* was already used frequently in the Old Testament to refer to God. About 500 years after Jesus Christ, a group of Jewish scribes called 'Massoretes' feared that Jewish people would lose their ability to read and speak Hebrew. So they began devising an elaborate system of markings—dots and dashes—to write into the consonantal text to indicate the vowel sounds. When they came to the name 'Yahweh', they wanted to encourage the practice of saying 'Adonai' instead of 'Yahweh', so they put the vowel markings for the word 'Adonai' with the consonants YHWH! People in their day understood their strategy. Several hundred years later, however, some Bible scholars looked at this combination and thought that the name for God was to be pronounced 'Jehovah'. As a result of this confusion about how to pronounce God's memoril name, early English translations simply translated it as 'LORD' or 'GOD' in all capital letters. Modern versions have followed this practice. This distinguishes it from the Hebrew title *Adonai*, usually translated as 'Lord' with lower case letters after the capital 'L'.

The key point is, whenever you see 'LORD' or 'GOD' in all capital letters in the NRSV or in most other English versions, you know that the Hebrew name for God in this instance is 'Yahweh'.

Coping with a violent God

Probably the most troubling aspect of Joshua and Judges for modern readers is God's sanction of violence. How could a God of love ever command his people to annihilate other people groups, including their women and children? The answer is rooted in Yahweh's character. While Yahweh's outstanding character quality is love and compassion, his character obligates him to judge evil (see the ratio of God's judgment on the third and fourth generations compared to his love to thousands in Exodus 20:5; 34:7). Yahweh cannot tolerate evil any more than a person allergic to penicillin can tolerate that particular drug, or than a person with hay fever can tolerate pollen. Still, Yahweh graciously withheld his judgment for 400 years until the sin of the Canaanites reached its full measure (Genesis 15:13, 16). Eventually, though, he called Israel to wipe out the Canaanites so that their false worship would not infect Israel (Deuteronomy 20:16–18).

We must remember that Yahweh did not act out of nationalistic interests. That is, he did not discriminate on the basis of race or nationality. In fact, he created Israel for the very purpose of blessing all the families of the earth (Genesis 12:1–3). The story of Rahab in Joshua 2 will demonstrate Yahweh's love for people of other cultures who turn to him. Furthermore, we will see that Yahweh's aversion to evil prompted him to deal severely with his own people, Israel (Joshua 7; Judges 2:14–15).

The stories of 'holy war' in Joshua and Judges provide no licence for Christians today who want to justify violence, particularly the violent disputes in the Middle East. The New Testament makes it clear that the law has only a shadow of the good things to come, and not the true form of these realities (Hebrews 10:1). In the Old Testament, the 'shadow' was actual warfare against nations thoroughly contaminated by evil. The coming of Jesus Christ brought the reality —warfare against evil itself through truth, righteousness, peace, faith, salvation, scripture and prayer (Ephesians 6:10–18).

Applying the text to life

This commentary will also provide leads for applying the message of Joshua and Judges to your life. The New Testament makes it clear that the Old Testament—including its stories!—can still teach followers of Jesus how to believe and live (2 Timothy 3:16–17; 1 Corinthians 10:11). Application of Old Testament narratives must do more than moralize ('I need to be more like Gideon'). Rather, it must focus on what the narratives teach us about the character of God—the main character in the drama of Joshua and Judges. As 'former prophets', the books of Joshua and Judges call us to clear up our picture of God and then to adjust our lives accordingly.

CANAAN *in the* TIME *of* JOSHUA & JUDGES

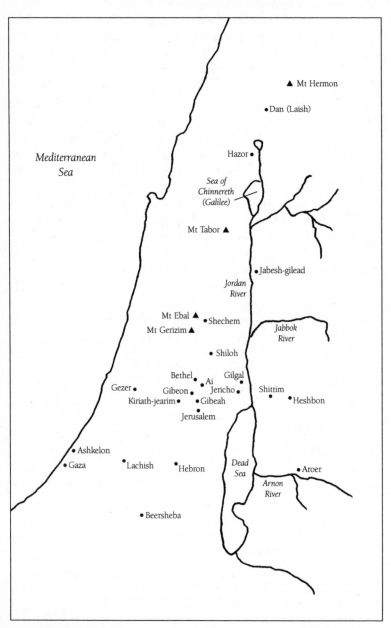

Mediterranean Sea

▲ Mt Hermon

• Dan (Laish)

Hazor •

Sea of Chinnereth (Galilee)

Mt Tabor ▲

• Jabesh-gilead

Jordan River

Mt Ebal ▲
Mt Gerizim ▲ • Shechem

Jabbok River

• Shiloh

Bethel • • Ai   Gilgal •
Gezer •   Gibeon •   Jericho •   Shittim •
Kiriath-jearim • • Gibeah   • Heshbon
Jerusalem •

• Ashkelon
• Gaza   • Lachish   • Hebron

Dead Sea   • Aroer

Arnon River

• Beersheba

LAND DISTRIBUTION *to the* TRIBES *of* ISRAEL

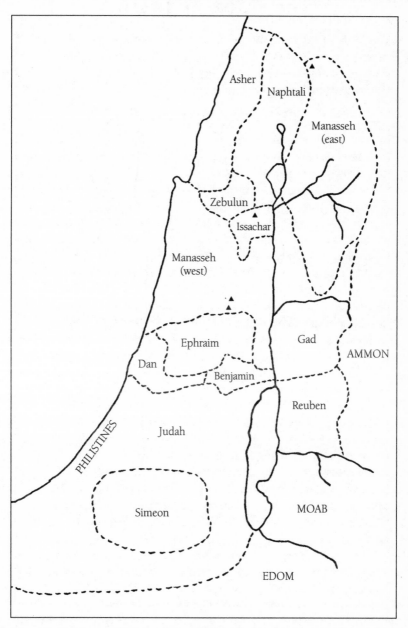

1 JOSHUA

The BOOK *of* JOSHUA

The book of Joshua covers a period in Israel's history from Moses' death to the settlement of Israel in Canaan under Joshua. As a former prophet (see Introduction), the book of Joshua uses the medium of historical narrative to offer a prophetic message.

Title and authorship

In both the Hebrew Bible and in English translations, this book takes its title from its leading human character, Joshua son of Nun. Originally, he went by the name 'Hoshea' (Hebrew for 'salvation') until Moses renamed him 'Joshua' (Numbers 13:16). The name 'Joshua' (Hebrew *Yehoshua*) means 'Yahweh is salvation'. In the Septuagint—the Greek translation of the Old Testament completed about 150BC—the name 'Joshua' appears as *Iesous*. This Greek name comes into English as 'Jesus'.

The book's author is anonymous, but Joshua himself probably wrote at least parts of it (see 8:32; 24:26). Ancient Jewish tradition holds that Joshua wrote most of the book, except for certain sections like the account of his death (24:29–33).

Some scholars have suggested linking the book of Joshua with the first five books of the Old Testament. Thus, Joshua forms the conclusion to the 'hexateuch'—a collection of six books consisting of Genesis to Joshua. However, the book of Joshua contains significant ties to the books that follow it. In the Jewish arrangement of scripture, Joshua heads the list of 'former prophets' (including Judges, Samuel, and Kings). Therefore, it is preferable to classify Joshua as the work of a 'Deuteronomistic historian' who sought to interpret Israelite history in light of the blessings and cursings found in the book of Deuteronomy. Whether or not the author of Joshua is the same person who composed the other former prophets, he at least worked from the same theological tradition shaped by the book of Deuteronomy.

The recurring expression 'until this day' suggests that a significant amount of time had passed between the events themselves and the completion of the book (see 4:9; 5:9; 6:25; 7:26; 8:28–29; 9:27; 13:13; 14:14; 15:63; 16:10). Completion of the book probably happened prior to the time of David because the book makes reference to the Jebusites living in Jerusalem (see 15:63). David drove the Jebusites out of Jerusalem when he took it as his capital city (see 2 Samuel 5:1–10).

Purpose, message and structure

The book of Joshua provides an official account of how Yahweh fulfilled his promise to Abraham (Genesis 15:7–21) and Moses (Deuteronomy 34:1–4) to give his people a land. The stories and records selected by the narrator emphasize God's faithfulness in fulfilling his promises (see 1:2–6; 21:45; 23:14). Thus, the prophetic message for a later generation of God's people is, 'It makes sense to trust and obey Yahweh when he leads you into new challenges, because Yahweh keeps his promises.'

Two major sections make up the book of Joshua. Chapters 1—12 narrate the *conquest* of the promised land of Canaan. Then, chapters 13—24 describe the *distribution* of this promised land.

The first section of Joshua breaks down into two parts: Israel's preparation for conquest (1:1—5:12) and Israel's military takeover of the land (5:13—12:24). The second section of the book also contains two parts: a series of lists which document the distribution of the land (13:1—21:45) and a series of farewell addresses from Joshua (22:1—24:33). While chapters 13—21 focus on Yahweh's loyalty to his people, chapters 22—24 challenge the people about their loyalty to Yahweh.

Relevance for today

The book of Joshua can help 21st-century believers who face new challenges and find their lives in transition. It challenges us to face the future with strength and courage because Yahweh, the God we serve, keeps his promises. The book of Joshua also encourages Christians today with the promise of rest. The rest secured by Joshua (see 1:13; 11:23; 14:15; 21:44; 23:1) was only partial (Hebrews 4:8). It only anticipated a 'complete' rest which is available in partnership with Jesus Christ (see Hebrews 3:1—4:11, especially 3:14).

FOR MEDITATION

Joshua 21:45 is the key verse of the book. Read it and give thanks to God that he keeps his word.

2

FACING *a* NEW CHALLENGE

The book of Joshua begins with Yahweh informing Joshua of Moses' death. This seems like an odd place for the narrator to begin his story, especially since the preceding book, Deuteronomy, closed with a complete account of Moses' death. Besides, a new chapter in Israel's life is beginning. After forty years of desert wandering, the people are poised to enter the promised land of Canaan. So why begin this book with a reminder of Moses' death? Yahweh is forcing Joshua to ponder the implication. Moses, the 'servant of Yahweh', has passed away from the scene, so Joshua, 'Moses' assistant', needs to take charge! To be sure, Joshua had served Moses successfully as a military leader (Exodus 17:13) and as a spy (Numbers 14:6–9, 30). But how could Joshua follow an act like Moses and lead the people in 'Operation Occupation'?

Be strong and courageous

The answer is for Joshua to 'be strong and courageous'. Three times Yahweh issues this command (vv. 6, 7, 9). The two terms work in concert to signal the 'strong courage' or 'courageous strength' that Joshua must exhibit as Israel's next leader. What readers often miss is that the second appearance of this command (v. 7) ties it to the purpose of obeying Yahweh's law. The Hebrew text literally reads, 'Only be strong and very courageous to be careful to do according to all the law…' Joshua's courage, then, must include the strength to flesh out Yahweh's commands in his life. His success will depend on it.

The importance of meditation

Joshua cannot live out what he does not know, however, so verse 8 requires him to know Yahweh's law intimately, framing the requirement negatively and positively. Stated negatively, God's law should not depart out of Joshua's mouth. Stated positively, Joshua must meditate on it day and night. To some people, meditation suggests a person sitting cross-legged on the floor, eyes closed, mumbling, and in some kind of trance. But the Hebrew term translated 'meditate' refers to repetition. Originally, the term referred to animals growling or moaning. Eventually, people used the term to describe any kind of repeated sounds, including the sound of a person reciting or reading. So, meditation, as the first line in verse 8 suggests, means repeated reading and reciting of Yahweh's law. In the 21st century, meditation—the repeated exposure to God's word—could take the form of daily Bible reading or listening to the Bible on audio tape while travelling to work. American evangelist Billy Graham recommends reading a chapter a day of Proverbs. Obedience to God's law begins with a relentless quest to know it by going over it again and again.

Yahweh's empowering presence

But how can Yahweh expect Joshua to exercise courageous strength when faced with such an enormous challenge? The answer is in Yahweh's empowering presence. The promise of Yahweh's empowering presence appears twice (vv. 5, 9). The first promise statement in verse 5 assures Joshua that he will experience Yahweh's presence as Moses did. When Yahweh interrupted Moses' sheep-tending job in the desert and commissioned him to lead Israel out of Egypt, Moses objected, 'Who am I that I should go to Pharaoh, and bring the Israelites out of Egypt?' (Exodus 3:11). Yahweh replied by saying, 'I will be with you.' Now, to Joshua, Yahweh uses identical language: 'I will be with you.' Then he adds further reassurance: 'I will not fail you or forsake you.'

Does the promise made to Joshua apply to modern believers when they battle cancer, begin a new career, or stand up for justice? Yes! The promise of God's presence is woven throughout the Bible. God made the same promise to his people suffering in captivity (Isaiah 41:10). Through Jesus, God made the same promise to his disciples as they faced the prospect of carrying on Jesus' ministry when Jesus ascended to heaven (Matthew 28:20). Even Paul needed this same promise when he received opposition in the city of Corinth (Acts 18:9–10). Like Joshua, God's people today need the assurance that where God guides, he provides his empowering presence so that his people can exercise courageous strength.

PRAYER

God of Moses and Joshua, help me to face today's challenges with courageous strength because of your awesome presence. Amen.

ISRAEL'S RESPONSE *to* JOSHUA

Joshua 1 consists of four speeches. After Yahweh's speech to Joshua (1:1–9), the narrator records Joshua's speech to the officers of the people (vv. 10–11), Joshua's speech to the tribes living east of the Jordan (vv. 12–15), and the people's reply to Joshua (vv. 16–18). The flow of the speeches keeps us in suspense. Yahweh has commissioned Joshua to lead the people into Canaan, and so Joshua gives the people their orders. But how will the people of Israel—especially those tribes already settled east of the Jordan—respond to this new challenge by a new leader?

Speech to the officers

Joshua's speech to the officers of the people (vv. 10–11) demonstrates his readiness to obey Yahweh's command. Joshua now issues a command to the officials—administrators who had previously been appointed to help Moses (see Deuteronomy 1:15, 16:18). Joshua commands them to pass through (literally 'cross in the middle of') the camp and command the people to get ready to cross the Jordan River. The time has come for Israel to take possession of the land Yahweh has given to them.

The term 'command' occurs seven times in Joshua 1 (vv. 7, 9, 10, 11, 13, 16, 18). Its prominence in Joshua's speech in verses 10–11 raises tension. Will the officers who previously served Moses now obey Joshua's command? Even if they do, will the people respond to the command delivered by Joshua through the officials?

Speech to the tribes east of Jordan

Before describing the people's response, the narrator records Joshua's speech to the tribes living east of the Jordan River. The Hebrew grammatical construction used to introduce this speech (v. 12) differs from the typical constructions used at the beginning of the other speeches (vv. 1, 10, 16). Essentially, the Hebrew construction pauses the main storyline to present this speech as important background information. Capturing the full force of the construction would require an English translation like this: 'By the way, you should know that Joshua also spoke specifically to the Reubenites, the Gadites, and the half-tribe of Manasseh, saying...' Now this does not mean that the speech in verses 12–15 is less important than the other speeches. Rather, the grammar sets it apart as something that happened in conjunction with the previous speech (vv. 10–11) and something that should be distinguished from the following speech (vv. 16–18).

This speech to the tribes east of the Jordan adds to the tension. Two and a half tribes had already found a 'place of rest' on the east side of the Jordan. As Joshua acknowledges, Moses had given these tribes the authority to do so (vv. 13–14). Perhaps the men of these tribes might be reluctant to help their brothers take the land west of the Jordan. Why should they go and fight after they had just got settled? So Joshua challenges the warriors in these tribes to 'cross over' and help their brothers. The stakes are high! If the tribes east of the Jordan do not recognize his authority, Joshua stands to lose appeal as a leader.

The people's reply to Joshua

The narrator resumes the action in verse 16 by reporting the reply of the people. We should note that this reply comes in response to Joshua's command to the whole nation in verses 10–11, not simply to his speech to the tribes east of the Jordan in verses 12–15. As we read the reply in verses 16–18, we realize that the crisis has been resolved favourably. The people pledge their allegiance to Joshua, promising to obey his commands even as they obeyed Moses in all things. They, too, recognize the need for Yahweh's presence in his life, and reiterate the need for Joshua to be strong and courageous (v. 18).

Joshua 1:9–18 establishes two ingredients needed for God's people to succeed when facing new challenges—obedience to God's commands and a commitment to community. God's people must work together to achieve success.

PRAYER

Lord God, I want to stand firm and prosper as you move me into new territory. Empower me and strengthen my commitment to obedience and to community. Help me to maintain the unity of the Spirit in the bond of peace.

ISRAELITE SPIES *in a* PROSTITUTE'S HOUSE

Joshua 2:1–7 contains both the 'exposition' and the 'crisis' of a new episode which runs through chapter 2 (see Introduction, p. 14, for a discussion of these terms). The central character is a Canaanite prostitute named Rahab.

Ominous details

According to verse 1, Joshua secretly sends two men from Shittim as spies to look over the Canaanite city of Jericho. Initially, these details seem ominous and raise tension. First, the last Israelite spy mission had ended in disaster, with ten out of twelve spies bringing back a bad report which led to forty years of wandering (see Numbers 13—14). Second, the last time the Israelites stayed at Shittim, the Israelite men had sexual relations with Moabite women (Numbers 25:1–3).

Furthermore, why are Joshua's spies entering the house of a prostitute? The narrator words his account carefully, though, to keep the spies above suspicion of sexual immorality. Rahab's house was probably an inn or hostel where travelling merchants or messengers could stay the night. Thus, it provided an obvious choice of lodging for spies.

Figures in hiding

Verse 2 indicates that the king of Jericho received intelligence information about these Israelite men and their mission. When the king of Jericho sent orders to Rahab to turn over the men, she hid them and then concocted a story about them leaving the city before the gate closed at dark (vv. 3–5). The narrator pauses the action in verse 6, however, to provide more details. Rahab had actually hidden the men among the stalks of flax on her roof. As verse 7 shows, the ruse worked. The pursuers left the city, and the gate was shut. This latter detail portrays a city expecting an attack.

Risking her life

As readers, we must understand that Rahab was risking her life to hide the spies. A law in the *Code of Hammurabi*, a Babylonian law code written a couple of centuries before Rahab, reflects the view of cultures in the ancient Near East towards such conduct: 'If outlaws have congregated in the establishment of a woman wine seller [i.e., an inn or tavern owned by a woman] and she has not arrested those outlaws and did not take them to the palace, that wine seller shall be put to death' (law 109). The reason Rahab risked her life will become clear as the story unfolds.

What about Rahab's lie?

Although the narrator shows no interest in commenting on Rahab's lie, this ethical issue concerns some modern readers. Was Rahab justified in telling a lie? Some Bible teachers say 'No'. They argue that God's laws or commands never conflict with each other. That is, a believer does not have to choose between telling the truth and saving a life. Rahab should have trusted God to provide for her a way to protect the spies that did not require lying (see 1 Corinthians 10:13). The New Testament, in Hebrews 11:31 and James 2:25, commends Rahab for her faith, not her lie.

However, other Bible teachers say 'Yes'. They believe that God's laws and commands sometimes conflict with each other because of humankind's fall into sin. For example, in Acts 5:29, the apostles had to disobey the government in order to obey God. The responsibility of the believer is to choose the higher law. In Rahab's case, her lie was part of her act of faith. While Hebrews 11:31 and James 2:25 do not explicitly condone Rahab's lie, neither do they qualify her actions. Apparently, withholding truth, skewing truth and practising deception in order to save a life may be justified in an extreme case such as warfare. In these situations, when normal human relationships have utterly broken down, believers may make a choice to preserve life (see also the example of the Hebrew midwives in Exodus 1:17–21). Of course, scripture does not allow believers to abandon the basic posture of submitting to authorities, telling the truth, and acting out of the fear of God.

FOR MEDITATION

Do you think Rahab was justified in telling a lie?
Read the scripture references cited in the above discussion
and then explain your viewpoint.

RAHAB'S FAITH

Rahab's intentions in hiding the spies become clear as the story begun in 2:1–7 continues. With the pursuers gone for the moment (2:7), Rahab approaches the hidden spies before they go to sleep and initiates a dialogue (v. 8).

A remarkable confession and request

Rahab's opening speech consists of a confession (vv. 9–11) and a request (vv. 12–13). In contrast to her earlier claim not to know the nationality of the spies (2:4), Rahab begins by confessing to the spies what she knows about their God (v. 9). In verse 10, she cites the cause of her knowledge. She and her people had heard about both the Red Sea deliverance and Israel's victory over the two Amorite kings. Rahab wraps up her confession by reiterating her people's intense fear and by admitting, 'The Lord your God is indeed God in heaven above and on earth below' (v. 9).

What a stunning admission from a foreigner! Rahab's people, the Canaanites, believed in a smorgasbord of gods and goddesses (see comment on Judges 2:11–13, pp. 126–127). The Canaanites would have acknowledged Yahweh, Israel's God, yet they would have adopted a 'my god is bigger than your god' attitude. Rahab, however, acknowledges Yahweh's sovereignty over the realms of heaven and earth—the very truth that Moses had commanded the Israelites to acknowledge and take to heart (Deuteronomy 4:39).

The words 'Now then' (literally, 'And now') at the beginning of verse 12 signal a new section of Rahab's speech. Here she moves from confession to request. Her request is for the Israelites to deal kindly with her as she has dealt kindly with them. The term 'kindly' is the Hebrew term *hesed*—a term signifying 'covenant love' or 'covenant loyalty'. Rahab also requests a sign of good faith that she and her family will be spared (v. 13).

To accept or not to accept?

According to verse 14, the spies made an oath to accept Rahab's request as long as she did not betray them. This raises a key question: were the Israelite spies wrong to enter into covenant with Rahab?

After all, Yahweh had commanded them through Moses to annihilate completely the nations in Canaan and not to make covenants with them (Deuteronomy 7:1–3; 20:16–18). However, in this case the Israelite spies acted appropriately. Rahab's confession of faith in Yahweh made her situation unique. She had converted from the worship of false gods and goddesses to the worship of Yahweh. In effect, her conversion fell in line with Yahweh's promise to bless all the families of the earth through Abraham's offspring (see Genesis 12:1–3).

Escaping Jericho

The remainder of the Rahab story describes the spies' escape from Jericho and their return to Joshua (vv. 15–24). A notable feature is the spies' insistence that Rahab tie a crimson cord in the window through which she let them down (v. 18). When the Israelites returned to conquer Jericho, this cord would identify Rahab's house as the hiding place of a family to be spared.

Unlike those involved in the previous spy mission (Numbers 13—14), these spies offer a unanimously favourable report upon their return, expressing confidence that Yahweh has given them the land (v. 24).

Message for today

In this story, the stage belongs to Rahab. Joshua, the lead character of the book, appears only briefly at the beginning and end of the story. Rahab's story testifies to the grace of God. God in his grace reaches out to people like Rahab who have sordid pasts and no connection to the people of God. Perhaps the name 'Rahab'—which means 'breadth, width, expanse'—emphasizes the wideness of God's mercy! Amazingly, Rahab becomes part of the royal line from which Jesus the Messiah emerged (Matthew 1:5). She also serves as a model genuine of genuine faith—a faith which is verified by action (see Hebrews 11:31; James 2:25).

PRAYER

Lord God, empower me to demonstrate by my daily deeds
that my faith is alive.

CROSSING *the* JORDAN RIVER

The story in Joshua 3 to 4 advances the theme of Joshua—Yahweh is a keeper of promises—by telling how Yahweh enabled Israel to cross the Jordan River (ch. 3) and how Israel memorialized this event (ch. 4). The river-crossing episode in Joshua 3 parallels the story of the crossing of the Red Sea (Exodus 14).

Initial instructions

The episode in Joshua 3 breaks down into three sections. The first section in verses 1–6 focuses on the people's responsibility to follow the ark of the covenant of Yahweh. This object served as the vehicle through which Yahweh related to his people (see Exodus 25:10–22). The ark consisted of a gold-plated box, about 110cm long by 66cm wide and 66cm high. On the lid of the ark were two figures—angels with spread wings, facing each other. In between those angels, Yahweh revealed his presence.

After camping for three days on the banks of the Jordan River, the officers commanded the people to follow the ark so that they would know which way to go (vv. 3–4). At the same time, the people were to maintain a definite distance from it—about two thousand cubits, or one kilometre (v. 4). This distance, like the distance the Israelites maintained from Mount Sinai when Yahweh gave the ten commandments (see Exodus 19, especially vv. 12, 23), reflected the need for Yahweh's people to respect his awesome majesty and holiness. Joshua's instruction for the people to sanctify themselves (v. 5) also parallels the scene at Mount Sinai. There, Yahweh told Moses to consecrate the people (Exodus 19:10, 14). The term 'sanctify' in Joshua 3:5 and 'consecrate' in Exodus 19:10 and 14 translate the same Hebrew root, *q-d-sh*, which means 'to be set apart, holy'. The purpose for the Israelites in sanctifying themselves was to prepare for Yahweh's display of 'wonders' among them (v. 5). These wonders are 'amazing acts' or miracles which will display the extent of Yahweh's power. Today, God still takes his people through crossings—that is, challenging circumstances—to show them how amazing he really is.

Additional instructions

The second section in the Joshua 3 episode (vv. 7–13) begins with Yahweh instructing Joshua. Yahweh will exalt Joshua, to show the people that his presence is with Joshua as it was with Moses (v. 7). Joshua's responsibility is to command the priests carrying the ark to walk into the Jordan River (v. 8). In verses 9–13, Joshua relays Yahweh's words to the people. He informs them that what will take place will confirm that Yahweh is a 'living God' in contrast to the gods of the seven people-groups mentioned in verse 10. Basically, when the priests carrying the ark step into the water, the upstream waters of the Jordan River will stop flowing and stand up in a heap—just as if they had been contained by a dam (v. 13).

The miraculous crossing

The third section in verses 14–17 is the most intriguing. Hebrew scholars have noted that the action slows down to a crawl as the narrator describes the actual miracle. Another 'Red Sea deliverance' takes place! Only two clauses advance the story line: 'the waters... stood' (v. 16) and 'the priests... stood' (v. 17). The Hebrew grammar in the remaining clauses slows down the story and adds description or further details. To imagine the effect of this material on the original readers, imagine watching a video of this event and viewing the material in verses 14–17 in slow motion or in a freeze-frame mode.

A couple of details deserve comment. First, verse 15 reminds the reader that the Jordan River was at flood stage. Ordinarily, the Jordan was only 18–30 metres wide, and only 1–3 metres deep. However, by the time of the barley harvest in late April or early May, spring rains would swell the river and send it raging down the Jordan Valley rift. This made crossing it dangerous. Second, the two cities mentioned in verse 16 indicates that the waters piled up about 15 miles north of the crossing. Like he did at the Red Sea, Yahweh has brought his people through a crossing that they cannot negotiate in their own strength.

PRAYER

Almighty God, you made the Jordan River stand up! I tremble at the thought of your power, but I rejoice that you use it to help your people get through difficult crossings.

7

A PILE *of* ROCKS

The first line of Joshua 4:1 is almost identical, in both Hebrew and English, to the final line of Joshua 3:17.

> '...*until the entire nation finished crossing over the Jordan*' (3:17).
> '*When the entire nation had finished crossing over the Jordan*' (4:1).

This repetition effectively links the two episodes into one story. The episode in Joshua 4 focuses on the memorial that Yahweh commanded the people of Israel to create after they crossed the Jordan.

Gathering rocks

Joshua 4 consists of two sections: verses 1–14 and verses 15–24. The first section consists of instructions (vv. 1–7) and a report of the people's obedience (vv. 8–14). When the crossing was completed, Yahweh told Joshua to have twelve men take twelve stones from the middle of the Jordan and lay them down in the Israelite camp (vv. 1–3). The verb 'carry' in verse 3 means literally 'cause to cross'. By using this verb, the narrator emphasizes the 'crossing' theme which has been prominent in the story. Similarly, the verb in the expression 'lay them down' (v. 3) literally means 'cause them to rest'. By using the verb 'rest' rather than a more common term for setting down something, the narrator links the rocks to the theme of rest.

According to verse 5, Joshua summoned twelve men, one from each of the twelve tribes, and offered instructions about taking up the stones. In the course of his instructions, he explains the purpose of this action. The twelve stones will serve as a 'sign'—that is, a marker which points back to a significant event. Similarly, in verse 7, the narrator refers to the stones as a 'memorial'. The expectation is that Israelite children in the future will ask, 'What do those stones mean to you?' (v. 6). The parent's reply, repeated twice in verse 7 for emphasis, will highlight how the waters of the Jordan were cut off.

Verses 8–14 describe the execution of this command. Perhaps the report seems tedious because it repeats a lot of detail already reported in verses 1–7. The narrator does this intentionally, however, to stress that Israel fulfilled God's command exactly as he had issued it. Also, verse 9 may confuse readers into thinking that Joshua set up an additional twelve stones in the middle of the Jordan. However, the Hebrew grammar of verse 9 indicates that the narrator has stopped the action to provide some background information. That is why the NRSV puts this verse in parentheses. Verse 9 simply describes the same stones referred to in verse 8. Initially, Joshua had set them up in the middle of the Jordan, but, as verse 8 indicates, the stones were carried to the camp. The final statement in verse 9—'and they are there to this day'—refers to the camp location, not the middle of the river.

Notice the emphasis on Israel's recognition of Joshua's authority. Verses 12–13 report the obedience of the two and a half tribes who lived east of the Jordan. About 40,000 of their warriors participated in the crossing as Moses had ordered (see Deuteronomy 3:12–20; Joshua 1:12–15). Moses' authority still looms over the people's responses (see vv. 10, 12), yet verse 14 informs us that now the people stood in awe of Joshua as they had stood in awe of Moses, and they revered Joshua for the rest of his life.

The Jordan returns to flood stage

The second section of Joshua 4 (vv. 15–24) reviews the aftermath of the crossing to provide some additional details. In verses 15–18, the narrator reveals that the Jordan resumed its flow and returned to flood stage once the priests left the river bed. The return to the topic of the memorial stones establishes it as the narrator's main interest in Joshua 4. Israel must use the memorial stones as a teaching tool for future generations. Israelite children need to know how Yahweh enabled Israel to cross the Jordan at flood stage. Joshua's statement in verse 23 clearly pictures the drying up of the Jordan as a miracle on a par with the drying up of the Red Sea. Creating memorials helps God's people to remember how he comes through for them when they face difficult crossings.

MEDITATION

What 'crossings' in your life deserve memorials? What stories of God's intervention in your life do you want to pass on to your children? What objects do you have—photos, receipts, letters, and so on—which remind you of how God brought you through a difficult situation in your life?

8 JOSHUA 5:1-12

The 'HILL of the FORESKINS'

The leaders of the city-states in Canaan are terrified of Israel (v. 1), so the time seems right for Israel to begin military operations. But Israel is not yet ready. More spiritual preparation needs to take place.

Why circumcision?

Yahweh's command to Joshua to circumcise the Israelites (v. 2) catches us by surprise. On the eve of a military campaign, it seems like a poor strategy. Circumcision, the removal of the foreskin from a male's penis, was normally performed when a baby boy was 8 days old. The procedure would cause considerable pain for an adult male and would require recovery time (see v. 8)—not the most strategic situation for a nation that has just entered enemy territory!

However, Yahweh had established circumcision as the sign of the covenant he had made with the Israelites, the offspring of Abraham (see Genesis 17:9–14). Furthermore, Yahweh certainly used the Canaanites' fear (v. 1) to keep them from attacking Israel at such a vulnerable time. Still we wonder, as modern readers, why God would choose such a radical procedure for a sign. Why not pierce an ear, use a tattoo, or even cut off an earlobe? Yahweh probably chose a surgical procedure on the most intimate part of a man's body because it reflects the intimate bond that Yahweh has with his people. Also, the surgical removal of the foreskin symbolized what Yahweh's people were to do to their hearts (Deuteronomy 10:16).

A second time

Verse 3 reports that Joshua obeyed Yahweh's command. He circumcised the Israelites at Gibeath-haaraloth—a Hebrew expression which means 'Hill of the Foreskins'. Then, in verses 4–7, the narrator stops the action and explains the reason for this event. The reference to circumcising the Israelites a 'second time' (v. 2) reflects the need for a new generation of Israelites to undergo circumcision. The previous generation, which had personally experienced deliverance from Egypt, had been circumcised, but they had not circumcised their offspring— the current generation—during their years of wandering in the wilderness.

Healing at Gilgal

The action resumes in verse 8 with the Israelites remaining in camp until the men had time to heal. According to verse 9, Yahweh responded to this act by rolling away the 'disgrace of Egypt'. This expression refers either to the disobedience of the previous generation that came out of Egypt or to the scorn that the Egyptians showed the Israelites by claiming that their forty years of wandering around in the desert would end in death (see Deuteronomy 9:27–28). The place name 'Gilgal' memorializes this declaration by Yahweh because it sounds similar to the Hebrew verb for 'roll'.

No more manna

Another significant event took place while the Israelites were camped at Gilgal: they celebrated Passover (v. 10; see Exodus 12; Leviticus 23:4–5). On the day after Passover, the day when the feast of Unleavened Bread was to begin (Leviticus 23:6–8), the Israelites ate the produce of the land (v. 11). On that same day, the 'manna' (Hebrew for 'what is it?') that Yahweh had been providing for years stopped coming. Now Yahweh provided the crops of Canaan for their food.

Message for today

'Being' comes before 'doing'. That is, when God places an opportunity or challenge before his people, he expects them to prepare themselves spiritually. He expects his people to deal first with the guilt and shame resulting from their disobedience. Spiritual preparation precedes the execution of any assignment that God has given to us.

What about circumcision today? Galatians 5:6 says, 'For in Christ Jesus neither circumcision nor uncircumcision counts for anything; the only thing that counts is faith working through love.' Christians have already experienced a spiritual circumcision—removal of the sinful nature—in Christ (Colossians 2:11).

PRAYER

Thank you, Father God, for rolling away the guilt and shame of my sin. Thank you for the circumcision you performed through Christ on my heart. Help me to pursue purity before I pursue service.

9 JOSHUA 5:13–15

ENCOUNTERING *the* COMMANDER *of* YAHWEH'S ARMY

The opening chapters in Joshua have been building up to an attack on Jericho (see 2:1–3; 3:16; 4:13, 19). Israel now appears to be ready, but the narrator shares a final incident in 5:13–15 which occurred before Yahweh's people made their advance on the city. The opening expression 'once' (literally, 'now it happened') introduces this new scene. The scene will consist almost entirely of dialogue between Joshua and the commander of the army of Yahweh.

A surprise encounter

In verse 13, the Hebrew term *hinneh* ('look, behold!') highlights the surprising sight that Joshua saw. The NRSV leaves the term untranslated, but a more literal translation would read like this: 'He looked up and saw, and behold, a man was standing before him with a drawn sword in his hand.' The expression 'with a drawn sword in his hand' is the very same expression used of the angel of Yahweh when he stood before Balaam's donkey (Numbers 22:23), and the only other occurrence of this expression comes in 1 Chronicles 21:16, where an angel is again the subject.

Interestingly, the man with the drawn sword deflects Joshua's question—'Are you one of us, or one of our adversaries?'—and addresses another issue. The NRSV's 'Neither' in verse 14 is a bit misleading. The Hebrew term is simply 'No.' The man is not claiming that he is neither on Israel's side nor on the side of Israel's adversaries. Rather, he is saying, 'No, that's not the issue here.' The issue is that this person has come as the commander of the army of Yahweh. This raises an additional question: what is meant by 'the army of Yahweh'? Does this refer to the Israelite army or to a heavenly army? The term 'army' (Hebrew *saba*) in this story provides a clue. It is often used in its plural form in the expression 'Yahweh of hosts (armies)'. In fact, the expression 'Yahweh of hosts' or 'Yahweh the God of hosts' occurs more than 270 times in the Old Testament, and refers to heavenly forces. So the reference is to a heavenly army. Furthermore, the man's identification of himself as commander of Yahweh's army hints that he is actually an angel or a divine being.

Worshipping before the commander

Joshua's response seems to confirm our suspicion that this man is actually an angel or a divine being. Upon learning the identity of the man, Joshua fell to the ground and worshipped—that is, prostrated himself (v. 14). Three details in Joshua's question at the end of verse 14 reveals his recognition of the commander's authority: he seeks a command or message; he calls himself 'your servant'; and he refers to the commander as 'my lord'.

Holy ground

The scene closes with the commander of Yahweh's army instructing Joshua to remove his sandals because 'the place where you stand is holy' (v. 15). The term 'holy' means 'set apart'. The place is holy because Yahweh is present. Perhaps the best definition of God's holiness comes from the English hymn 'Holy, holy, holy' by Reginald Heber (1783–1826). One of the stanzas says, 'Only Thou art holy—there is none beside Thee, perfect in power, in love and purity.'

The commander's instructions to Joshua resemble Yahweh's instructions to Moses at the burning bush (Exodus 3:5). Like Moses, Joshua must come to grips with Yahweh's holiness before setting out on the mission Yahweh has assigned to him. With the privilege of Yahweh's presence comes the responsibility to respect Yahweh's holiness.

This brief episode reminds God's people today that worship comes before service. To put it another way, God's people must respond to God's holiness before they carry out the mission that God has given them to complete. Because God is holy, he expects his people to pursue holiness in their lives (Leviticus 11:45; 19:2; 1 Peter 1:15–16).

MEDITATION

Scottish pastor Robert Murray M'Cheyne, who died before reaching his thirtieth birthday, once said, 'My people's greatest need is my personal holiness.' In what areas of your life do you need to pursue holiness before God so that you can serve him effectively?

10 JOSHUA 6:1–21

The BATTLE *of* JERICHO

The time has finally come for Israel to advance against the city of Jericho and begin the process of conquering the land of Canaan. But like the Jordan River (see Joshua 3), the city of Jericho presents a real challenge to Israel. Verse 1 pictures Jericho as a city ready for an attack. The city gates have been completely shut—a fact verified by the lack of any traffic in and out of the city. Ancient fortified cities, with walls as high as 6 metres and as thick as 2.5 metres and with double or triple gates, could withstand an attack for months if they had enough food in storage and a sufficient water supply. Guards were usually stationed high upon the walls in guard towers. They were ready to shoot arrows, pour hot oil, or dump boulders on any enemy warriors who tried to scale the wall or whack it with a battering ram. Verse 1, then, effectively creates suspense. How will Israel capture this city which is ready for an attack?

An unusual strategy

Yahweh's instructions to Joshua catch us by surprise (vv. 2–5). Israel is supposed to form a ceremonial procession consisting of warriors, the ark, and seven priests with seven trumpets made of rams' horns. This procession will circle the city once a day for six days. Then, on the seventh day, the procession will march around the city seven times with trumpets blaring. A long trumpet blast will signal the people to shout, and then the city wall will fall, giving the people an opportunity to charge straight into the city. This unusual strategy reflects Yahweh's intention to hand over the city to Israel as a gift (v. 2). Like the Jordan River, the city of Jericho presented no obstacle to Yahweh's mighty power!

Verses 6–11 record Joshua's relay of the instructions to the people. A few new details emerge: the priests will precede the ark of the covenant; a group of armed men will precede these priests while another group serves as a rear guard; and the people must not speak or shout until they receive instructions from Joshua on the appointed day. Furthermore, three occurrences of the Hebrew term 'cross over' in verses 7–8 (translated by the NRSV as 'Go forward… pass on… went forward') keep the crossing theme prominent in the reader's mind. Yahweh uses his power to bring his people through crossings that they are unable to handle in their own strength.

The walls fall down!

The narrator describes the action in verses 12–21 in a way that highlights Israel's obedience. There are no surprises. Israel precisely follows Yahweh's instructions on the first six days (vv. 11–14) and on the seventh day (vv. 15–20). When the people 'raised a great shout'—literally, 'shouted a great shout'—the city wall fell down as Yahweh had promised (v. 20). Then, the people rushed in to capture the city, and they completely destroyed all its inhabitants (vv. 20–21).

An interesting feature of this account is Joshua's instruction to the people about the 'things devoted to destruction'—the translation of the Hebrew term *herem* (vv. 17–19). This instruction reflects the command in Deuteronomy 20:16–18 to wipe out entire towns so that Israel might not learn the corrupt practices of the pagans in them. Thus, the Israelites are to put the inhabitants of the city to death and to put all the valuables into the treasury of Yahweh. The lone exception is Rahab and her family. She was spared because she had hidden the Israelite spies (v. 17)—an act that verified her conversion to Israel's God, Yahweh.

Message for today

We cannot hold up the strategy used by Israel at Jericho as a paradigm. In other battles in the book of Joshua, Israel had a military role —setting ambushes, making surprise attacks, and engaging in siege warfare against the fortified cities. What this story teaches is that God fights for his people. His power wins battles. No doubt God selected the unusual strategy for this inaugural conquest because it highlighted this theme. Ordinarily, God commands human effort (see Philippians 2:12), but he still wants us to know that victory comes ultimately from his power (see Philippians 2:13). We should also note that the writer of Hebrews offers this story as an example of faith (Hebrews 11:30).

PRAYER

Father God, you are a warrior who fights for your people.
Thank you for providing victory through your power.

The AFTERMATH of JERICHO'S FALL

The conclusion to the Jericho story in verses 22–27 explores three issues related to the city's destruction: Rahab's rescue, Joshua's curse on the city, and Yahweh's presence with Joshua.

Rahab's rescue

Joshua's command in verse 22 indicates that he recognized the oath that the two spies had made to Rahab during an earlier spying mission (see Joshua 2). Joshua's mention of 'the prostitute's house' and his reference to her as simply 'the woman', instead of a reference to her by name, reflect her status as an undeserving pagan. The mercy and grace that Joshua and the Israelites extend to her seem all the more remarkable given her background.

The narrator supplies an interesting detail in verse 23. When Rahab and her family were brought out of Jericho, they were set 'outside the camp of Israel'. The favourable statements in verse 25 about Rahab's place in Israel suggest that this detail should not be understood as a negative reflection on Rahab. Perhaps her family's placement outside the camp reflects a need for a temporary period of purification before entering the camp (see Deuteronomy 23:10–11 for a possible parallel). Or, this placement may simply reflect Rahab's status of being unattached to any particular Israelite tribe. By verse 25, though, Rahab and her family seem to be fully assimilated into the nation of Israel.

At any rate, verses 24–25 set Rahab's rescue in stark contrast to the destruction of the city. The narrator even notes that she 'has lived in Israel ever since'—that is, she was still living in Israel when the narrator wrote this account. However, the NRSV has chosen to translate the pronoun 'she' as 'her family'. This reflects the possibility that the statement about Rahab's being present in Israel at the time of the narrator's writing refers to the descendants of Rahab—the house of Rahab—and not necessarily to Rahab herself. Now for the second time in this story, the narrator mentions the motive for Rahab's rescue: 'she hid the messengers whom Joshua sent to spy out Jericho' (v. 25; see 6:17).

Joshua's curse on Jericho

Following the discussion of Rahab's rescue, the narrator records Joshua's pronouncement of an oath (v. 26). The oath takes the form of a curse. The recipient of this curse is identified as 'anyone who tries to rebuild this city—this Jericho!' The nature of the curse is harm upon the cursed person's offspring—from firstborn to youngest. Intriguingly, the curse comes true a few hundred years later when a man during King Ahab's time, Hiel of Bethel, loses his oldest and youngest sons when he rebuilds Jericho (see 1 Kings 16:34). The language of the curse covers the entire process of building or rebuilding a city. Laying the foundations happens first, while setting up the gates is the final step in the process.

Readers may wonder about the purpose of such a strong curse. Why was it necessary? Deuteronomy 13:12–16 appears to set a precedent for not only destroying towns involved in idol worship but then forcing them to remain as perpetual ruins, never to be rebuilt.

Yahweh's presence with Joshua

The narrator closes the account with the notice that Yahweh was with Joshua (v. 27). This reality causes Joshua's fame. Some scholars look at the grammatical construction that begins verse 27 and suggest that it serves as an introduction to the story in chapter 7 rather than as a conclusion to the story in chapter 6. Whatever the case, the statement certainly serves as a contrast to the following story.

The conclusion to the Jericho story reveals God's attitude towards sin and sinners. He shows grace and mercy to the Rahabs who turn from their sin to acknowledge his sovereign power. Yet he calls his people to abhor sin and to remove the corrupting influences that destroy their intimacy with him. Today, God does not call Christians to wipe out evil cities. Rather, he calls us not to conform to evil culture but to pursue purity in our lives (see Romans 12:1–2; 2 Corinthians 7:1).

MEDITATION

Read 2 Corinthians 7:1. Identify some ways in which you can cleanse yourself from the defilements that corrupt your purity and rob you of intimacy with God.

12 JOSHUA 7:1–5

DEFEAT *at* AI

After the victory at Jericho, Israel experiences a major upset when attacking the city of Ai. The men of Ai rout the Israelite army, and 36 Israelites lose their lives. Earlier, the hearts of the Canaanites melted with fear (2:9, 11, 24). Now, the hearts of the Israelites melt and turn to water (v. 5).

The reason for the defeat

The narrator supplies some information at the beginning of the story which explains why Israel experienced defeat. As it turns out, an Israelite named Achan had acted unfaithfully. In the Old Testament, the expression 'broke faith' (v. 1) describes the breaking of a trust between two parties. For example, the expression appears in Numbers 5:12, 27 where it describes a wife's adultery. However, it usually refers to a person breaking trust with God. In this case, Achan broke faith by violating Yahweh's clear command not to take any loot after the battle. Any valuable articles were supposed to go into Yahweh's treasury (see 6:18–19).

Prefacing the story with this information is an interesting strategy. Often, the writers of Old Testament narratives practise 'strategic delay'. That is, they tell stories in the way that Sir Arthur Conan Doyle tells his tales of Sherlock Holmes. Doyle often withholds key pieces of explanation—such as the identity of the culprit—for later in the story. This keeps readers in suspense. To create a dramatic effect, the narrator could have withheld the information contained in verse 1 and let it emerge in verses 18–21. However, he provides this privileged information—which is unknown to the characters at this point in the story—to shape the way we understand the action that follows. By identifying Achan and his sin at the outset of the story, the narrator indicates that the plot does not turn on 'who committed the sin' or 'why Israel suffered defeat'. Rather, the story focuses on what happens when God's people break trust with him. It also focuses on why God's people would have the audacity to violate a clear command of the Lord.

Yahweh's face gets hot

As a result of Achan's sin, Yahweh's anger burned against the children of Israel (v. 17). Literally, the Hebrew text says that 'Yahweh's nose burned'. The picture comes from a bearded Hebrew male whose red-flushed nose betrays his anger. The Old Testament makes it clear, however, that Yahweh's outstanding character quality is his loyal love. In contrast with his anger, which he expresses to the third and fourth generations of those who disobey him, he shows his loyal love to the thousandth generation of those who love and obey him (Exodus 20:5–6; 34:6–7). Yet anger is a real part of God's character. His anger is not an out-of-control temper, but a measured outrage against evil (Romans 1:18). Through the death of Jesus Christ, God's righteous anger has been satisfied (see Romans 3:25, where the 'propitiation' or 'sacrifice of atonement' involves the satisfaction of God's wrath; see also 1 Thessalonians 5:9). However, even the writer of Hebrews motivates new covenant believers to obedience by reminding them that 'our God is a consuming fire' (Hebrews 12:29).

A lack of faith

A careful reader will also detect a lack of trust in Yahweh on the part of the spies (v. 3). Unlike an earlier group of spies sent by Joshua into Canaan (see 2:24), this group does not factor Yahweh into the equation. Rather, their report resembles the majority report of Moses' spies more than forty years earlier: it exhibits a lack of faith. The lack of trust in Yahweh on that occasion was due to doubt and fear. In the spying of Ai, the lack of faith stems from self-reliance. There is no hint of trust in Yahweh's deliverance—the lesson that the battle of Jericho intended to teach. If Israel had sought Yahweh's help, would Yahweh have revealed Achan's sin before Israel headed into battle and got routed?

Whatever the answer, the story makes it clear that the sin of one member of the community of faith has a devastating effect on the whole community. This principle still stands today. Sin in a church needs to be identified and dealt with to keep God's people spiritually healthy (1 Corinthians 5).

PRAYER

O Father God, holiness is what I long for, holiness is what I need.
Transform my mind and conform my will to yours.

UNABLE *to* STAND

In the wake of the devastating defeat at Ai, Joshua tears his clothes and falls face down in front of the ark of Yahweh (v. 6). The ark was the place Yahweh had chosen to reveal his presence. The elders of Israel did the same and even sprinkled dust on their heads—a dramatic expression of grief. The scene that follows consists of a dialogue: Joshua's lament (vv. 7–9), and then Yahweh's response (vv. 10–15).

A grief-stricken leader

Joshua's prayer of lament begins with 'Ah'—a cry which is used fifteen times in the Old Testament at the beginning of a statement or prayer to express either alarm or grief. He addresses God as 'Sovereign Yahweh' (Hebrew *Adonai Yahweh*).

At this point, Joshua is unaware of what the reader already knows: the reason for Israel's defeat is the anger of Yahweh, which was incited by Achan's sin (7:1). So, Joshua questions the wisdom of crossing the Jordan and entering the land of Canaan. Joshua questions Yahweh's wisdom ('Why have you brought this people across the Jordan…?') as well as his own decision ('Would that we had been content…'). Ultimately, Joshua shows concern for Yahweh's reputation as well as the nation's well-being (v. 9).

To stand or not to stand

Yahweh's reply to Joshua employs a series of wordplays. First, Yahweh forms a wordplay with the term 'stand'. He challenges Joshua to 'Stand up!' (v. 10), and then observes a few statements later that 'the Israelites are unable to stand before their enemies' because of sin (v. 12). The question that Yahweh poses after commanding Joshua to stand—'Why have you fallen upon your face?'—indicates that Joshua has no reason to offer a complaint or lament. Rather, he needs to answer for Israel's sin. Thus, the summons to stand initiates a lawsuit that Yahweh is bringing against his people.

An inappropriate 'crossing'

Next, Yahweh charges that Israel has 'sinned' and 'transgressed' his covenant with them (v. 11). To 'sin' is to 'miss a mark or a way'. The term 'transgressed' is actually the Hebrew term 'cross over' which has been prominent in the previous stories. Thus, Yahweh's use of it here amounts to another wordplay. The people whom Yahweh enabled to 'cross over' the Jordan River (see 1:2; 3:14, 17; 4:1, 23) and 'cross over' against Jericho (see comments on 6:7, p. 38) had the audacity to 'cross over' the boundaries of the covenant that Yahweh had made with them.

Israel now devoted for destruction

A third wordplay appears in Yahweh's comments in verse 12. Because the people of Israel took some of the 'devoted things' (*herem*, v. 11), they themselves have become a 'thing devoted for destruction' (*leherem*).

In the remainder of Yahweh's speech, he instructs Joshua to 'sanctify' the people and to call them to 'sanctify' themselves in preparation for an encounter with Yahweh on the following day (v. 13). The term 'sanctify' translates the Hebrew verb *qadesh* which means 'to set apart, make holy'. Furthermore, Joshua is to inform them about their sin and its long-term consequences if they do not deal with it (v. 13). Then, he is to tell them that they will come before Yahweh the next morning, tribe by tribe (v. 14). Yahweh will expose the guilty person by narrowing his identity down to his tribe, then to his clan, then to his household, and finally to the individual himself. According to his statement in verse 15, the one who did this 'outrageous thing' would be burned by fire, along with everything that belonged to him (see the commentary on Judges 19:23–24, p. 209, for a discussion of the Hebrew term *nebalah* which is used here in verse 15).

Dealing with sin

This scene reveals the seriousness of blatantly disobeying Yahweh's commands. It challenges communities of faith to deal with the sin of their members, since that sin jeopardizes the well-being of the entire community (see Matthew 18:15–20; 1 Corinthians 5:1–13; 2 Thessalonians 3:14–15).

PRAYER

Wash me thoroughly from my iniquity,
and cleanse me from my sin.

Psalm 51:2

The TROUBLE *with* SIN

Tension runs high in the final scene of chapter 7 as Joshua rises early in the morning to begin the process of identifying the guilty person (v. 16). The details leading up to the identification of Achan (vv. 17–18) may seem tedious to the reader, but these details add to the tension as the process of elimination narrows the focus to the tribe of Judah, to the clan of the Zerahites, to the family of Zabdi, and finally to Achan.

Yahweh's glory at stake

Joshua's instructions to Achan reveal what is at stake. The overriding concern is Yahweh's glory. The Hebrew term 'glory' (*kabod*) literally means 'heaviness, weightiness'. When used in reference to God, it refers to the weightiness of his character—that is, the sum total of all God's character qualities. God's concern throughout the Bible is to put his glory on display (Exodus 14:4; Psalm 96:3; Isaiah 48:11; 1 Corinthians 10:31; Ephesians 1:12, 14, 18). In this scene, Achan will bring glory to Yahweh by confessing his sin. The expression 'make confession' literally means 'give public acknowledgment'.

The seduction of coveting

As noted previously, this story provides insight into why God's people have the audacity to disobey his clear commands. Achan explains his sins with the verbs 'saw', 'coveted' and 'took' (v. 21). These same three verbs appear in Genesis 3:6 in the description of the first sin by a human being, Eve. (By the way, the term 'Shinar' refers to Babylon.)

The underlying sin amounted to coveting—*hamad* in Hebrew. This very term appears in the tenth commandment, 'You shall not covet your neighbour's...' (Exodus 20:17). Coveting is a person's strong desire to possess what does not rightfully belong to him or her. When God's people lust for what does not rightfully belong to them, it can lead them to pursue actions that make no sense—actions as ridiculous as disobeying God's clear commands.

Double trouble

After Achan's confession, Joshua sent messengers who ran to Achan's tent and discovered the loot. Once the items were recovered, Israel 'spread them out' before Yahweh (v. 23)—an act which amounted to returning these items to Yahweh. Then, Joshua and the people took Achan, the stolen items, his family and all his possessions to the Valley of Achor (v. 24). The term 'Achor'—similar in sound to 'Achan' —means 'trouble'. In fact, Joshua's indictment, offered in the form of two questions, turns on the word 'trouble'. Because Achan brought trouble on Israel because of his sin, Yahweh was now bringing trouble on Achan. The account of the actual execution is swift and startling. Achan and his family are stoned to death, burnt, and covered with a pile of stones. Like the stone memorial at Gilgal, this pile of stones remained even until the time the narrator wrote this account (v. 26). While the stones at Gilgal testified to Yahweh's deliverance, this pile of stones testified to Yahweh's judgment. After Israel dealt with the sin in the camp, Yahweh's burning anger subsided.

Message for today

This story offers a prophetic message that sin brings nothing but trouble and that communities of faith must deal with sin in their midst in order to experience God's blessing.

Still, the punishment upon Achan seems unusually harsh to us as modern readers. Why did God deal so harshly with Achan when others, like David (2 Samuel 11—12), received a second chance? On a few occasions throughout biblical history, God released the full fury of his wrath against people who rebelled—Nadab and Abihu (Leviticus 10:1–3); Uzzah (2 Samuel 6:6–7); and Ananias and Sapphira (Acts 5:1–11). Apparently, God used these selective occasions as opportunities to show his people the seriousness of sin. If God always dealt with his people on this basis, none of his people would be alive! Without these occasional, dramatic reminders, however, we might be tempted to think that God is soft on sin. The fact is that the gracious, compassionate God we serve is a holy God who cannot tolerate sin.

PRAYER

Help me, Lord, to be holy as you are holy. Help me never to take for granted the fury of your wrath against sin.

A SECOND ATTACK *on* AI

Now that the Israelites have dealt with Achan's sin, they can resume the task of conquering the land. The next step is to launch another attack against Ai. In case of any lingering fear or discouragement from the previous defeat at Ai, Yahweh commands Joshua not to fear or be dismayed (v. 1a). Yahweh also emphasizes the certainty of victory by promising to give to Joshua the king of Ai, his people, his city and his land (v. 1b).

Revised instructions

Yahweh instructs Joshua to do to Ai and its king as he did to Jericho and its king, but with two exceptions. First, Yahweh has lifted the ban on the devoted things which had been in effect at Jericho. Now, Israel can take booty for themselves. Second, Yahweh dictates a different strategy. This time, he instructs Joshua to set an ambush behind the city.

Preparing to set an ambush

The details in verses 3–9 show us that Joshua is taking Yahweh's instructions quite seriously. To begin with, Joshua sends 30,000 warriors at night, under the cover of darkness, to hide behind the city (vv. 3b–4). The plan is for Joshua to lure the residents of Ai away from their city by leading another group of Israelites against the city and then pretending to flee. When the residents of Ai pursue them, the 30,000 Israelite warriors hiding behind the city will rise up and take the city. Joshua is careful to emphasize that Israel's seizure of the city will result from Yahweh their God giving it into their hands (v. 7b). Israel's responsibility is simply to do what Yahweh has ordered (vv. 7a, 8). Verse 9 may seem to add unnecessary repetition, but once again it assures us that both Joshua and the warriors of Israel carried out Yahweh's instructions.

Carrying out the ambush

The actual description of the ambush seems confusing (vv. 10–17). On first reading, it appears as though Joshua sent another 5,000 warriors—a third group—to set a second ambush west of the city between Bethel and Ai (v. 12). This additional ambush force would presumably handle any help that came to Ai from Bethel (see v. 17). However, verse 9 indicates that the original group of warriors assigned to ambush the city from the rear had already positioned itself to the west of the city between Bethel and Ai. Why would the narrator identify the 5,000 as an additional group of warriors if they set up an ambush at the same spot as the first group? Furthermore, the summary statement in verse 13 speaks only of two groups—the main contingent north of the city and the rear guard stationed to the west of the city.

A solution is to read verses 11–13 as a review of the events already described in verses 3–9. In fact, the Hebrew grammar at the beginning of verse 11 pauses the action momentarily to provide a piece of background information: all the fighting men who were with Joshua had gone up. Perhaps the story line stays in a 'review' mode until the beginning of verse 14. Otherwise, verse 13 requires a second night's stay for Joshua in the valley.

The main problem with reading verses 11–13 as a review is the apparent contradiction between the number of soldiers assigned to ambush the city: 30,000 (v. 13) as opposed to 5,000 (v. 12). One of the more plausible solutions is that the 5,000 may have been a 'special force' within the 30,000. This 'special force' took the lead in setting the ambush while the remaining 25,000 provided support from behind the front lines. Whatever the case may be, the details in this account confirm that Israel was careful to follow Yahweh's instructions.

Finally, the report in verses 14–17 assures us that the strategy worked. The narrator is careful to emphasize that the king of Ai was unaware that an ambush had been set (v. 14). Then, after reporting that 'all the people' were lured away from the city (v. 16), the narrator emphasizes this fact by restating it negatively: there was not a man left in Ai or Bethel who did not go out after Israel (v. 17).

MEDITATION

The balance in this story between Yahweh's power (v. 7b) and
Israel's need to act (vv. 7a, 8) reflects a similar balance in the
Christian life. Believers work out their salvation (Philippians 2:12)
because God is the one supplying the power (Philippians 2:13).

16 JOSHUA 8:18–29

VICTORY *at* AI

The account of the ambush against Ai continues with Yahweh telling Joshua to stretch out his sword towards the city (v. 18a). The Hebrew term translated 'sword' by the NRSV (and 'spear' or 'javelin' by other English versions) actually indicates a sword with a heavy, curved blade. Yahweh follows this command by offering a reason, which he introduces with the term 'for' (Hebrew *ki*): he will give Ai into Joshua's hand (v. 18b).

The outstretched sword

To English readers, the final clause in verse 18 probably seems unnecessary. The narrator could simply say 'And Joshua did so' instead of repeating the very words that Yahweh used when issuing his command to Joshua. However, this kind of repetition is a deliberate technique used by the narrator to inform us that Joshua obeyed exactly what Yahweh had asked him to do.

Notice that the 'command clause' (v. 18a) and the 'reason clause' (v. 18b) both contain the expression 'in(to) your hand'. This links the ideas in the two clauses together. Joshua's act of stretching out the sword that is in his hand represents the fact that Yahweh will be the one who gives the city of Ai into Joshua's hand.

Once Joshua stretched out his hand, the ambush troops rushed into the city, took possession of it, and set it on fire (v. 19). When the men of Ai turned and looked, they saw a startling sight. The Hebrew particle *hinneh* (usually translated 'look' or 'behold', but left untranslated here by the NRSV) introduces the startling sight: 'the smoke of the city was rising to the sky' (v. 20). The narrator then uses grammatical forms to pause the action and inform us that the people of Ai were powerless to escape because Joshua's group which had pretended to flee now turned back against the people of Ai. Verses 21–22 describe the thorough slaughter that followed. The narrator again stops the action in verse 23 to inform us that the Israelites took the king of Ai alive and brought him to Joshua. This creates a bit of suspense. What will Joshua do with the king of Ai?

Verses 24–25 show the completeness of the Israelite victory. After slaughtering the inhabitants of Ai in the open wilderness, the Israelites returned to the city to complete the slaughter—presumably of the women and children who had remained (v. 24). For the record, Ai's entire population of 12,000 fell that day (v. 25). As modern readers, we struggle with such a brutal slaughter of people. However, we must remember that Yahweh has called Israel to wipe out the Canaanites so that their evil does not infect Israel (Deuteronomy 20:16–18). Furthermore, we must remember that God withheld his judgment for 400 years until the sin of Canaanites reached its full measure (Genesis 15:13, 16).

Once again, in verse 26, the narrator pauses the action to highlight Joshua's act of stretching out his sword. He did not draw his hand back until the mission was accomplished. The outstretched sword motif in this story reminds us of two previous situations in which Yahweh delivered his people. First, Yahweh created a crossing through the Red Sea by parting the waters while Moses lifted up his staff and stretched out his hand over the sea (Exodus 14:16, 21). Yahweh also instructed Moses to stretch his hand over the sea to bring the water back upon the Egyptians (Exodus 14:26). Then, in Exodus 17:8–16, Joshua defeated the Amalekites while Moses held up his hands. In each of the three situations, the uplifted or outstretched arms signified Yahweh's control over the battle and his supply of power to help the Israelites achieve victory.

A hanging and a heap of stones

As the narrator draws the story to a close, he is careful to note that Israel followed Yahweh's instructions when taking booty from the city (v. 27). The final scene is a vivid one. Joshua hanged the king of Ai on a tree. Then, in the evening, the king's body was thrown down at the entrance of the city gate and, like Achan's body (see 7:26), was covered with a pile of stones (v. 29). These actions, as brutal as they seem, reflect Joshua's care to follow Yahweh's instructions for the execution of a criminal (see Deuteronomy 21:22–23). In the end, the prophetic message of this story is that success flows from obedience to God.

PRAYER

I cling to your decrees, O Lord; let me not be put to shame.

Psalm 119:31

REAFFIRMING YAHWEH'S COVENANT

This story shows Israel making a priority of knowing Yahweh's word. In the previous episode, Israel's success stemmed from its obedience to Yahweh's word (8:1–29). Such obedience can spring only from a thorough knowledge of Yahweh's instructions. While Yahweh has provided specific details to Joshua about each new venture or battle (for example, see 3:7–13; 4:1–3; 6:2–7; 8:1–2), the law of Moses contains the heart of Yahweh's instructions for his people (see Deuteronomy 11:31–32; Joshua 1:7).

Obeying Deuteronomy 27

Like Joshua (see 1:8), the Israelites needed a means of keeping the law of Moses fresh in their minds. In Deuteronomy 27, Yahweh had spelled out a procedure for reviewing the law once the Israelites crossed the Jordan. This procedure parallels treaties or covenants made by great kings with subject nations. In such treaties, the great kings stipulated that the subject nations must make provision for a periodic reading of the terms of the treaty.

Joshua's act of building an altar to Yahweh on Mount Ebal (vv. 30–31a) begins the process of obeying a command that Yahweh had issued through Moses in Deuteronomy 27:5–7. Interestingly, this episode contains only three verbs which advance the main story line: 'they *offered*... and *sacrificed*... Joshua *wrote*' (vv. 31b–32). Everything that precedes or follows provides important background details to these activities.

Joshua makes a stone copy

The description in verse 32 of Joshua writing a copy of the law of Moses provides intriguing insight into the process of preserving Scripture. Writing materials such as plastered stones (see Deuteronomy 27:2) required effort to produce and were not always durable over time. Furthermore, the general populace did not read or write. Joshua ensures that Israel will continue to have a copy of the law given through Moses by writing a copy of a previously written copy.

Between two mountains

With the whole nation gathered, half in front of Mount Gerizim and half in front of Mount Ebal, Joshua read 'all the words of the law', including its blessings and cursings (vv. 33–35). The mention of the 'alien as well as citizen' (v. 33) reflects the presence of foreigners, like Rahab and her family, who had converted to faith in Yahweh. If verse 35 seems redundant to us as modern readers, we must remember that it is the narrator's way of emphasizing that Joshua left nothing out: no one in Israel missed the opportunity to hear the book of the law read.

The location of this event is significant. As prescribed in Deuteronomy 11:29 and 27:11–13, the people gathered in front of Mount Gerizim and Mount Ebal—hills to the south and the north of Shechem. The valley between these hills was about three miles long and provided a natural amphitheatre with excellent acoustics. This spot was located about twenty miles from Ai, so it required a major trek through Canaanite country—enemy territory! Why did Yahweh instruct his people to go there? Perhaps he sent them there because it was the site where he first appeared to Abraham (then known as Abram) in the land of Canaan (Genesis 12:6–7). This raises another question, though. How could the Israelites have gathered on the slopes of Mount Gerizim and Mount Ebal without any resistance from the Canaanites? Perhaps Israel's previous ties with Shechem resulted in a friendly relationship (see Genesis 12:6–7; 33:18–20; 35:4; 37:12–14). Furthermore, the aliens referred to in verses 33 and 35 might have included Shechemites.

Knowing scripture

This episode highlights the need for God's people to review God's commands and keep them fresh in their memory. After all, success flows from obedience, and obedience requires an intimate knowledge of Scripture. Today, the challenge for God's people is a bit different. We have ample Bible translations and a wide variety of study helps—including commentaries like this one. But God's people still have to discipline themselves to read and reflect on Scripture rather than neglecting it. Ignorance happens when God's people ignore his word.

PRAYER

I will never forget your precepts, for by them you have given me life.

Psalm 119:93

DECEIVED *by the* GIBEONITES

Beginning with this episode, the effort to conquer the land takes on a new twist. Previously, what the Canaanites heard about Israel caused their hearts to melt (2:9–11; 5:1). Now, what they have heard has led them to co-operate with each other to fight against Joshua and Israel (vv. 1–2). Exactly what did they hear? The expression in verse 2, 'heard of this', is vague. The Hebrew text does not supply an object, but simply says that they 'heard'. Here, the narrator expects us to fill in the details. Obviously, these Canaanite leaders have heard about the conflict at Ai, including Israel's initial defeat. Now, they no longer believe that Israel was invincible.

A cunning scheme

Joshua 9:1–2 effectively serves as the heading for the remaining conquest stories in chapters 9—11. But it also sets up the story in 9:3–27. In contrast to the group of city-states who gathered to fight Israel, the inhabitants of Gibeon chose another tactic—a cunning scheme. As the story develops, the nature of their ruse will emerge. They hope to deceive Israel into making a peace treaty. Gibeon was located about six miles south-west of Ai and about five miles north-west of Jerusalem. No doubt the Gibeonites suspected that they might be Israel's next target.

Before identifying the nature of their scheme, the narrator raises our curiosity by describing in detail their elaborate preparations (vv. 4–5). The key expression is 'worn-out'. They gathered an assortment of items that travellers would possess—all of them worn out, some being torn, mended, and patched. Even their food supply was dry and mouldy.

The nature of their scheme begins to unfold as they approach Joshua, claim to be from a far country, and request a treaty (v. 6).

Israelite suspicion

The response of the Israelites in verse 7 betrays their suspicion. They are concerned that this contingent seeking a peace treaty might consist of locals and not people from a far land. But what difference does this make? Here, we encounter one of the amazing features of this story. The Israelite response in verse 7 makes it clear that they understood Yahweh's law and were taking it seriously. Their recent review of the law of Moses (8:30–35) would have reminded them that they were to treat differently the towns nearby and the towns in distant areas. According to Deuteronomy 20:10–18, Israel could offer peace to towns very far from them; but they were to annihilate the towns close to them—the towns of the Hittites, Amorites, Canaanites, Perizzites, Hivites and Jebusites. At the beginning of verse 7, the narrator provides a startling piece of information for his readers: the people of Gibeon to whom the Israelites were replying were Hivites! Joshua, too, asks questions that reflect his suspicion (v. 8). The Gibeonites offer a passionate, plausible story about how they have heard of the name of Yahweh and the victories he accomplished for Israel (vv. 9–11). Then, they point to their worn-out items as proof of their 'very long journey' (vv. 12–13).

Making an unfortunate treaty

The narrator concisely summarizes Israel's response. With each clause, the situation deteriorates. First, they sampled the provisions (v. 14a). But then, they failed to ask direction from Yahweh (v. 14b). What a damning revelation! Literally, the text reads, 'the mouth of Yahweh they did not ask'. Finally, Joshua made a peace treaty with the Gibeonites (v. 15). The consequences of this action will become clear in the next scene (9:16–27).

While not as chilling as the Achan story, this episode still has a sobering effect on us as readers. How troubling that believers who know God's word can still make the wrong decision! Joshua's motives were pure, but his decision was ill-advised. The fact is that we set ourselves up for failure when we don't consult with God. We often pray for God's provision, but this story challenges us to pray for God's direction as well.

MEDITATION

What current decisions do you face, which you should take to God in prayer for consultation?

WOOD CUTTERS & WATER CARRIERS

It took three days for the Israelites to discover their huge mistake (v. 16). As a result of failing to ask direction from Yahweh (9:14), the leaders of Israel concluded that a group of Hivites from nearby Gibeon were residents of a very far country. Therefore, Joshua made a peace treaty with them (9:15). But three days after the treaty, Israel discovered that they had made a treaty with their neighbours who were living among them (v. 16). This was clearly a violation of Deuteronomy 20:16–18.

Investigating and grumbling

The story continues with the Israelites setting out for the Hivite cities (v. 17). Their mission was to verify or disprove what they had heard— the report that the people with whom they had made a peace treaty lived nearby. The four Hivite cities mentioned in verse 17 were located in territory allotted to the tribe of Benjamin in an area about 6–12 miles south-west of Ai and 5–10 miles north-west of Jerusalem. Once the Israelites discovered that they had made a treaty with the leaders of these cities, they did not attack them. The decision not to attack them stemmed from the oath they had sworn by Yahweh, the God of Israel (v. 18a).

However, this decision resulted in the congregation murmuring against the leaders (v. 18b). The term 'murmured' (Hebrew *lun*) in verse 18 is used frequently in Exodus and Numbers to refer to Israel's complaining in the wilderness. Unlike those contexts, in which the grumbling was directed against Yahweh, the Israelites now have just cause to be upset. The use of such a strong term here suggests an attitude of anger bordering on rebellion. It is astounding how a failure to ask direction from Yahweh (see 9:14) can cause so much disruption and hostility among God's people. Interestingly, Joshua is not mentioned in this section of the story. Certainly he is as culpable as the other leaders for the failure to inquire of Yahweh. Perhaps the lack of reference to Joshua says something about the legitimacy of the people's murmuring. They were not directing it towards Yahweh; nor were they singling out Joshua, Yahweh's appointed leader. They were legitimately outraged at the failure of their leaders.

What to do with the Gibeonites?

The leaders handle the situation sensibly, however. In verse 19, they verbalize what the narrator has already shared with us in verse 18: they have ratified the treaty by swearing by Yahweh, the God of Israel. The reference to 'Yahweh, the God of Israel' calls to mind his faithfulness in keeping his covenant with his people. Breaking an oath made in Yahweh's name would amount to profaning or polluting his reputation (Leviticus 19:12). The leaders of Israel recognized that a violation of the oath would incur Yahweh's wrath (v. 20). They were right. During the monarchy (period of the kings), Israel faced a three-year famine as the consequence for King Saul's violation of this very oath (2 Samuel 21:1–2).

But the leaders still have another dilemma. What will they do with the Gibeonites and the residents of the other Hivite cities with whom they have made a peace treaty? Once again, the leaders find a biblical solution. Their decision to make these people wood cutters and water carriers finds its precedent in Deuteronomy 29:11—a statement linking these occupations with the 'aliens who are in your camp'.

Joshua's interrogation

Joshua's interrogation of the Gibeonites uncovers the motive for their ruse (vv. 22–25). As it turns out, they had heard about Yahweh's promise to Moses to give Israel the land, and so they were terrified. They tricked Israel into a treaty because they feared for their lives. The narrator's report in verse 26 is ironic. Rather than saving the Israelites from the Gibeonites, Joshua—whose name means 'Yahweh is salvation'—saved the Gibeonites from the Israelites! Still, even in the wake of Israel's failure, the Gibeonites certainly experience Yahweh's grace and end up with a future serving Israel ('for the congregation', v. 27) as well as Israel's God, Yahweh ('for the altar of Yahweh', v. 27).

PRAYER

Lord God, I call upon you because you are worthy of praise.
You are a God who has saved me from my enemies. Help me
not to forget to seek your face when I face decisions,
challenges and opportunities. Amen.

20   JOSHUA 10:1–15

The MOST AMAZING DAY

In Joshua 10, the narrator describes Israel's conquest of southern Canaan. The first section, verses 1–15, describes Israel's victory over the Amorites who attacked Gibeon. In the narrator's opinion, it was the most amazing day that Israel had ever experienced (v. 14).

Five kings attack Gibeon

The narrative begins by describing the fear of King Adoni-zedek of Jerusalem (vv. 1–2). Basically, he feared the alliance between Israel and Gibeon, a large city full of mighty warriors. So he called on four other kings of Amorite city-states south-west of Jerusalem to attack Gibeon (vv. 3–5).

Slaughter by hailstones

On the basis of its recent peace treaty with Israel, Gibeon called upon Joshua for help in fighting off the Amorite kings (v. 6). Joshua responded with Yahweh's assurance of victory, and inflicted a 'great slaughter on them' (vv. 7–10). Once again, Yahweh won the victory for Israel. First, he threw the enemy into a panic when Israel suddenly arrived (vv. 9–10). Then, when the Amorites fled, Yahweh hurled down hailstones on them (v. 11). The narrator even notes that more enemy soldiers died from the hailstones than from Israelite swords.

Sun and moon stand still

At the end of the account, the narrator reveals something astounding that had taken place on the day of the battle (v. 12). It turns out that Joshua had addressed Yahweh in the sight of the people. The NRSV nicely captures Joshua's six-word 'prayer' (in Hebrew) in two lines of poetry at the end of verse 12. Joshua's request was granted. According to verse 13, the sun stood still and the moon stopped until Israel took vengeance on the enemy. The narrator adds two important clauses in verse 13. The first mentions that this event is described in the 'Book of Jashar'—an extra-biblical work which has not survived. Based on the two references to this book in the Old Testament (the other is 2 Samuel 1:17–18), the book must have contained songs or poems commemorating events in Israel. The final clause in verse 13 describes the sun as stopping in the middle of the sky and not going down for about a whole day.

This raises the question, what actually happened? In what way did the sun and moon stand still? The traditional interpretation is that Yahweh performed a miracle. The sun and moon stopped where they were in the sky until the battle ended. In other words, the earth stopped or slowed its rotation to provide additional daylight. Other variations of this interpretation offer non-miraculous explanations: the sun stopped shining either because of a solar eclipse or because of the cloud cover related to the hailstorm. Another possible interpretation takes its cue from Habakkuk 3:10–11 and reads verses 12–13 as a poetic, figurative expression of the battle described earlier in the chapter. In this case, Yahweh's victory would be so overwhelming that the sun and moon would stand still in awe. To suggest this view is not to deny Yahweh's miraculous power—unless one also denies the crossing of the Jordan (Joshua 3) or the fall of Jericho's walls (Joshua 6). Yahweh has already miraculously cast down nation-specific hailstones (v. 11).

Yahweh 'obeys' Joshua

For the narrator, the most outstanding feature of this day is not the sun and moon standing still. According to verse 14, this has been the most amazing day in Israel's history because Yahweh 'heeded [obeyed] a human voice'. The language here—literally 'when Yahweh listened to the voice of a man'—employs a technical expression in the Old Testament which refers to obedience. For example, when the Old Testament uses this wording to describe how Yahweh's people should respond to him, it is translated as 'obey my voice' (for example, see Exodus 19:5; Deuteronomy 9:23, 13:4). The end of verse 14 explains that Yahweh 'obeyed' Joshua by fighting for Israel.

This story captures the wonder of prayer. How incredible that Yahweh, the sovereign God of the universe, responds to the prayer of his people!

MEDITATION

The prayer of the righteous is powerful and effective.

James 5:16

The FATE of the FIVE KINGS

While the Israelites inflicted a great slaughter on the Amorites, the five Amorite kings fled and hid themselves in the cave at Makkedah (v. 16). When Joshua heard about this (v. 17), he took steps to seize the kings. In a 'holy war' designed to purify the land of evil, the mission was certainly not accomplished until the leaders had been destroyed as well as the army.

A successful pursuit

Joshua's instructions in verses 18–19 contain language that reflects the previous battle (10:9–15). Yahweh had destroyed Amorite troops with hailstones described as 'huge stones' (Hebrew *abanim gedoloth*). Now, Joshua uses the exact same Hebrew expression when he commands his warriors to roll 'large stones' (*abanim gedoloth*) against the mouth of the cave (v. 18). Furthermore, when Joshua says, 'Do not stay there' (v. 19), he uses the same Hebrew verb, *amad*, that appears in Yahweh's assurance that 'not one of them shall stand [*amad*] before you' (10:8). This verb appeared as well as in 10:13, in the report that 'the moon stopped [*amad*]'. In addition, the command, 'Do not let them enter their towns' in verse 19 employs the Hebrew verb *bo*, which appeared in the statement in 10:14 that the sun did not hurry 'to set'. These linguistic connections tie the two accounts together. Joshua's concern to prevent the enemies from entering their towns reflects the difficulty of destroying them once they got inside a fortified city with its stone walls, guard towers, and gate system.

Verses 20–21 describe the success of this operation. The Israelites did inflict a great slaughter and returned safely, although some Amorites survived and entered the fortified towns. The crowning detail, though, appears at the end of verse 21: 'No one dared to speak against any of the Israelites.' Literally, the expression reads, 'And no one sharpened his tongue against any of the sons of Israel.' To sharpen one's tongue is to offer criticism. The mission was so successful that no Israelites offered criticism of their leaders (as they did in 9:18), and no Canaanites or Amorites offered words of threat or opposition. Conditions in southern Canaan were ripe for peaceful settlement!

The execution of the five kings

In verse 22, the focus returns to the five kings. Joshua issues orders for the kings to brought from the cave, and the Israelites obey. Throughout this account, modern readers may find the repetition of details tedious, as the narrator repeats the language of the command when he describes Israel's obedience of it (see vv. 22–24). However, this emphasizes Israel's commitment to do exactly what Joshua commanded them to do.

Joshua has arranged the events of the execution to make a statement. Instructing the Israelite military leaders to put their feet on the necks of the Amorite kings served as an image of victory (v. 24). Likewise, hanging them on five trees provided intimidation and served notice that Israel had triumphed over the Amorites (v. 26). While brutal, this action was carried out according to the law of Moses—including the removal of the bodies before sunset (Deuteronomy 21:22–23; see also Joshua 8:29). The story that began with the five Amorite kings hidden in the cave of Makkedah ends with these same kings hidden in the same cave (v. 27). But this time, the cave turns out to be a burial chamber, not a place of refuge. Once again, large stones seal them inside, never to be removed.

The key to understanding this account is Joshua's command in verse 25. Echoing the instructions he received from Yahweh months before (see 1:6–7, 18) and even days before (see 8:1), Joshua calls the people to exhibit courageous strength rather than fear or dismay. The reason is that the act of standing on the kings' necks pictures what Yahweh will do to Israel's enemies. The present episode encourages God's people that Yahweh is a warrior who fights for his people, destroying the evil that threatens their peace.

MEDITATION

But the Lord is with me like a dread warrior; therefore my persecutors will stumble, and they will not prevail. They will be greatly shamed, for they will not succeed. Their eternal dishonour will never be forgotten.

Jeremiah 20:11

22   JOSHUA 10:28–43

The CONQUEST of the SOUTH

This section completes the account of Israel's conquest of southern Canaan. It also marks a shift from detailed descriptions of victories, like those at Jericho, Ai, and Gibeon, to brief, fast-paced summaries. Specifically, this section reports the conquest of seven towns: Makkedah (v. 28), Libnah (vv. 29–30), Lachish (vv. 31–32), Gezer (v. 33), Eglon (vv. 34–35), Hebron (vv. 36–37), and Debir (vv. 38–39). Then, the narrator closes with a summary (vv. 40–43).

The conquest of seven cities

The brief reports of the conquest of seven southern cities (vv. 28–39) each follow a similar pattern, yet they are not identical to each other. A few details deserve comment. First, later accounts in Joshua reveal that Israel conquered additional southern cities (see 12:13–15), so the number of the towns in this account—seven in all—seems deliberate and suggests completeness. Second, the variation of language and details in each account suggests that Israel perhaps used different tactics in each victory. For example, only two accounts mention the use of siege warfare (Lachish and Eglon). Five accounts specifically mention the destruction of the city's king (Makkedah, Libnah, Gezer, Hebron and Debir). In fact, some Bible scholars suggest that the variation in details verifies the authenticity of the accounts. Using the exact same formulae might have suggested fictitious accounts. Third, the account about Gezer (the fourth and middle one in the list) differs significantly from the others. Israel took the offensive against the other six cities, but Gezer took the initiative against Israel by coming to help Lachish (v. 33).

Summary of victory

The summary of Israel's conquest of southern Canaan is quite thorough (vv. 40–43). First, the narrator describes the conquest using geographical terms (v. 40). Next, he summarizes it by using political terms—that is, place names (v. 41). Finally, he describes the conquest by using a time reference: Joshua took these kings and lands 'at one time' (v. 42). The point is that these victories happened as part of one campaign. Joshua's return with all Israel to the camp at Gilgal signals the close of this campaign in the south (v. 43). The concern of the narrator has been to provide the 'big picture' of Israel's success in the south. Certainly, he does not intend to imply that every last person or city was conquered (see 10:20, for example). Even in modern times, the conquest of a nation or region does not mean that every pocket of resistance has been subdued. The point is that Israel has taken control over southern Canaan, making it ready for settlement.

What about 'holy war' today?

As noted in the Introduction (pp. 16–17), 'holy war' in the Old Testament was rooted in Yahweh's aversion to evil. He used Israel as an instrument of judgment against nations whose evil had reached its full measure and whose false worship posed a threat to Israel.

But how should Christians today apply 'holy war' passages like this one to their lives? After all, the New Testament makes it clear that the Old Testament—including its stories—can still teach followers of Jesus how to believe and live (2 Timothy 3:16–17; 1 Corinthians 10:11). The starting point is the New Testament's insistence that the provisions in the law of Moses are shadows of what is to come, and the reality is found in Jesus Christ (Colossians 2:17; Hebrews 10:1). So how has 'holy war' been brought to its real expression in Jesus Christ? In the New Testament, God's people wage holy war against the forces of evil by demolishing false ideas about Jesus Christ (2 Corinthians 10:3–5) and by standing firm against evil schemes through the resources God has provided—truth, righteousness, peace, faith, salvation, scripture and prayer (Ephesians 6:10–18).

MEDITATION

For our struggle is not against enemies of blood and flesh, but...
against the spiritual forces of evil in the heavenly places.

Ephesians 6:12

The WAR with the NORTH

In chapter 11, the focus shifts from the south to the north. When the Israelites crossed the Jordan River and moved into Canaan, they conquered cities, Jericho and Ai, which were located in the geographic centre of the land from north to south. Then, they conquered the land in southern Canaan (ch. 10). Now, chapter 11 describes Israel's conquest of northern Canaan.

Aggression by the king of Hazor

Verse 1 begins with the same wording that begins the previous narrative in 10:1 (see also 5:1). The formula used in both places is: 'Now it came about that when X, king of X, heard…' This signals another attempt by a king of a Canaanite city-state to gather allies and attack the Israelites. This time, the leader is King Jabin of Hazor, the leading city in northern Canaan at the time (see v. 10). Hazor, a name meaning 'settlement' or 'village', was mentioned in 19th century BC Egyptian texts, in 18th century texts from the Old Babylonian city of Mari, and also in the 14th century BC Amarna letters—correspondence found in Amarna, Egypt, between Egyptian pharaohs and the rulers of city-states in Canaan.

The cities and regions mentioned in verses 1–3 are all located in northern Canaan. The name 'Chinneroth' (v. 2) is a reference either to the Sea of Galilee or to a city located on its north-western shore. The meaning of 'Naphoth-Dor' is unknown, but it certainly relates to the town of Dor on the Mediterranean coast.

This northern coalition sent an army against Israel which put Israel in the most impossible situation it had yet faced in the conquest of the land (vv. 4–5). First, the northern coalition held a definite numerical advantage, with the number of their troops resembling the sand on the seashore. Second, they held an overwhelming technological advantage, with horses and chariots.

Exact obedience

Once again, Yahweh commands Joshua not to fear and then promises victory over the enemy. Yahweh also instructs Joshua to 'hamstring their horses, and burn their chariots with fire' (v. 6). This would prevent the use of these resources in the future. Why did Israel lack horses and chariots? Earlier, Yahweh had commanded Israel not to multiply horses but instead to depend on his power for deliverance (Deuteronomy 17:16; 20:1).

Joshua responded by leading a sudden attack on the northern coalition by the waters of Merom—located north-west of the Sea of Galilee and west of Hazor. The expression 'fell upon' at the end of verse 7 indicates success. Then, verse 8 credits the success to Yahweh who 'handed them over to Israel'. The mention of specific place names in verse 8, as well as the narrator's summary at the end of the verse, confirms the completeness of Israel's victory. They invaded all the territory ruled by the northern kings and struck down the fleeing warriors. Verse 9 emphasizes Joshua's obedience to Yahweh's command. The initial statement to this effect is confirmed by the word-for-word repetition of the command (v. 6) in verse 9's report of its fulfilment.

In verses 10–15, the northern campaign draws to a successful conclusion. First, the narrator provides a brief account of Joshua's destruction of Hazor. Then, he stops the action (as is apparent from the grammatical constructions he uses) and provides further details about the destruction of the other towns. Why did Israel burn Hazor but not the other northern cities? By burning the most prominent city in the region (v. 10), Israel was making a vivid statement about the fate of those who tried to resist Israel's occupation of the land. Once again, the narrator's concern is to stress Joshua's complete obedience to Yahweh's commands through Moses. Verse 15 emphasizes Joshua's obedience with a pair of opposite statements: 'Joshua did' and 'he left nothing undone' (v. 15). Moses was the great 'law-giver' in Israel. Joshua appears here as the great 'law-keeper'.

MEDITATION

Read Deuteronomy 26:16–19 and 28:58–68 to appreciate the sense of urgency that surrounds obedience to Yahweh's commands. Obedience would bring overwhelming blessing, while disobedience would bring overwhelming affliction.

The CONQUEST COMPLETED

This section serves as a narrative conclusion to the first half of the book of Joshua. All the major battles have taken place, and Israel has conquered the land of Canaan. The narrator focuses on Joshua, the human hero, and on Yahweh, the hero ultimately responsible for Israel's victories.

Joshua takes the land

The account begins with a summary statement that 'Joshua took all the land'. Grammatically, the remainder of verses 16–20 provides background information that elaborates on this statement. To begin with, verses 16–17 describe the conquered territory. The southern region is described by references to the hill country (south of Jerusalem), to the Negeb (the desert region south of the hill country), to the land of Goshen (a region between the hill country and the Negeb which was named after the region of Goshen in Egypt), to the lowland (the foothills between the Mediterranean coast and the hills of Judah), to the Arabah (the Jordan River plain), and to Mount Halak (a smooth, bald mountain located somewhere south of the Dead Sea on the border of Seir or Edom). The reference to Mount Halak in the south is balanced by the reference to Baal-gad at the foot of Mount Hermon in the north. These details, tedious as they are to read, inform us that Joshua conquered land from about 40 miles north of the Sea of Galilee to about 5–40 miles south of the Dead Sea (depending on the exact location of Mount Halak).

Next, verse 18 reminds us that Joshua's conquest took a 'long time'—literally 'many days'. Verse 19 notes that with the exception of the Hivites who lived in Gibeon (see Joshua 9), no other peace treaties were made. Rather, all the towns were taken.

Yahweh the hardener of hearts

In verse 20, the narrator shares the reason for Joshua's success in taking all the land from the Canaanites. The Hebrew text literally reads, 'because it was from Yahweh to harden their hearts'. Just as he did to Pharaoh (Exodus 4—14), Yahweh is hardening the hearts of people who show stubborn resistance to himself and his people.

Yahweh's capacity to show mercy to the nations has been established by Israel's response to Rahab. The point, then, is that Yahweh is not hardening the hearts of innocent people. He is simply strengthening and accelerating their resolve to show evil resistance.

Wiping out the Anakim

The action resumes in verse 21 with a report that Joshua wiped out (literally, 'cut off') the Anakim from the hill country. Survivors remained only in the coastal cities of Gaza, Gath and Ashdod—cities eventually occupied by the Philistines (v. 22). What an appropriate way to close the conquest narrative. The Anakim (from the Hebrew term *anak*, 'long-necked') were a race of gigantic warriors. They were the cause of the original spies' fear (see Numbers 13:21–33). This fear led to disobedience, specifically fear and complaining, which resulted in forty years of wandering in the wilderness (Numbers 14). By the end of the conquest, however, Israel has come full circle in its approach to the Anakim. Rather than being a people to be feared, the Anakim have become one more defeated enemy. Now the land has rest from war (v. 23).

The New Testament implies, however, that Joshua did not provide the people of Israel with complete rest (Hebrews 4:8–9). A greater measure of rest is available in partnership with Jesus Christ (see Matthew 11:28; Hebrews 3:1—4:11). This rest is a life of satisfaction and enjoyment of God's gifts. While God's rest comes as a gift, Joshua 11:16–23 reminds us that experiencing God's gift of rest requires obedient participation on the part of his people.

PRAYER

Father, I come to you weary and burdened.
Please let me find true rest in you.

25

An ITEMIZED LIST of VICTORIES

At first glance, Joshua 12 looks like one of the most boring chapters in the Bible. It is more likely to elicit a yawn from a reader than to trigger a sense of excitement. When understood properly, however, Joshua 12 is exciting. It provides an itemized list of the victories whose stories were told in Joshua 1—11. It resembles a score summary in a newspaper, accompanying a story about a victory by a cricket or soccer team.

Defeated kings east of the Jordan River

The chapter breaks down into two sections: a list of defeated kings east of the Jordan River (vv. 1–6), and a list of defeated kings west of the Jordan River (vv. 7–24). The first section highlights the leadership of Moses, while the second highlights the leadership of Joshua.

In the first section, verses 1–6, the narrator lists the victories over the two kings who controlled the east-Jordan region: King Sihon of the Amorites and King Og of Bashan. Verse 1 establishes the general boundaries of the land that Israel took from these kings. Obviously, the Jordan River forms the western border. The Wadi Arnon, which runs from east to west into the Dead Sea, marks the region's southern border. The term 'wadi' refers to a river bed which is dry during parts of the year. Mount Hermon, about forty miles north of the Sea of Galilee, constitutes the northern border. Verses 2–5 provide considerable geographic details about land controlled by King Sihon to the south and King Og to the north.

Both kings were defeated under Moses' leadership of Israel. The defeat of Sihon is described in Numbers 21:21–32 (see also Deuteronomy 2:24–37). *En route* to the promised land of Canaan, Israel requested permission from King Sihon of the Amorites to pass through his territory. Israel had promised to stay on the King's Highway and not to take any produce or water from the fields, vineyards or wells. However, Sihon did not grant permission. In fact, he attacked Israel while they were in the wilderness. But Israel destroyed him and took possession of his land. The defeat of Og is described in Numbers 21:33–35 (see also Deuteronomy 3:1–11). He, too, tried to fight Israel when they attempted to pass through his territory. But

Yahweh gave him into Moses' hands. As a result, there were no survivors left, and Israel took possession of his land too.

Verse 6 concludes the first section with the summary report that Moses, the servant of Yahweh, and Israel defeated these kings. Furthermore, Moses gave this conquered land east of the Jordan to two and half tribes: Reuben, Gad and the half-tribe of Manasseh. This summary once again highlights the obedience of Moses and the people. Obedience to Yahweh brings blessing and success.

Defeated kings west of the Jordan River

Now, the focus in verses 7–23 shifts to the kings whom Joshua defeated on the west side of the Jordan. After detailing the geographic boundaries of the land of Canaan, the narrator provides a list of 31 kings defeated by Israel. Readers will recognize the names of cities whose stories of defeat have already been told, including Jericho, Ai, Lachish, Gezer, Hazor and so on. However, about half of the cities have not been mentioned previously in the book of Joshua—cities such as Geder, Hormah, Arad, Adullam, Lasharon, Taanach and Megiddo. This reminds us that the narrator's intent was not simply to preserve a historical summary of each battle. Rather, the narrator purposefully selected stories of certain battles to communicate a prophetic message to a later generation of Yahweh's people.

A list of thanks

What can God's people today learn from Joshua 12? This chapter sets a precedent for producing an itemized list of God's blessings at major points in our journey of faith. This is the essence of 'giving thanks'. In Psalm 105, for example, the psalmist calls Yahweh's people to give thanks to him. The remainder of the psalm provides a specific listing of what Yahweh had done for his people. Thanksgiving fails when we settle for generic expressions like, 'Thank you, Lord, for all your blessings.' Instead, in the words of an old hymn, the challenge is: 'Count your blessings, name them one by one. And it will surprise you what the Lord has done.'

MEDITATION

Take a few minutes and identify specific ways which God has blessed your life. How has he kept his promises to you? How has he provided for your needs? Write down a specific list.

26 JOSHUA 13:1-7

From CONQUERING *to* DIVIDING *the* PROMISED LAND

The narrator's report about Joshua's old age in verse 1 marks the transition to a second major section of the book. Readers will notice several differences between the first section (chs. 1—12) and the second section (chs. 13—24). In terms of *theme* or subject matter, the focus shifts from the conquest of the land to the distribution of the land. As far as *literary style* is concerned, the narrator switches from telling stories to providing lists and legal descriptions.

Admittedly, readers often find this section of Joshua boring or at least laborious to read. However, readers should view this material like a will or a title deed to a piece of property. While such documents do not employ an exciting style, the contents provide assurance, joy and even excitement. Like a will or title deed, chapters 13—24 verify Israel's possession of the land.

An urgent situation

Joshua 13:1-7 consists mainly of Yahweh's command to Joshua to divide the land. Yahweh's speech begins with an observation about Joshua's old age (v. 1b). Yahweh then follows this observation with a second observation: 'very much of the land still remains to be possessed' (v. 1c). Coupled with the two statements about Joshua's old age—the narrator's (v. 1a) and Yahweh's (v. 1b)—this second observation raises tension and creates a sense of urgency. How will the people of Israel gain possession of the unconquered portions of land, especially since their leader has grown old?

The description of the unconquered land in verses 2–6a creates even more tension. There is still an overwhelming amount of territory remaining to be possessed. Yahweh gives a specific description of unconquered territory, beginning in the south and moving northward. The first region, described in verses 2–3, consisted of lands to the south under the control of the Philistines and the Geshurites (v. 2). The Philistines had settled in five cities along the Mediterranean coast of southern Canaan (v. 3; see Judges 3:3). The Geshurites were inhabitants of the wilderness that ran south of the Philistine cities to the border of Egypt. A second key region, described in verse 4, consisted of land in the north-west along the Phoenician coast. Finally, the third key region, described in verses 5–6a, consisted of land in the north-eastern hill country of Lebanon.

Yahweh's solution

The 'crisis' created by Joshua's old age and the unconquered land is solved by Yahweh's promise in verse 6b: 'I will myself drive them out from before the Israelites.' The NRSV's translation—'I... myself'—nicely captures Yahweh's emphasis. Hebrew verbs are inflected to indicate the subject—'I', 'she', 'you', and so on—but Yahweh adds an additional pronoun for emphasis. So the Hebrew text literally reads: 'I, I will drive them out.' Yahweh, then, has taken upon himself the responsibility for completing the conquest.

Yahweh's lengthy speech to Joshua arrives at its point in verses 6b–7. Yahweh wants Joshua to distribute the land. The importance of this command is reflected by several features. First, it is preceded by the term 'only', which limits what Joshua is to do. Second, the command is stated in verse 6b and then restated in verse 7. Third, Yahweh's initial statement ends with the words 'as I have commanded you' (v. 6b). Finally, the term 'Now' (literally, 'And now') at the beginning of verse 7 commands attention. Yahweh will take care of further conquest. Joshua must divide the land among the remaining tribes of Israel. Two and a half tribes had already received their inheritance east of the Jordan River. The time has come for the tribes west of the Jordan to receive their portion. This section reminds us that the God who makes promises is also the God who provides.

MEDITATION

Father, I ask you to provide for people who have no land. I pray for peace and healing for all caught in the crossfire of those fighting today for control of the promised land.

The EAST-JORDAN TERRITORIES

After recording Yahweh's speech to Joshua (13:1–7), the narrator reports Moses' prior act of giving an inheritance to the two and a half tribes who settled east of the Jordan River (13:8–33). Verses 8–14 function as an introduction to this report. Bible scholars have noted that the transition from the end of Yahweh's speech (13:7) to the reference to the two and a half tribes in verse 8 is rather abrupt grammatically. The narrator seems eager to link what Joshua is about to do for the remaining nine and a half tribes to what Moses did previously for the two and a half tribes who now occupy the territory east of the Jordan River. These tribes consist of the half-tribe of Manasseh, the Reubenites, and the Gadites.

Describing the east-Jordan territory

In verses 9–12, the narrator provides a specific, verifiable description of the boundaries of the east-Jordan territory by citing geographical features (such as the Wadi Arnon, the tableland, and Mount Hermon), specific cities (such as Aroer and the cities of King Sihon), and ethnic regions (such as the regions of the Geshurites and Maacathites and the kingdom of Og). The Arnon River served as the southern border, while the region of Bashan and Mount Hermon provided the northern border. The Jordan River obviously served as the western border, and the territory extended east as far as the desert, including the mountain region of Gilead. The region of Gilead extended from the north end of the Dead Sea to Bashan in the north. Stretching about 60 miles long and 20 miles wide, the region was fertile, with trees and crops flourishing on its western slopes. The region also produced spices, balm and myrrh (see Genesis 37:25; Jeremiah 8:22; 46:11).

Alert readers will notice the narrator's allusion to Israel's past victories over King Sihon of the Amorites and King Og of Bashan. As noted previously in the commentary on Joshua 12:1–24 (pp. 68–69), both kings were defeated under Moses' leadership when Israel attempted to pass through their lands.

A hint of failure?

Verse 13 contrasts the fact that Moses defeated and drove out the inhabitants of the east-Jordan territory (v. 12) with an observation that 'the Israelites did not drive out the Geshurites or the Maacathites'. What should we make of this observation? Does it serve as a reminder that Israel did not fully obey Yahweh's command to drive out the people-groups in the land of Canaan? Or, since the Geshurites and Maacathites were not specifically listed among the people-groups to be driven out of the land (Deuteronomy 7:1–4; 20:16–18), should we refrain from blaming Israel for this? The scope of Yahweh's commands to Israel in Deuteronomy 20:16–17 ('You must not let anything that breathes remain alive' and 'You shall annihilate them') suggests that the list of nations to be destroyed was representative, not exhaustive. The Geshurites and Maacathites do not seem to qualify as 'towns that are very far from you' which could be offered a peace treaty (Deuteronomy 20:15). Thus, verse 13 reflects a failure by Israel to drive out these people from their midst.

No inheritance for the tribe of Levi

Verse 14 brings the introduction to a close by reminding the reader that the tribe of Levi did not receive a land-grant. Rather, this tribe's inheritance consisted of 'the offerings by fire to the Lord God of Israel' (v. 14). Later in the chapter, the narrator describes the Levites' inheritance as Yahweh himself (13:33; see Deuteronomy 10:9; 18:2). The Levites had the privilege of standing and serving the people in Yahweh's name (Deuteronomy 18:5). Instead of receiving a portion of land from which they could make a living, the Levites would receive wages in the form of produce or meat which Israel brought to sacrifice to Yahweh (Numbers 18:20–24).

Whether through a land-grant or through 'wages' from the sacrificial offerings, Yahweh graciously provided what his people needed to make a living.

MEDITATION

My flesh and my heart may fail, but God is the strength of my heart and my portion for ever.

Psalm 73:26

28 JOSHUA 13:15–33

The EAST-JORDAN INHERITANCES

The narrator now describes in detail the inheritances given to the Reubenites (vv. 15–23), to the Gadites (vv. 24–28), and to the half-tribe of Manasseh (vv. 29–31). Each of the three sections begins with the same introductory formula: 'Moses gave an inheritance to the tribe of the X, according to their families' (vv. 15, 24, 29; the term 'clans' in v. 15 translates the same Hebrew word rendered 'families in vv. 24 and 29). A fourth section summarizes the east-Jordan distribution, mentioning again the unique circumstances surrounding the tribe of Levi (vv. 32–34).

The amount of detail seems overwhelming to most readers. Once again, we must remember that we are reading material that resembles legal property descriptions, not simple mailing addresses. The specifics confirm that the tribes of Israel received actual gifts of land, not just vague claims to territory.

The inheritance of Reuben

The description of Reubenite territory (vv. 15–23) locates this tribe in the region east of the northern half of the Dead Sea. It is the furthest south of the east-Jordan tribes. Most of the towns mentioned lie on a line between the towns of Aroer to the south and Heshbon to the north. This is the fertile 'tableland' which forms the eastern border of Reuben's inheritance. The Jordan River forms the border to the west (v. 23). The mention of cities like Bamoth-baal (literally, 'the heights of Baal') and Beth-baal-meon (literally, 'the house of Baal-meon') reflect Yahweh's power over the gods and goddesses of Canaan.

The narrator's allusion to Balaam provides another reminder of Yahweh's power over Canaanite deities. Balaam son of Beor was the infamous pagan diviner (v. 22). He had been hired by the Moabite king Balak to curse the Israelites, but every time Balaam opened his mouth to curse Israel, he uttered words of blessing (see Numbers 22—24). Eventually, though, he counselled Moabite women to seduce the Israelite men into sexual immorality (Numbers 25:1–9; 31:16). Balaam was later killed by the Israelites in their battle against the Midianites (Numbers 31:8).

The inheritance of the Gadites

The description of Gadite territory (vv. 24–28) locates this tribe in the region just north of the Reubenites. Generally, the cities listed in verse 25 establish the eastern border, and the cities listed in verse 27 establish the western border along the Jordan River as far north as 'the lower end of the Sea of Chinnereth' (that is, the Sea of Galilee). The listing of cities in verse 26 moves from south to north. The towns apparently refer to fortified, walled cities, while the villages refer to the unwalled settlements in the outlying areas (v. 28).

The inheritance of Manasseh

The description of the territory allotted to the half-tribe of Manasseh locates it to the north of the Gadites, east of the Sea of Galilee. The reason for the designation 'half-tribe' stems from the decision by half of the tribe of Manasseh to join Reuben and Gad in settling east of the Jordan River (see Numbers 32:33–42; 34:13–15). The other half of Manasseh stayed with the other nine tribes who would inhabit the land west of the Jordan River.

Yahweh: the people's portion for ever

The account of land-grants to the tribes who decided to settle east of the Jordan closes with a note about the tribe of Levi. In the introduction to this account, the narrator described the Levites' inheritance as the offerings that the other Israelites brought to Yahweh (13:14). Now, however, the inheritance of the Levites is described as 'the Lord God of Israel'—Yahweh himself (v. 33). While the land was a wonderful gift, the greatest treasure of all was the giver of the land, Yahweh (see Psalm 16:5–6). Even more amazing is the fact that Yahweh's portion or inheritance is his people (Deuteronomy 32:9). Intimacy with God, then, is the believer's greatest provision, strength, and joy in life.

PRAYER

I cry to you, O Lord; I say, 'You are my refuge, my portion
in the land of the living.'

Psalm 142:5

The WEST-JORDAN INHERITANCES

This paragraph introduces the land-grant descriptions in chapters 14—19. Now that the distribution of land to the two and a half tribes living east of the Jordan River has been reviewed (see 13:8–33), the narrator turns his attention to the division of land to the nine and a half tribes who would settle west of the Jordan (see 13:7). Much of the material in chapters 14—19 consists of legal property descriptions. However, the narrator weaves in four stories or 'land-grant narratives' which emphasize Israel's zeal in taking possession of the land. These stories recall the efforts of Caleb (14:6–15), Achsah (15:18–19), the daughters of Zelophehad (17:3–6), and the tribe of Joseph (17:14–18).

While the introductory paragraph (vv. 1–5) contains some details which are repetitious, persistent readers will discover three significant themes: Eleazar's role in the distribution of land; the role of casting lots; and the role of obedience.

The role of Eleazar

Eleazar the priest appears for the first time in the book of Joshua here in verse 1. Eleazar was a son of Aaron (see Exodus 6:23, 25) who eventually succeeded his father as Israel's high priest (see Numbers 20:25–28). His involvement in the distribution process signifies that the land distribution was a 'spiritual matter' tied deeply to Israel's relationship with Yahweh.

The role of casting lots

Eleazar's involvement was necessary because the distribution happened by the casting of lots. The narrator makes it clear that Yahweh had commanded this means of distributing the land (v. 2). This should not surprise us, since Yahweh had previously commanded lot-casting for the selection of the goats used on the Day of Atonement (Leviticus 16:8–10). While lot-casting may seem to be 'decision by chance', Proverbs 16:33 observes that the outcome of lot-casting rests with Yahweh. Even Jesus' disciples used lot-casting to determine God's choice to take the place of Judas Iscariot among the twelve apostles (Acts 1:24–26). However, the practice of casting lots to determine God's will appears nowhere else in Acts or in the remainder of the New Testament. Apparently, the coming of the Holy Spirit made the practice unnecessary since the Spirit himself provided guidance (see Acts 8:29; 11:12; 13:2; 15:28; 16:6).

Anyway, the point of lot-casting in the distribution of land was to keep the process under Yahweh's control. In Egypt, the Pharoah or the temples held title to all the land (see, for example, Genesis 47:20–26). In the Canaanite city-state system, the kings or rulers of cities controlled much of the land. But now, Yahweh is gifting the land to the people themselves—tribes, and families within these tribes. No person or class seems to have special privileges—apparently not even Joshua (see 19:49–50).

The narrator provides a couple of details to explain how the tribes numbered twelve (vv. 3–4). The number twelve comes, of course, from the twelve sons of Abraham. The descendants of Joseph, however, split into two tribes named after Joseph's two sons, Manasseh and Ephraim. This brought the total to thirteen tribes, but the fact that the Levites were not given a land-grant kept the number at twelve for the purposes of land-distribution. So where did the Levites live? They were given towns and pasture land within the various tribes (v. 4; see Joshua 21).

The role of obedience

Verses 1–5 also stress the role of obedience. The expression 'as the Lord commanded Moses' appears twice (vv. 2, 5). Yahweh has specified a process which will keep the land-distribution process free from corruption. Israel's obedience assures a successful process of dividing the land among the tribes. Such obedience is always in the best interests of God's people (see Deuteronomy 5:33).

MEDITATION

You must follow exactly the path that the Lord your God has commanded you, so that you may live, and that it may go well with you, and that you may live long in the land that you are to possess.

Deuteronomy 5:33

CALEB'S COURAGEOUS REQUEST

The distribution of land to the tribes settling west of the Jordan River begins with the tribe of Judah. The account of Judah's inheritance runs from 14:6 to 15:63. A 'land-grant narrative' featuring Caleb stands at the beginning of this account (vv. 6–15). As noted previously (see commentary on 14:1–5, pp. 76–77), four 'land-grant narratives' appear amid the legal descriptions in chapters 14—19 to emphasize Israel's zeal in taking possession of the land. The Caleb narrative consists of two sections: Caleb's speech (vv. 6–12) and Joshua's response (vv. 13–15).

Caleb's speech to Joshua

In verse 6, Caleb begins his speech by describing an event recorded in Numbers 13—14. The event involved Caleb and Joshua, the man before whom Caleb is now making his request. Readers may wonder why Caleb goes over details which, by his own admission, Joshua knows intimately (v. 6). The key is that Caleb is making a formal request to Israel's leader. He appeals to something that Yahweh had said to Moses about Caleb and Joshua.

Caleb and Joshua were two of the twelve spies (one from each tribe) who had been sent by Moses from Kadesh-barnea to spy out the promised land of Canaan 45 years earlier (see v. 10). Caleb claims, 'I brought him an honest report' (v. 7). Literally, the Hebrew text of his claim reads, 'I brought him a word just as it was in my heart.' This signals Caleb's truthfulness. By contrast, Caleb claims that his companions, with the exception of Joshua, 'made the heart of the people melt' (v. 8). Then, he follows this with one more assertion of his integrity: 'Yet I wholeheartedly followed the Lord my God.' According to Numbers 13:30, Caleb had quietened the people who were apparently upset by the report of giants in the land and said, 'Let us go up at once and occupy it, for we are well able to overcome it.' In verse 9, Caleb recalls the promise that Moses had made to him about receiving an inheritance in the land (see Numbers 14:24; Deuteronomy 1:36).

In verse 10, Caleb's words 'And now' signal a turn in his attention from the past to the present. Caleb is now 85 years old. He was forty when he spied out the land (v. 7), and 45 years have elapsed since then (v. 10). Yet he insists that he is just as strong for fighting and travelling as he was then (v. 11). This brings Caleb to his request, which he introduces with the expression, 'So now' (v. 12). His request is, 'Give me this hill country of which the Lord spoke on that day.' Armed with Yahweh's presence, Caleb intends to drive out the Anakim—the leftover giant warriors. According to 11:21–22, Joshua had driven out the Anakim from the hill country. Survivors remained only in three cities on the Mediterranean coast—Gaza, Gath and Ashdod. Presumably, some of these survivors migrated back to the hill country where they had previously lived. Caleb's final words in verse 12 reveal that his intention is based on Yahweh's word to him earlier.

Joshua's response to Caleb

Joshua responds to Caleb by blessing him and by giving him Hebron as an inheritance (v. 13). By not reporting the actual words of Joshua's blessing, the narrator allows Caleb's speech to remain the centrepiece of the narrative. The city of Hebron, located about twenty miles south of Jerusalem and twenty miles west of the Dead Sea, became Caleb's inheritance because of his whole-hearted devotion to Yahweh (v. 14). Ironically, this was a city formerly named for Arba, one of the greatest Anakim warriors (v. 15). Kiriath-arba, the former name of Hebron, meant 'city of Arba'. Now, the city receives the name Hebron, meaning 'community' or 'alliance', and becomes a place of rest from war. Sadly, Hebron has again become a place of war and violence in the 21st century.

The prophetic message of this story is that God honours people who fully follow him. By contrast, people who do not take a proactive approach to God's promises take what is left over (see Joshua 18).

PRAYER

Heavenly Father, the temptation is to play it safe. Help me, though, to act on your promises with courageous strength so that I can experience the blessings you want to give me.

The BOUNDARIES of JUDAH

At first glance, this section describing the boundaries of Judah looks like another tedious list of hills, valleys, springs, wilderness areas, and wadis. However, the description is alive! It traces the boundary of Judah with active verbs, giving the reader the sensation of watching the line being drawn on a map on television or on a computer screen. Bible scholars have noted that the boundary description for Judah here in verses 1–12 is the most detailed of all the boundary descriptions in chapters 14—19. This is not surprising, given the prominence of the tribe of Judah in the Bible.

The significance of boundaries

Before looking at the actual boundary descriptions, we should notice the significance of the term 'boundary' (Hebrew *gebul*). After all, it occurs 21 times in verses 1–12. The NRSV translates the term as 'boundary' nineteen times. One of its occurrences, in verse 4, is left untranslated. Another occurrence, in verse 12, is translated as 'coast'. People in the ancient Near East took boundaries seriously, believing that boundaries stood under the protection of the gods of the land. The people of Israel understood that Yahweh, the Most High, set the boundaries of all peoples on the earth (Deuteronomy 32:8). To violate a boundary would amount to violating something that God had established.

Tracing the boundaries of Judah

The description of Judah's boundary starts with the southern desert and moves anti-clockwise. Verses 1–4 cover the southern boundary, while the eastern boundary is simply described in verse 5a as the Dead Sea. Verses 5b–11 track the northern boundary, while verse 12 lists the western border as the Mediterranean Sea coast. Historically, this territory has played a prominent role. It formed the bulk of the southern kingdom once the nation of Israel divided after Solomon's reign. In New Testament times, the northern part of this region formed the Roman division of Judea. Today, in the 21st century, this territory includes the southern part of Israel, the southern part of the West Bank, and also the Gaza Strip.

What stands out about this description of Judah's boundary, as well as later descriptions of other tribal boundaries, is the sensation of watching the boundary line being traced. The narrator accomplishes this by using eight different verbs with the term 'boundary' as their subject. Accordingly, the boundary performs the following actions:

- 'goes out'   Hebrew *yasah*   (vv. 3, 4, 11)

- 'passes along'   Hebrew *abar*   (vv. 3, 4, 6, 7, 10, 11)

- 'goes up'   Hebrew *alah*   (vv. 3, 6, 7, 8)

- 'makes a turn' / 'circles'   Hebrew *sabab*   (vv. 3, 10)

- 'comes to' / 'ends'   Hebrew *hayah*   (vv. 4, 7, 11)

- 'turning'   Hebrew *panah*   (v. 7)

- 'extends' / 'bends'   Hebrew *ta'ar*   (vv. 9, 11)

- 'goes down'   Hebrew *yarad*   (v. 10)

These eight verbs appear almost 30 times in verses 2–11. Some of them occur more than once in a particular verse. Furthermore, the NRSV chooses not to translate some of them, perhaps because translating them every time they appear would sound redundant in English. The point is that these verbs create the effect of tracing a boundary line around the territory of Judah.

The summary statement in verse 12b conveys a sense of security. A boundary has been established. The term 'lot' in verse 1 ties this border to Yahweh's command to distribute the inheritance by lot (14:2). Thus, the boundary is recognized and protected by Yahweh (see Exodus 23:31). For today's believers, this section serves as a strong testimony to the goodness of God. He provides security for his people.

MEDITATION

The Lord is my chosen portion and my cup; you hold my lot.
The boundary lines have fallen for me in pleasant places;
I have a goodly heritage.

Psalm 16:5–6

ACHSAH'S REQUEST

A second 'land-grant narrative' about Caleb's inheritance appears here between the tribe of Judah's boundary list (15:1–12) and a listing of Judah's cities (15:20–63). Like the previous Caleb story, this one highlights an Israelite's efforts to take possession of the land. The focus of this story, however, is Achsah, a woman whose zeal to receive an inheritance matches the zeal of her father, Caleb. Interestingly, the narrator of Judges uses this exact story near the book's beginning.

Caleb's conquest and challenge

Verse 13 summarizes material already conveyed in 14:13–15. Grammatically, verse 13 serves as background information to the action that starts in verse 14. The story begins, then, with Caleb driving out three descendants of Anak (see the commentary on 14:12, p. 79). The narrator stresses their Anakite heritage by identifying them as 'sons of Anak' before giving their names, and as 'descendants of Anak' following their names. From Hebron, Caleb advances against Debir, a city whose ancient name was Kiriath-sepher. Instead of taking the city himself, Caleb issues a challenge. He promises to give his daughter, Achsah, as a wife to anyone who attacks and captures Kiriath-sepher (v. 16). Othniel, Caleb's nephew and a member of the next generation, accepts the challenge (v. 17a). Caleb then gives his daughter, Achsah, to Othniel as a wife (v. 17b).

Achsah takes action

Rather than being passive, though, Achsah takes action herself. She urges her husband to ask her father for more land. The Hebrew verb translated 'urged' in verse 18 means 'to incite, prompt, instigate'. When her father, Caleb, questions her about her wish, she asks for a present, or literally 'a blessing'. The blessing she seeks amounts to a field with water resources. She needs this because of her land's location in the Negeb, a desert region. Caleb grants her request, giving her 'the upper springs and the lower springs' (v. 19).

Hebrew narrative generally shows us, rather than telling us, about a character's traits, and this story is no exception. The narrator portrays Othniel and Achsah as Israelites determined to gain their full inheritance. Like Caleb, both Othniel and Achsah model the courage and determination needed by the people of Israel to experience the blessings that God had promised.

A theology of desire

This episode, along with the one in 14:6–15, can help modern believers to form a proper theology of desire. Somehow, we have read the biblical mandate to 'be content' (see Philippians 4:11–12; 1 Timothy 4:6–8; Hebrews 13:5) as a warning against desire. However, what the Bible warns against in these contexts is misplaced desire, not desire itself. Specifically, these passages warn against focusing our desires on material goods, as if money and property could ever satisfy our deepest longings. Still, Caleb declared, 'Give me this hill country' (14:12), and his daughter, Achsah, insisted, 'Give me springs of water as well' (v. 19). What were they seeking if not property? Essentially, they were seeking the full life that Yahweh had promised them—a life tied specifically to the land of Canaan.

Today, a full life for Christians is tied not to rest in the land of Canaan, but to rest available through connection to Jesus Christ (Matthew 11:28–30; Hebrews 3:1—4:11). Furthermore, this full life is ultimately tied to a heavenly kingdom, not just an earthly one (see Hebrews 11:16, 29–31, 39–40; 12:28). Our problem, then, is not that we desire too much, but that we desire too little. To say it another way, the greatest enemy of holiness is not passion, but apathy. Caleb and Achsah teach us the appropriateness of what Saint Augustine called a 'holy longing' or what G.K. Chesterton called 'divine discontent'. This means pursuing God's promise and blessing with a passion—even though the pursuit involves effort and risk

PRAYER

Oh Lord, help me to experience the freedom of desire,
not freedom from desire. Help me to pursue with passion
the interests of your kingdom and your righteousness. Help me to
pursue the dreams you have instilled in me, including opportunities
to serve you and to know you intimately.

CITIES *of* JUDAH

A mind-numbing list of cities waits for the reader in verses 20–63. But this section, which ends the discussion of Judah's inheritance, contributes to the argument of the book. The list of cities cries out, 'Look what Yahweh has provided for the tribe of Judah!' Yahweh has certainly kept his promise to provide his people with the gift of the land in which they can settle. The size of this list—by far the largest listing of cities given to an Israelite tribe—testifies to the tribe's prominence and importance. In the commentary on this section, we will survey the details first and then explore the message conveyed by this material.

Significant details about the city list

Between the heading in verse 20 and the concluding observation in verse 63, the list of cities breaks down into four parts. First, verses 21–32 list cities in the extreme south, toward the boundary of Edom. Second, verses 33–47 enumerate cities in the 'lowland' (v. 33) or the western foothills region. Summary tabulations at the end of verses 36, 41, and 44 effectively divide this second part into four groupings of cities. The third part, running from verse 48 to 60, documents cities in the hill country—that is, the central spine of mountains stretching from south to north in Israel. The fourth part, verses 61–62, cites cities in the wilderness or desert. These particular cities were grouped in the desert between the north-western half of the Dead Sea and the eastern slopes of the central spine of mountains.

One puzzle for Bible scholars concerns the summary reference to 'twenty-nine towns, with their villages' in verse 32. Alert readers will count 36 names cited in verses 21–32. Why the discrepancy? Some scholars suggest that a copyist made an error. Others think that seven names in the list refer to villages rather than towns. Thus, seven villages and 29 towns equals 36. This accounts, then, for the reference to 'twenty-nine towns with their villages'. An easier puzzle to solve is the reference to 'fourteen towns with their villages' in verse 36. The names in verses 33–36 actually total fifteen. However, the name 'Gederothaim' (Hebrew for 'two walls') in verse 36 refers to a place associated with the city of Gederah. The Septuagint—the Greek translation of the Old Testament completed about 150BC—translates 'Gederothaim' as 'her dwelling places'.

Some of the cities in the list are familiar—for example, Beer-sheba (v. 28; see Genesis 21:14, 31–33), Adullam (v. 35; see Genesis 38:1), Lachish (v. 39; see 10:31–35), Ekron (v. 45; 13:3), Timnah (v. 57; see Judges 14:1–5), and En-gedi (v. 66; see 1 Samuel 24:1). However, about half of the cities listed are not mentioned anywhere else in the Old Testament.

Inability to drive out the Jebusites

The observation in verse 63 forms a rather ironic conclusion to the account of Judah's inheritance (14:6—15:63). Despite Yahweh's gift of an inheritance and the efforts of people like Caleb and his daughter, Achsah, the tribe of Judah failed to take possession of the whole land. Incidentally, the reference in Judges 1:21 to *Benjamin* failing to dislodge the Jebusites is not a contradiction. While Jerusalem was allotted to Benjamin (Joshua 18:16, 28), it was a border town between Benjamin and Judah. Anyway, this note of failure serves as a prophetic warning against leaving evil inhabitants in the land. These inhabitants would remain as 'barbs' in the Israelites' eyes and 'thorns' in their sides (Numbers 33:52–55).

Message for today

What does this section contribute to the message of the book of Joshua? First, it continues the emphasis on God's goodness in giving his people a place to live. Second, it reminds believers of the need to deal with evil in their communities of faith. As Proverbs 16:17 says, 'The highway of the upright avoids evil; those who guard their way preserve their lives.'

Sadly, in the 21st century, this very region that God intended to be a source of blessing has become a source of bitter conflict and bloodshed.

PRAYER

Father, I pray for the peace of Jerusalem and the land
of promise. Bring healing to this war-torn land.
May those who counsel peace have joy.

JOSEPH'S INHERITANCE:
the TRIBE *of* EPHRAIM

The narrator shifts the focus from the tribe of Judah in chapters 14—15 to the tribes of Joseph in chapters 16—17. Although the descendants of Joseph consisted of the tribes of Manasseh and Ephraim (see v. 4), their inheritance consisted of one allotment. The need to share this territory eventually led to a complaint (see 17:14–18).

Tracking the southern boundary

Verses 1–4 track the southern boundary of the two tribes of Joseph. Once again, the narrator's use of action verbs—'went', 'going up' (v. 1), 'going', 'passes along' (v. 2), 'goes down', 'ends' (v. 3)—creates the effect of watching the boundary line being traced on a map. By linking the two tribes together for the moment (see v. 4), the narrator highlights the favoured status that they had as sons of Joseph. The large allotment they received in the centre of the land certainly matches the blessing given to Joseph by his father, Jacob (see Genesis 49:22–26).

Yahweh's strange sovereignty

Despite listing the two tribes of Joseph in the order of the sons' birth—Manasseh and Ephraim—in verse 4, the narrator begins his description of Joseph's inheritance with the tribe that originated with the younger son, Ephraim (vv. 5–10).

By starting with the inheritance for the tribe of the younger son, the narrator provides a subtle reminder of the events of Genesis 48. Joseph had brought his two sons, Manasseh and Ephraim, to his father, Jacob (Genesis 48:1). Joseph had placed the two boys before Jacob so that Jacob could place his right hand on the head of Manasseh, the older son, and his left hand on the head of Ephraim, the younger son (Genesis 48:13). In such a case, the son getting priority would receive his father's right hand—the hand of power—on his head. According to the customs of the day, priority went to the firstborn son. However, Jacob crossed his hands and placed his right hand on the head of Ephraim, the younger son (Genesis 48:14). This displeased Joseph, so he attempted to switch his father's right hand from Ephraim's head to Manasseh's head (Genesis 48:17–18). Jacob refused this attempt, however, and said: 'I know, my son, I know; he [Manasseh] also shall become a people, and he also shall be great. Nevertheless his younger brother [Ephraim] shall be greater than he, and his offspring shall become a multitude of nations' (Genesis 48:19). The narrator of Joshua intends for the reader to recall these events by discussing Ephraim's inheritance before Manasseh's inheritance.

Inability to drive out the Canaanites

After verse 5 has traced Ephraim's southern boundary, verses 6–8 trace Ephraim's northern boundary as it runs towards the east (vv. 6–7) and towards the west (v. 8a). A summary statement (vv. 8b–9) reveals that some of Ephraim's towns were located within territory given to Manasseh. Once again, the narrator may be alluding to Ephraim's privileged position. Finally, verse 10 reveals the failure of the Ephraimites to drive out a pocket of Canaanites living in Gezer. While the Ephraimites pressed these Canaanites into forced labour, this did not meet Yahweh's expectations set out in Deuteronomy 20:16–18. This is the second time in chapters 14—19 where the narrator notes a tribe's failure to remove the inhabitants of the land (see commentary on 15:63, p. 85).

What do modern readers learn about God's ways from Joshua 16? By highlighting the surprising reversal of the younger son over the first-born, the narrator highlights Yahweh's 'strange sovereignty'. Yahweh is the God of the unexpected who goes against human conventions and expectations. He showers his blessing on the undeserving and on those who do not have priority by human standards. God will bless people and use people whom we least expect, including ourselves (see 1 Corinthians 1:26–29; James 2:5).

MEDITATION

God chose what is low and despised in the world, things that are not, to reduce to nothing things that are, so that no one might boast in the presence of God.

1 Corinthians 1:28–29

JOSEPH'S INHERITANCE:
the TRIBE *of* MANASSEH

The second allotment of territory given to the Josephites goes to the tribe of Manasseh, the firstborn son of Joseph. Half of the tribe of Manasseh had already received a portion east of the Jordan along with Reuben and Gad (see 13:29–31).

Tribal families receiving allotments

In verses 1–2, the narrator begins the account of Manasseh's inheritance by listing the tribal families that received allotments. Machir, the firstborn son of Manasseh, received the land of Gilead and Bashan east of the Jordan River. Machir was actually Manasseh's only son (Genesis 50:23; Numbers 26:29). He was allotted Gilead—presumably named after his son—and Bashan because he was a warrior (v. 1, literally 'a man of war'). This refers to Machir's earlier success in driving out the Amorites from this region (Numbers 32:39). Through this reference, the narrator reinforces a theological idea prominent in chapters 14—19: Yahweh honours those who take the initiative to possess what Yahweh has promised them.

The rest of the tribal families are listed in verse 2. These tribes would have settled west of the Jordan River. Their names derive from the sons of Gilead, the son of Manasseh (see Numbers 26:29–32).

The request of Zelophehad's daughters

Verses 3–6 contain the third of four 'land-grant narratives' found in chapters 14—19. These brief stories emphasize Israel's zeal in taking possession of the land. In this story, Zelophehad, a descendant of Manasseh, had daughters but no sons (v. 3). In the ancient Near East, the inheritance of property passed through the line of male relatives, so Zelophehad's family faced the prospect of seeing its inheritance diverted to another male relative. According to Numbers 27:1–11, Zelophehad's daughters had approached Moses about this problem to argue their case and request 'a possession among our father's brothers' (Numbers 27:4). This was a bold request considering the customs of the day. However, Moses brought the case before Yahweh, and Yahweh responded favourably towards the daughters of Zelophehad (Numbers 27:5–11). He allowed them to possess an inheritance, and he established a priority list for distributing the inheritance in the case of a man who has no son, no daughter, no brothers, and so on.

Anyway, Zelophehad's daughters now appeal to Joshua, Eleazer the priest, and the other leaders to follow through on what Yahweh had previously commanded Moses about giving them an inheritance. Once again, Joshua acts in obedience to Yahweh and gives these daughters of Zelophehad an inheritance.

Tracing the boundary of Manasseh

Like previous land-grant accounts, the Manasseh account in verses 7–13 includes a section that traces the boundary lines of the tribe's territory. Verse 7a sets the basic parameters, observing that the territory reached from Asher in the north to Michmethath in the south. Then, verses 7b–10a elaborate on the southern boundary, while verses 10b–11 trace the boundary in the northern and north-eastern part of Manasseh's territory. Verses 12–13 describe Manasseh's failure to drive out the Canaanites from its cities. This has become a recurring theme in chapters 14—19 (see 15:63; 16:10).

This narrative provides more than historical data. Rather, by shaping his account to include a reference to Machir, the 'man of war' (v. 1), the story of Zelophehad's daughters (vv. 3–6), and a reference to Joshua's obedience (v. 4), the narrator has communicated a prophetic message. Essentially, this material declares that Yahweh blesses those men and women who make an effort to possess what he has promised them. Men and women of faith act in boldness and confidence to pursue what God has in store for them. Furthermore, as this account demonstrates, the consequences of failing to obey God fully may not show up immediately. Verses 12–13 specify no immediate effects of the failure to drive out the Canaanites, but this failure sets the stage for later disaster described in the book of Judges.

PRAYER

Father, help me to act boldly and courageously on your promises.

The SONS of JOSEPH COMPLAINT

The fourth 'land-grant narrative' found in chapters 14—19 (see commentary on 14:1–5, p. 76) appears here in verses 14–18. However, unlike the previous three land-grant narratives (14:6–15; 15:18–19; 17:3–6), the request in this story takes the form of a complaint rather than a legitimate request. The story consists of a dialogue between the sons of Joseph and Joshua. The sons of Joseph initiate this dialogue with a request (v. 14). Then, the speeches alternate.

Joseph lodges a complaint

The story begins in verse 14 with a speech by the tribe of Joseph (literally, 'the sons of Joseph') to Joshua. Two features of this speech lead us as readers to view it as a complaint rather than a legitimate request. First, the request does not appeal to Yahweh's promises like the requests of Caleb and Zelophehad's daughters in two earlier land-grant narratives (14:6–15; 17:3–6). Second, the request challenges the result of casting the lot, a process commanded and controlled by Yahweh himself (14:2; see also Proverbs 16:33). The sons of Joseph argue that 'one lot' is not sufficient for 'numerous people'. They hint that Yahweh is not really blessing them in their current circumstance.

Joshua's challenge

Joshua replies to the sons of Joseph by issuing a challenge (v. 15). He takes their description of themselves as a 'numerous people' and uses it against them. As a 'numerous people', they should be able to clear out some space in enemy territory—a forest area occupied by the Perizzites and Rephaites. The narrator does not specify the location of this forested area, although it presumably lies within territory allotted to the sons of Joseph, perhaps within the hill country of Ephraim.

Joseph's counter-complaint

Verse 16 records the rebuttal of the sons of Joseph to Joshua's challenge. Their rebuttal makes two points. First, they argue that the hill country 'is not found for us' (a literal translation of the Hebrew text of v. 16a). This can mean either that the hill country is 'not big enough for us' or that it is 'not available to us'. While the NRSV's translation reflects the former idea, the latter idea seems to fit best with the context—that is, with their next statement (v. 16b) and with Joshua's reply (vv. 17–18). Second, the sons of Joseph argue that the Canaanites in the plain possess iron chariots. (The reference is probably to chariots plated with iron.) This gave the Canaanite warriors a technological edge. Iron made the chariots durable and difficult for enemy arrows and spears to penetrate. Iron was stronger than copper or bronze, and Israel at this time did not possess the ability to work with it (a fact reflected in 1 Samuel 13:19–22).

Joshua's counter-challenge

Joshua's counter-challenge appears in verses 17–18. He still insists that the sons of Joseph have the 'people power' needed to take the hill country and drive out the Canaanites despite their technological edge and their strength. Once again, he uses the Josephites' expression 'numerous people' to make his point. While some Bible scholars see a difference between the 'one lot' in verse 17 and the 'hill country' in verse 18, it is likely that the hill country is part of the lot. If this is the case, Joshua is insisting that the sons of Joseph will have to take full possession of the territory within their allotment rather than receiving additional territory. They apparently hoped for additional territory with fewer forests and fewer enemies!

While God honours those who boldly pursue the life he has offered (see 14:6–15; 15:18–19), God's people must accept what God in his grace has given and what God in his grace has not given. The fact is that God has provided 'everything needed for life and godliness' (2 Peter 1:3).

PRAYER

Thank you, God, for your power and your promises. You are all I will ever need to live an effective, fruitful life. Help me to make the effort to act in the power you have provided.

A TASK *to* COMPLETE

This unit of text stands at the very literary centre of both the land-grant descriptions (chapters 14—19) and the second half of the book of Joshua (chapters 13—24). By placing this material at the literary centre of these sections, the narrator has also placed it at the theological centre. That is to say that verses 1–10 provide the key for understanding the events of the surrounding chapters—and this key is the presence of Yahweh among his people. Chapters 18—19 form a subsection that describes the allotment of land to the remaining seven Israelite tribes. The references to the tent of meeting here in 18:1 and again in 19:51 function like bookends or brackets which enclose their contents. Bible scholars refer to this literary device as an *inclusio*.

The tent of meeting at Shiloh

Up until this time, Israel's base of operation has been Gilgal. Now, however, the congregation assembles at Shiloh (about fifteen miles north-west of Jericho) and set up the 'tent of meeting' there (v. 1). The verb forms of 'assembled' and 'set up' indicate that the first two clauses of verse 1 advance the story line. The third clause, however—'the land lay subdued before them'—pauses the action and serves as an important piece of background information for what comes next.

This is the first of two times in the book of Joshua where the expression 'tent of meeting' occurs (see also 19:51). The 'tent of meeting'—or 'tabernacle' in some translations—was a portable tent about 14 metres long and 4.5 metres wide. It served as a place where Yahweh would reveal his presence to his people through the priests (see Exodus 26 for its construction and Exodus 29:42–46 for its purpose). By locating the tent of meeting in Shiloh, Shiloh became the place of Yahweh's dwelling in the midst of his people (Leviticus 26:11–12; Deuteronomy 12:5, 10–14). Shiloh remained the place of Yahweh's dwelling until the Philistines captured the ark of the covenant from it during the time of Eli (1 Samuel 4).

Finishing the mission

After pausing the action to mention that 'the land lay subdued before them' (v. 1), the narrator resumes the action in verse 2, revealing that seven tribes had not yet received their inheritance. Joshua's initial statement to the Israelites in verse 3 appears to be a rebuke. The verb translated 'be slack' occurs two other times in Joshua, and these occurrences help us to understand its emphasis. First, it appears in Yahweh's promise to Joshua, 'I will not fail you' (1:5). Then, it appears in the Gibeonites' plea to Joshua, 'Do not abandon your servants' (10:6). By using this term, then, Joshua implies that the remaining tribes are in danger of failing to occupy the land Yahweh had gifted to them.

Joshua continues his speech by spelling out a procedure for following through with the task of possessing the land (vv. 4–7). Three men from each tribe would form an expedition whose mission was to divide the remaining land into seven pieces. Joshua's reference to the territories of Judah and the house of Joseph (v. 5), as well as his mention of the east-Jordan tribes (v. 7), emphasizes the unity of the twelve tribes. The command to provide a written description (vv. 4, 8) signals the seriousness of the task.

Verses 8–10 indicate that the expedition carried out Joshua's instructions and thus fulfilled its mission. With a description of seven territories, Joshua began casting lots to determine which tribes would receive which territories (v. 10). The narrator emphasizes Yahweh's involvement in this process by including three references to Joshua's casting of lots in the presence of Yahweh (in the reporting of Joshua's speech in verses 6 and 8, as well as in the narrator's own report in verse 10).

Message for today

This narrative emphasizes the centrality of God's presence. God has positioned himself at the centre of his people's lives. The proper response to God's presence is to follow through on the commands and responsibilities he has issued.

MEDITATION

Lord God, thank you for your Holy Spirit who makes your presence real to me today. Empower me to keep in step with the Spirit as he leads me to accomplish your will for my life.

The INHERITANCE of BENJAMIN

Benjamin was the first of the remaining tribes to receive its allotment. Some Bible scholars attribute the tribe's prominence—reflected by its place in the lottery and by the length and detail of its territorial description—to its geographical location between Judah to the south and Ephraim to the north (see v. 11). It is more likely, however, that the tribe's prominence stems from its heritage. After all, Benjamin was one of two sons, along with Joseph, born to Jacob's favourite wife, Rachel (Genesis 35:18, 24). Furthermore, in the ancient Near East, fathers were often most fond of sons born in their old age.

Tracing Benjamin's boundary line

After an introductory statement in verse 11, verses 12–20 trace the boundary line of Benjamin. This tracing begins in the north-eastern corner of its territory at the Jordan River and moves in an anti-clockwise direction (v. 12). Verses 12–13 describe the northern boundary line as it moves from east to west. Benjamin's northern border also served as Ephraim's southern border (see 16:1–5). All the places found in 16:1–5 occur here in verses 12–13, with the addition of Beth-aven, an unknown region in the desolate wilderness between Jericho and Luz, that is, Bethel.

Roughly halfway between the Jordan River and the Mediterranean Sea (on an east-to-west plane), Benjamin's boundary line turns south (v. 14). This line, running from north to south, forms the western border of the territory.

Benjamin's southern boundary line gets extensive attention in verses 15–19. The line gets traced from the outskirts of Kiriath-jearim in the south-west of its territory (v. 15) to the northern bay of the Dead Sea in the south-east of its territory (v. 19). One important detail along the way is the boundary line's route 'south of the slope of the Jebusites' (v. 16). In other words, the city of Jerusalem, occupied at this time by the Jebusites, is actually part of the territory of Benjamin.

Why does the narrator offer such a detailed description of Benjamin's southern boundary? Perhaps because this border is shared with Judah, Israel's most important tribe. Benjamin's southern boundary is Judah's northern boundary. In fact, the description of Benjamin's southern boundary here in verses 15–19 matches closely the description of Judah's northern boundary in 15:5–11.

In verse 20, the narrator briefly mentions that the Jordan River forms the eastern boundary, and then he offers a summary statement identifying the previous details as 'the inheritance of the tribe of Benjamin'. The territory within the boundary lines consists of a section of hill country which is roughly 26 miles wide from east to west, and about twelve miles long from north to south. This probably explains why a Benjaminite named Saul later called his tribe 'the least of the tribes of Israel' (1 Samuel 9:21). By 'least', he apparently meant smallest in size, not smallest in importance.

Benjamin's town list

The account of Benjamin's inheritance concludes with a town list in verses 21–28. The two enumerated summaries represent different geographical groupings. The 'twelve towns' of verse 24 form an eastern district, while the 'fourteen towns' in verse 28 comprise a western district. A quick scan of this list reveals the presence of towns which have been or will become prominent in Israelite history. Jericho (v. 21), of course, was the first city conquered by the Israelites when they entered the promised land of Canaan. Jebus, or Jerusalem, will become the nation's 'holy city' (Nehemiah 11:1; Isaiah 52:1). Gibeah will produce Saul, Israel's first king (1 Samuel 9—10), and Kiriath-jearim will host the ark of the covenant for twenty years (1 Samuel 7:1–2).

The concept of inheritance

Like the surrounding inheritance accounts, the account of Benjamin's inheritance reminds us that God provides what his people need to live a full, productive life. Today's believers find their inheritance not in land but in a union with Jesus Christ (1 Peter 1:3–5).

PRAYER

*Loving Father, thank you for the inheritance
kept in heaven for me—an inheritance that is imperishable,
undefiled and unfading.*

39 JOSHUA 19:1–23

The INHERITANCES of SIMEON, ZEBULUN & ISSACHAR

In Joshua 19, the narrator continues describing the results of the lot-casting at Shiloh (see 18:10). Verses 1–23 present the allotments for the tribes of Simeon (vv. 1–9), Zebulun (vv. 10–16) and Issachar (vv. 17–23).

Simeon's inheritance

The second lot cast went to the tribe of Simeon. Here, the reader encounters a surprise. Rather than finding a boundary description, we are informed that Simeon's inheritance will lie 'within the inheritance of the tribe of Judah' (v. 1). The narrator then specifies cities within Judah's territory which belong to Simeon (vv. 2–8). Two-thirds of the eighteen listed cities have already appeared in Judah's list: Beer-sheba (v. 2; see 15:28), Moladah (v. 2; see 15:26), Hazar-shual (v. 3; see 15:28), Ezem (v. 3; see 15:29), Eltolad and Hormah (v. 4; see 15:30), Ziklag (v. 5; see 15:31), Beth-lebaoth (v. 6; possibly the same as 'Lebaoth' in 15:32), Ain and Rimmon (v. 7; see 15:32), Ether and Ashan (v. 7; see 15:42).

The first and third clauses of verse 9 raise a key issue: why did Simeon obtain an inheritance within Judah's territory? The middle or second clause provides the answer. Judah's portion was too large for them.

Readers familiar with the Old Testament will recognize another underlying reason for the tribe of Simeon receiving a group of towns within another tribe's inheritance. When Jacob offered a prophecy regarding his sons shortly before his death, he took note of the violence of two of them, Simeon and Levi (Genesis 49:5–6). This violence probably included the slaughter of the men of Shechem—an attempt to avenge the rape of their sister, Dinah (see Genesis 34). The end of the prophecy in Genesis 49:7 reads:

> Cursed be their anger, for it is fierce,
> and their wrath, for it is cruel!
> I will divide them in Jacob,
> and scatter them in Israel.

This prophecy seems to find its fulfilment in the land allotments to the tribes. The inheritances received by both Simeon and Levi (see Joshua 21) amount to cities within the territory of other tribes.

Zebulun's inheritance

The third lot cast went to the tribe of Zebulun. Verses 10–16 describe Zebulun's inheritance with a boundary description. Zebulun's territory lies in the north, centred between the Sea of Galilee to the east and Mount Carmel near the Mediterranean coast to the west. While the description does not contain a formal list of towns, the narrator tallies the towns listed in the boundary description—a number he identifies as 'twelve'. However, the number of towns listed totals fifteen. Perhaps the number was miscopied at some point in the process of copying from one manuscript to anther.

Issachar's inheritance

The fourth lot cast went to the tribe of Issachar. The description of Issachar's territory is brief, running from verse 17 to 23. It consists mainly of a list of thirteen cities (vv. 18–21). The fleeting reference to its boundary mentions three more cities as well as the Jordan River (v. 22). Zebulun's inheritance consisted of a small territory to the southeast of the tribe of Zebulun and to the south-west of the Sea of Galilee.

By this point in the book, readers may be growing weary of the endless boundary descriptions and lists of cities. However, these lists serve the narrator's strategy. He has provided them to give concrete shape to the promises of Yahweh. The boundary descriptions and city lists, though tedious to read, affirm that Yahweh has made good on his promise to give the offspring of Abram a land (see Genesis 15:7–21; Deuteronomy 34:1–4). Therefore, his people can trust him whenever he leads them into new challenges.

PRAYER

Lord God, I praise you and trust you because you keep the promises you make to your people.

The INHERITANCES of ASHER, NAPHTALI & DAN

In this section, the narrator completes his report of the lot-casting results at Shiloh. He describes the allotments for Asher (vv. 24–31), Naphtali (vv. 32–39), and Dan (vv. 40–48). A brief report about Joshua's inheritance follows (vv. 49–50). Then, a summary statement concludes the distribution of inheritances at Shiloh (v. 51).

Asher's inheritance

The fifth lot cast went to the tribe of Asher (v. 24). The narrator describes Asher's territory by tracing its boundary line in reference to clusters of cities (vv. 25–30). Asher's territory consisted of a long strip of land, from north to south, along the Mediterranean Sea. It was located, then, in the far north-western part of the land.

Naphtali's inheritance

The sixth lot cast went to the tribe of Naphtali. Verses 32–39 describe its inheritance with a boundary description (vv. 33–34) and a list of cities (vv. 35–37). Naphtali's territory, then, consisted of a long strip of land, from north to south, just east of the tribe of Asher's allotment. The Sea of Galilee was located within its borders. Bible scholars describe the Galilee region as a rich, forested land.

Dan's inheritance

The seventh and final lot cast went to the tribe of Dan (v. 40). Based on the city list in verses 41–46, as well as the location of the other tribes, we can figure out its territory. The Mediterranean Sea served as its western border, while the tribe of Benjamin was located to the east. Ephraim and Manasseh bordered it to the north, while Judah bordered it to the south.

Verse 47 indicates, however, that the Danites were unable to possess their territory. Eventually, they migrated north and captured the city of Leshem, which they renamed 'Dan'. Judges 18 tells the story of Dan's migration to the north. Unfortunately, the narrator of Judges uses the story to illustrate Israel's religious decay.

Joshua receives an inheritance

At the end of the land distribution to the tribes, Joshua received an inheritance (v. 49). The narrator specifies that the Israelites gave this to Joshua 'by command of the Lord'—literally, 'by the mouth of the Lord' (v. 50). We are unsure about the details of this command since the Bible does not discuss it anywhere else. The location of Joshua's territory in the hill country of Ephraim was appropriate since Joshua was a member of the tribe of Ephraim (Numbers 13:8). This brief description of Joshua's inheritance serves as an appropriate summary of the entire inheritance distribution to the tribes west of the Jordan River (chs. 14—19). The account began with the giving of an inheritance to Caleb (14:6–15) and now closes with the giving of an inheritance to Joshua (vv. 49–50). The two serve as positive counterparts emphasizing the Yahweh's faithfulness in fulfilling his promise to both (see Numbers 14:30).

Mission accomplished

Verse 51 provides a formal conclusion to the account in chapters 18—19. The land distribution at Shiloh to the remaining seven tribes has been completed. Verse 51 also brings closure to chapters 14—19. The full names of the characters involved in the land distribution, 'the priest Eleazar and Joshua son of Nun', appear here in verse 51 and in 14:1. These references provide the introduction (14:1) and the conclusion (v. 51) to the section. A final formal summary will appear in 21:43–45, once the Levites receive towns for an inheritance (ch. 21). With the bulk of the land distribution finished, however, Yahweh has shown himself to be a promise-keeper, as well as a giver of good gifts to his people.

MEDITATION

Every generous act of giving, with every perfect gift, is from above,
coming down from the Father of lights, with whom there is
no variation or shadow due to change.

James 1:17

CITIES *of* REFUGE

At this point in the book of Joshua, each tribe has received its inheritance except for the tribe of Levi. The Levites' situation is unique, so chapters 20—21 describe their inheritance. Chapter 20 deals with the appointment of cities of refuge, while chapter 21 describes the allotment of towns to the Levites. Although chapter 20 seems unrelated to the Levites, previous instructions given through Moses called for six cities of the Levites to be designated as cities of refuge (Numbers 35:6).

Yahweh issues instructions

Yahweh commands Joshua to appoint cities of refuge according to the instructions given previously to Moses (vv. 1–2). These instructions appear in Exodus 21:12–14, Numbers 35:6–34, and Deuteronomy 4:41–43 and 19:1–13. The purpose of these cities was to provide asylum for a person who killed someone else 'without intent or by mistake' (v. 3a). For example, if two men were cutting wood in a forest, the head of one man's axe might fly off, strike the other man, and kill him (Deuteronomy 19:5–6). This would qualify as a case of unintentional manslaughter.

A person who unintentionally killed another person needed a place as a refuge from the 'avenger of blood' (v. 3b). The term 'avenger' translates the Hebrew term *goel*. The same term is translated 'kinsman' in the book of Ruth. The *goel* was basically the protector of family rights—the one who redeemed any loss sustained by a family. In the book of Ruth, the redemption related to property. Here in Joshua 20, another issue emerges. One of the *goel*'s primary responsibilities was to avenge his relatives for the killing of one of their own. We should note that Yahweh does not command the avenging of blood. Rather, Yahweh has made a provision for his people who lived in a culture where 'blood-vengeance' was the norm. The provision reflects Yahweh's mercy, as well as his value of life.

In the case of an unintentional killing, then, the slayer flees to one of the cities and explains his case to the elders (v. 4), presumably to establish that he acted 'without intent or by mistake'. In such a case, the elders will grant him a place of protection from the avenger (v. 5).

(If the elders determined that the slayer committed an act of intentional murder, Deuteronomy 19:11–12 instructed them to hand the culprit over to the avenger of blood.) The slayer then remains in the city of refuge until his trial in his home town (v. 6a; see also Numbers 35:22–28). If the trial establishes his innocence, he can return to the city of refuge. This will afford him protection in case the avenger still seeks vengeance for the blood of the slain relative. However, verse 6 mentions another fascinating provision for the slayer who is acquitted. He can return to his home town to live—the town in which the deed was done—if the high priest dies. Apparently, the high priest's death provided atonement (that is, the legal satisfaction of justice) for the sin of the slayer.

Executing Yahweh's instructions

According to verses 7–9, Israel carried out Yahweh's instructions. They appointed three cities west of the Jordan (v. 7) and three cities east of the Jordan (v. 8). On each side of the Jordan, a city of refuge existed in the northern, central and southern regions of the land. No place in the land was more than a day's journey from one of these cities.

Message for today

The atonement provided by the high priest's death points forward to the atonement provided by Jesus, our 'merciful and faithful high priest' (Hebrews 2:17). By his death, he obtained 'eternal redemption' and the forgiveness of sins by offering himself as a single sacrifice (Hebrews 9:11—10:18). In Joshua 20:9, the recognition that the provisions in verses 1–9 apply to the alien as well as to the Israelite anticipates the wideness of God's mercy. His salvation extends to all who believe, non-Jewish as well as Jewish people (Romans 1:16).

PRAYER

Father, I pray for those who have unintentionally taken the lives of others by causing a road crash, an accident on a building site, or a tragedy in the home. Heal their pain and help them to find refuge in you.

42

CITIES *for the* LEVITES

The division of the promised land of Canaan concludes with the distribution of cities to the Levites. Levi did not inherit a particular region. Rather, the tribe received 48 cities and accompanying pasture land within territories allotted to the other tribes (see vv. 41–42). As noted in the previous study, six of these cities were designated as cities of refuge (see Numbers 35:6–8).

Understanding the Levites

Why were the Levites a landless tribe? The answer has its roots in Jacob's curse upon his sons Simeon and Levi for their violence (Genesis 49:5–7; see commentary on Joshua 19:1–23, pp. 96–97). However, Yahweh eventually chose Moses and Aaron from the tribe of Levi to free Israel from the land of Egypt (Exodus 6:13, 16–20, 26–27). The Scripture is silent about Yahweh's motive. Later, the sons of Levi responded to Moses' challenge—'Who is on the Lord's side? Come to me!'—in the aftermath of the golden calf incident (Exodus 32:25–26). After the Levites had obeyed Moses' instructions to kill their fellow Israelites who were engaging in idol-worship (Exodus 32:27–28), Moses said, 'Today you have ordained yourselves for the service of the Lord, each one at the cost of a son or a brother, and so have brought a blessing on yourselves this day' (Exodus 32:29).

So, while the Levites' landless status started out as a punishment, it eventually aided them in their ministry. As Moses noted in his blessing, the Levites were to be teachers of Yahweh's law, as well as priests who would offer sacrifices for the people (Deuteronomy 33:8–11). Being scattered throughout the land enabled the Levites to fulfil these functions for all the other tribes.

The allotment of cities

The account begins in verses 1–3 with an introduction describing the Levites' initiative in asking to receive what Yahweh had promised them. Both the Levites' request and Israel's response happen in accordance with Yahweh's word.

Then, verses 4–8 provide an overview of the division. It happened by the casting of the lot, just as in the land distribution for the other tribes. Three groups of cities were allotted to the descendants of Aaron's three sons: Kohath (vv. 4–5), Gershon (v. 6), and Merari (v. 7). The Kohathites received 23 towns—thirteen to the descendants of Aaron and ten to the remaining descendants. The Gershonites received thirteen towns, while the descendants of Merari received twelve. The total equals 48, agreeing with the summary tally in verse 1.

Verses 9–20 provide the specific details. The inheritance of the Kohathites is described in verses 9–26, including cities for the priests (vv. 9–19) and for the non-priests (vv. 20–26). Not all the Levites served as priests, though all the priests were Levites. The inheritance for the Gershonites is described in verses 27–33, while the inheritance for the Merarites is described in verses 34–40. As in the previous allotment descriptions, the details here assure us that Yahweh controlled the process and that the Levites received an actual inheritance—not just a vague promise.

The repetition of this Levitical city list in 1 Chronicles 6:54–81 a few centuries later shows the important role that the Levites had in Israel.

Priests today

This section of Joshua shows God's heart for placing spiritual leaders among his people. Today, God has placed spiritual leaders in the Church to equip Christians to do their part in developing a community of people who live and serve like Jesus (see Ephesians 4:11–16). A key difference exists, however, between ministry under the covenant with Moses and ministry under the new covenant. Under the covenant with Moses, only Levites could serve as priests. Under the new covenant, all believers are priests who can offer praise, thanksgiving and service before God (1 Peter 2:5, 9; Revelation 1:6).

MEDITATION

Reflect on God's care for the Levites. What steps can you take to do a better job of appreciating and providing for the spiritual leaders whom God has placed over you today?

No Falling Words

This grand summary concludes the entire land distribution account in chapters 13—21. Verses 43–45 form the 'theological heart' or the 'jugular vein' of the entire book. These verses conclude from the raw data in chapters 13—21 that none of Yahweh's promises failed. Rather, all came to pass.

Yahweh keeps his promises

Like the ending of a Beethoven symphony, these verses swell with a crescendo. Verse 43 affirms that Israel received the *land* promised by Yahweh to Israel's ancestors. These ancestors include Abraham—the original recipient of the promise (Genesis 12:1–3; 15:7–21)—and Moses (Deuteronomy 34:1–4). Verse 44 affirms that Israel also received the *rest* promised by Yahweh to Israel's ancestors (Deuteronomy 12:10; 25:19). This affirmation is complemented by a pair of opposite statements affirming the defeat of Israel's enemies. Stated negatively, no enemies withstood Israel (v. 44b). Stated positively, Yahweh gave all of the people's enemies into their hands (v. 44c).

Verse 45 provides the climax to the crescendo with a pair of opposite statements. First, stated negatively, not one of Yahweh's good promises failed (v. 45a). The language here is significant. Three occurrences of the Hebrew root *d-b-r* place the focus on what Yahweh has said. The noun *dabar* ('word') occurs twice, while the verb *dabar* ('speak') occurs once. Note these three occurrences in the following literal translation of the Hebrew text of verse 45a: 'A word (*dabar*, noun) of every good word (*dabar*, noun) which Yahweh spoke (*dabar*, verb) to Israel did not fall.' There is an image suggested here of a warrior slain in battle and falling to the ground. Verse 45a is saying that none of Yahweh's words fell to the ground in this way. To say that Yahweh's words do not fall is to say that Yahweh's words do not fail.

A second statement affirms the same concept in positive terms: 'all came to pass' (v. 45b). Literally, the final statement reads, 'all entered'. The term 'entered' (Hebrew *bo*)—the fourth most frequently used term in the Old Testament—is a term of movement. Rather than falling to the ground, Yahweh's words move. They happen. They arrive at the point of completion. This affirms the theme of the book of Joshua: *Yahweh keeps his promises.*

Six uses of the term 'all' (Hebrew *kol*) in verses 43–35 underscore this emphasis. According to verse 43, Yahweh gave Israel 'all (*kol*) the land'. In verse 44, Yahweh gave Israel 'rest on every (*kol*) side'. In fact, 'not one of all (*kol*) their enemies' withstood them; rather, Yahweh 'gave all (*kol*) their enemies into their hands'. According to verse 45, 'not one of all (*kol*) the good promises' Yahweh made failed; instead, 'all (*kol*) came to pass'.

Was the conquest really complete?

While the six uses of 'all' bring the summary to a thrilling conclusion, however, they also raise a troubling question in the reader's mind. Was the conquest really complete? Did Yahweh really give Israel *all* the land? Did he really give *all* of Israel's enemies into their hands? Several hints throughout the book have suggested that the conquest was incomplete (see 13:13; 15:63; 16:10; 17:12–13).

We must give the narrator enough credit to assume that he had not forgotten his prior statements about an incomplete conquest when he wrote the words in verses 43–45. In fact, he is holding two facts in tension: Yahweh followed through on his promises; but Yahweh's people did not do their part in completely driving out all enemies from the land (see commentary on 13:13, p. 73). From a macro-perspective (the big picture), Israel did occupy the entire land. Yet from a micro-perspective (the details), there were some pockets of resistance that the Israelites had not cleared. This prepares us as readers for the book of Judges—the story of Israel's slide into rebellion. This rebellion stemmed from a failure to drive the pagan inhabitants of Canaan out of the land.

However, the partial failure of God's people should not detract from the joyful message sounded in this grand summary: *Yahweh is a God who keeps his promises.*

PRAYER

Thank you, Father, for keeping the promises you make.
Though I live in a world littered with people's broken promises,
I can count on you to keep your word.

The EAST-JORDAN TRIBES DEPART

Joshua 22 begins the second part of the second major section of the book. Before looking at the text, we should pause to get our bearings. The first major section of Joshua, chapters 1—12, focused on the conquest of the promised land. The second section of Joshua, chapters 13—24, has been focusing on the *distribution* of the land. The first part of section two, chapters 13—21, provided a series of lists which documented the distribution of the land. Now, the second part of section two, chapters 22—24, closes the second section, as well as the book, with a series of farewell addresses from Joshua. Each of the final three chapters begins with the report that 'Joshua summoned' part or all of Israel (22:1; 23:2; 24:1). The focus has shifted from a statement about Yahweh's loyalty to his people (chs. 13—21) to a challenge about the people's loyalty to Yahweh (chs. 22—24).

A call to loyalty

The time had come for the tribes who had been allotted territory east of the Jordan River to head for home. Verses 22:1–8 contain Joshua's farewell speech to these tribes—the Reubenites, the Gadites, and the half-tribe of Manasseh (see v. 1). Joshua begins his speech by commending these tribes for their obedience. The term 'all' (Hebrew *kol*) appears twice in verse 2, stressing the completeness of their obedience both to Moses, the servant of Yahweh, and to Joshua. Joshua also commends them for not forsaking their 'kindred'—that is, the other tribes (v. 3). The language in verse 3, 'You… have been careful to keep the charge', is vivid. Both the verb and the object come from the Hebrew root *sh-m-r*, 'guard, keep, watch'. Translated literally into English, it might sound something like, 'you have kept what you were supposed to keep' or 'you have guarded what you were supposed to guard'. The east-Jordan tribes have kept Joshua's charge in 1:12–15. Now that Yahweh has given rest to the tribes living west of the Jordan, Joshua instructs the tribes who had been allotted territory east of the Jordan to return home (v. 4).

At this point, Joshua offers a further charge to the east-Jordan tribes before they depart for home. His words, recorded in verse 5, ring with passion and intensity. The NRSV's opening words, 'Take good care', are probably not strong enough to capture the emotion of the Hebrew text. A more appropriate translation would be, 'Only be extremely careful.' Then, Joshua piles on expressions that reflect the repeated calls to loyalty in the book of Deuteronomy, particularly Deuteronomy 6:5–6, which calls Israel to obey and love Yahweh. The expression 'hold fast' (Hebrew *dabaq*) provides a vivid picture. The term is used throughout the Old Testament to describe the sticking together of physical objects. Bones hold fast to skin. Dirt clods hold fast to each other after it rains. A warrior's hand holds fast to his weapon after a day of fighting. A husband and wife hold fast to each other. In similar fashion, Yahweh's people must cling to him!

Joshua's blessing

After calling the tribes to obey, love, hold fast to, and serve Yahweh (v. 5), Joshua blesses them and sends them on their way (v. 6). Verse 7 is a parenthetical statement which once again explains the unique situation of the tribe of Manasseh Then, verse 8 contains the actual words of Joshua's blessing. He instructs the east-Jordan tribes to divide the spoils with their fellow tribes and to return home.

Love and obedience

A key issue for consideration by today's believer is the connection between love and obedience. In verse 5, the instruction to love Yahweh is preceded and followed by instructions to obey his commands. This reflects the close connection between the two concepts in the book of Deuteronomy (see Deuteronomy 6:5–6; 11:1, 13, 22). Believers may sometimes wonder how they can tangibly express love to a God they cannot touch or see or hear physically. Obedience, though, provides a tangible expression of a believer's love for God. As Jesus said, 'They who have my commandments and keep them are those who love me' (John 14:21).

PRAYER

Lord God, draw me close to you. My desire is to love, obey and hold fast to you.

The CONTROVERSIAL ALTAR

The story of the east-Jordan tribes' return to their territory takes an unexpected turn. A misunderstanding brings the west-Jordan and east-Jordan tribes to the brink of civil war!

The threat of civil war

With Joshua's charge fresh in their minds, the east-Jordan tribes began the trip home (v. 9). Before crossing the Jordan from Canaan to the east-Jordan region, the two and a half tribes built an altar which the narrator describes as, literally, 'an altar of great appearance' (v. 10). As a result of hearing about this (v. 11), the Israelites living west of the Jordan gathered to make war against the Israelites living east of the Jordan (v. 12). This crisis catches the reader off guard. In fact, the narrator withholds details for the moment to keep the readers in suspense. Why did the altar upset the west-Jordan tribes? How can a nation united come to the verge of civil war?

Understanding the controversy

According to verses 13–20, the Israelites west of the Jordan sent a delegation to confront the east-Jordan tribes about the altar. This delegation consisted of Phinehas (the priest who dealt with Israel's disobedience at Peor in Numbers 25:6–13) and ten leaders from the nine and a half west-Jordan tribes. This delegation accused the east-Jordan tribes of committing treachery by turning away from following Yahweh (vv. 16–17). Literally, the Hebrew text of verse 16 reads, 'What is this trespass which you have trespassed against the God of Israel?' The delegation also describes it as an act of rebellion (vv. 16, 19). The statements in verse 19 help us understand the heart of the controversy. The Israelites west of the Jordan interpreted the building of this altar as an attempt to abandon and replace the authorized place of worshipping Yahweh—Yahweh's tabernacle. Yahweh had specified an authorized place of worship for Israel in Deuteronomy 12:5, 11, 13–14 (see also Leviticus 17:8–9).

Two statements made by the delegation reflect the seriousness of this matter. First, they compare the act of building an altar both to Israel's sin at Peor (Numbers 25) and to Achan's more recent sin at

Jericho (Joshua 7). Second, the delegation even suggest that the east-Jordan tribes should move west and share their land if it will keep them from worshipping at an unauthorized altar.

Clarification

In verses 21–29, the east-Jordan tribes explain what they have attempted to accomplish by building the altar. Their opening confession—'Yahweh, God of gods! Yahweh, God of gods!'—reveals their hearts (v. 22). They had no intention of rebelling or acting unfaithfully against Yahweh by offering sacrifices on the altar. Rather, they built it as a witness to the unity between them and the west-Jordan tribes (v. 27) and as a copy or replica of the real altar of Yahweh (v. 29). They feared that future generations living west of the Jordan might prohibit the east-Jordan tribes from coming to worship. In fact, the altar's location verifies its intended use. The east-Jordan tribes would certainly have built it on their side of the Jordan, the east side, if they had really intended to offer sacrifices on it.

Phinehas and the delegation expressed satisfaction with this explanation (vv. 30–31) and so they returned to report their findings to the Israelites (vv. 32–34). The tension is fully dissolved when the Israelites are declared pleased with the report and drop any talk of going to war against their east-Jordan relatives. Finally, the narrative closes with the east-Jordan tribes calling the altar 'Witness'. Their intent was for the altar to symbolize national unity and to affirm that Yahweh is God!

Message for today

This narrative reminds today's believers that neither unity alone nor purity of worship alone is enough. The two must be wedded together for God to be honoured. Christians cannot sacrifice purity of worship to achieve unity. Nor can they dispense with unity in the name of pure worship.

PRAYER

Father, grant your people today that courage to walk before you in purity and in unity.

FAREWELL *to the* LEADERS

The time had come for Joshua to offer his farewell speech. Consider-able time had elapsed since Yahweh had given rest to Israel, and Joshua was now an old man (v. 1). So he issued a final address to the leaders of Israel (ch. 23), and then a final address to the entire nation (ch. 24). In his farewell speech to the leaders, Joshua has nothing new to say. He revisits key themes that Yahweh has impressed on Israel throughout the conquest and distribution of the land.

It is difficult to trace a clear pattern or organizational scheme used by Joshua in this speech. Rather, he seems to repeat certain themes and ideas. This does not mean, however, that Joshua's address amounts to a rambling, disorganized jumble of thoughts. In fact, there is a definite movement from a tone of encouragement to a tone of warning as the speech progresses. Unlike Moses, who delivered his farewell address in poetry (see Deuteronomy 32—33), Joshua deliv-ers his speech in prose. His prose seems to consist of three cycles or movements of thought: verses 3–8, verses 9–13, and verses 14–16. In each cycle, Joshua reviews what Yahweh has done for the people and then offers some instructions. Several key themes emerge from his address.

Yahweh fights for his people

The first theme to emerge in Joshua's farewell address to the leaders is that Yahweh fights for his people. This theme surfaces in verse 3, and then again in verse 10. As a warrior, Yahweh 'drives out' the enemy despite the enemy's strength (vv. 9, 13). Thus, one Israelite warrior can send a thousand enemy warriors on the run (v. 10).

Love and obedience

Another theme that appears in Joshua's farewell address to the leaders concerns Israel's responsibility to love and obey Yahweh. In verse 6, Joshua challenges the leaders to 'observe and do all that is written in the book of the law of Moses, turning aside from it neither to the right nor to the left'. This echoes the challenge that Yahweh had issued to Joshua at the outset of Joshua's career as Israel's leader (see 1:7). Yet this obedience was to happen in the context of a loving relationship with Yahweh (v. 11). In the ancient Near East, people typically obeyed and served their gods in an attempt to manipulate them to provide fertility or a good harvest. However, Israel had the privilege of serving a personal God whom they could love.

Separation from the gods of Canaan

Related to the theme of loving and obeying Yahweh was the theme of remaining separate from the gods of the Canaanite culture. Joshua explicitly warned Israel about mentioning the names of these gods, swearing by them, serving them, or bowing down to them (v. 7). Separation from the Canaanite gods and goddesses required separation from the Canaanites who worshipped them.

Yahweh's judgment

Finally, Joshua's farewell address to the leaders warns them about Yahweh's judgment. The fact that Yahweh keeps his promises cuts two ways. In addition to his promise to bless his people (see vv. 5, 10, 14), he also promises to bring judgment on his people for their disobedience (vv. 15–16). The Israelites will perish quickly and face destruction if they violate the covenant that Yahweh has made with them. Although Yahweh is a God of love, his character prompts him to respond in anger against sin (v. 16; see Exodus 34:5–7). Yahweh's anger is not an out-of-control temper, but a measured outrage against evil (see commentary on 7:1–5, p. 43).

Summary

Like any other good speech or sermon, Joshua's farewell address does more than offer some 'random thoughts'. Rather, the ideas in his speech work together to express a central idea: when you hold fast to Yahweh, he fights for you; when you hold fast to the gods of your culture, he fights against you.

PRAYER

Loving God, help me to hold fast to you. Help me to be faithful to show you love and obedience.

YAHWEH'S GRACE

Joshua's farewell to the entire nation takes the form of a covenant renewal ceremony (24:25). Joshua 24, as well as the law of Moses, resembles the format of Hittite treaties made by great kings (suzerains) with people they had subjected (vassals). This covenant renewal ceremony takes place at Shechem (v. 1), the site of an earlier covenant renewal ceremony (see 8:30–35). Shechem was also the place where Yahweh first promised to give the land of Canaan to Abraham's offspring (Genesis 12:6–7).

The first section of Joshua's speech, verses 2–13, presents the word of Yahweh to the people. It resembles the beginning of a Hittite 'suzerain-vassal treaty' by offering a preamble which identifies the great king (v. 2a) and then a historical prologue which surveys the previous relationship between the great king and the subject people (vv. 2b–13). Ideally, a review of the past history between the two parties would convince the subject people that such a relationship would benefit them. The preamble section of Yahweh's address simply identifies him as 'Yahweh, the God of Israel' (v. 2a).

Abraham and the patriarchs

The historical prologue begins in verses 2–4 with Abraham. Perhaps the most striking details here concern Abraham's past. He was simply another pagan living in the ancient Near East when Yahweh took him from beyond the Euphrates River and led him to the land of Canaan. The picture is that Yahweh pulled Abraham away from his former gods as well as from his former homeland. A quick survey of Abraham's descendants and the mention of Jacob's move to Egypt bring the focus to the next significant event.

Moses and the exodus from Egypt

In verses 5–7, the focus shifts to Moses and Aaron and the deliverance of Israel from Egypt. Yahweh briefly mentions the plagues (v. 5a), but devotes most of his brief survey to the Red Sea deliverance (vv. 5b–6). This reveals his main concern—reminding Israel that he had provided deliverance for them. The exodus stands as the critical event in Israel's history. It was to the Israelite what the cross is to today's Christian—God's salvation of his people from bondage.

This section closes with a sweeping reference to Israel's time in the wilderness.

The conflict with the Amorites

The historical prologue now moves to the conflict that Israel had with the Amorites on the eve of their entrance into the promised land of Canaan (vv. 8–12). Here, Yahweh reminds the Israelites of how he delivered them from Balaam (Numbers 22—24), how he handed the citizens of Jericho over to them (see Joshua 6), and how he drove out the two kings of the Amorites—an obvious reference to the defeats of Sihon and Og (see the commentary on Joshua 12:1–24, pp. 68–69, for a discussion of these defeats, which are recorded in Numbers 21:21–35). The reference to Yahweh sending 'the hornet' ahead of the Israelites probably symbolizes the terror or panic that Yahweh sent, although some have taken it as a symbolic reference to Egypt or to literal insects (see also Exodus 23:28; Deuteronomy 7:20).

A gift of Yahweh's grace

The survey of Israel's history leads to a summary conclusion which affirms that Israel received the land of Canaan as a gift from Yahweh (v. 13). The people received land they had not worked, towns they had not built, and produce from vineyards and orchards they had not planted. In other words, they received undeserved favour, the grace of Yahweh.

This historical survey reminds us that the life we have in Jesus Christ is a gift of God's grace. Israel's story is essentially your story! At some point, God broke into your pagan way of life (as he did with Abraham), saved you (as he did in the Exodus event), and blessed you with a life of victory (as he did in driving out the Amorites). Salvation is solely a gift of grace (Ephesians 2:8–10).

MEDITATION

For by grace you have been saved through faith, and this is
not your own doing; it is the gift of God—not the result of works,
so that no one may boast.

Ephesians 2:8–9

The PEOPLE'S CHOICE

Joshua's farewell address now shifts from a review of the past to a challenge for the present. The address continues to resemble a Hittite treaty made by a great king (suzerain) with the people he subjected (vassals). Following the preamble (24:2a) and the historical prologue (24:2b–13), Joshua's address now contains a section of stipulations that describe the responsibilities of the vassal to the suzerain (vv. 14–24).

The choice of whom to serve

The 'stipulations section' of Yahweh's treaty with his people takes the form of a challenge from Joshua. Basically, he challenges them to serve Yahweh. This is the proper response to his gracious gift of the land (24:2–13). The term 'serve' (Hebrew *abad*), which occurs eighteen times in Joshua 24, expresses exclusive allegiance and devotion to someone or something.

Joshua's challenge to 'choose this day whom you will serve' (v. 15) is one of the most well-known statements in the entire book. It appears on plaques and artwork hanging in modern homes. But most people have not considered the alternatives provided by Joshua. He challenges the people to choose between serving the old gods ('the gods your ancestors served') or the new gods ('the gods of the Amorites in whose land you are living') if they are unwilling to serve Yahweh. Can Joshua be serious? Actually, he is using a touch of sarcasm to jolt them into seeing the foolishness of serving anyone but Yahweh. Yahweh is the one whom Joshua and his household choose to serve.

Joshua challenges Israel's response

The people of Israel offer an overwhelming response to Joshua's challenge, promising to serve Yahweh as their God and to avoid the sin of abandoning him for other gods (vv. 16–18). As readers, we are shocked, then, when Joshua challenges this commitment and claims that Israel is unable to serve Yahweh (vv. 19–20). The key to understanding Joshua's odd challenge is his description of Yahweh as a 'holy' God (see commentary on 5:15, p. 37) and a 'jealous' God. The term 'jealous' refers to a 'strong desire to possess something'. Because Yahweh has such a strong claim on his people whom he created and delivered, he cannot tolerate anything less than exclusive allegiance to him. This helps us to understand the strong statement that Yahweh would not forgive the people's transgressions or sins (v. 19). The statement seems to contradict other statements in the Old Testament which picture Yahweh as a God who does forgive sin (see Exodus 34:5–7). However, the picture in verse 20 is that Yahweh does not forgive people when they are serving foreign gods. It does not suggest that Yahweh withholds his forgiveness when his people turn back to him.

Joshua's challenge, then, is not an attempt to dissuade Israel from serving Yahweh. After all, he has made the same commitment for himself and his household (v. 15). Joshua simply wants the people of Israel to consider the gravity of making such a commitment. In the end, they are still adamant about committing themselves to serving Yahweh (vv. 21–24).

Final treaty elements

Joshua's actions in verses 25–27 reflect additional elements in the suzerain–vassal treaties of the Hittites. His act of writing the words in the book of the law of God (v. 26a) reflects the custom of depositing the text and providing for its periodic public reading. The 'book of the law of God' refers to Israel's copy of the law of Moses. Furthermore, by setting up the large stone as a witness (vv. 26b–27), Joshua reflects the custom of recognizing witnesses to the treaty. Usually, the Hittite treaties recognized gods as witnesses. In accordance with Israel's exclusive devotion to Yahweh, however, Joshua selected an object rather than an idol.

The covenant renewal ceremony closes in verse 28 with Joshua sending the people back to their inheritances.

MEDITATION

Think about how you experience the temptation to serve 'false gods'. How can God's gifts such as work, wealth, happiness and pleasure become gods that undermine our allegiance to him?

THREE BURIALS *in the* LAND

The book of Joshua concludes with the report of three burials and a notice about Israel serving Yahweh during Joshua's life and after Joshua's death. This conclusion brings the book to a peaceful end, confirming the Israelites' possession of the land and their faithfulness to Yahweh. Through this material, the narrator declares a prophetic message that choosing to serve Yahweh brings stability to people's lives.

Joshua's death and burial

The notice of Joshua's death and burial is brief, yet profound. The details make some key points. To begin with, Joshua is called 'the servant of the Lord' (v. 29a) for the first time in the book of Joshua. Until now, this title had been reserved for Moses and applied to him fourteen times in the book (1:1, 13, 15; 8:31, 33; 11:12; 12:6 [twice]; 13:8; 14:7; 18:7; 22:2, 4, 5). This detail places Joshua on the same level as Moses in terms of Joshua's faithfulness in leading Yahweh's people. Second, the narrator informs us that Joshua had lived 110 years (v. 29b). This detail declares that Joshua has lived a full life. Third, the narrator reports that Joshua was buried in his own inheritance (v. 30). This confirms that Joshua and Israel received the inheritance that Yahweh had promised to them.

Israel's faithful service

The information provided in verse 31 affirms the quality of Joshua's leadership. Israel served Yahweh during all of Joshua's days as well as during all the days of the elders who lived past Joshua and knew what Yahweh had done for his people. The double occurrence of the word 'all' (Hebrew *kol*) in verse 31 leaves no doubt about the scope of Israel's obedience. They did, in fact, follow through with the commitment they had made to join Joshua in serving Yahweh (see 24:24).

The burial of Joseph's bones

The notice about Joseph's bones being buried at Shechem (v. 32) brings closure to a promise that Joseph's brothers had made a few hundred years earlier. The entire scene in Genesis 50:24-26 is worth revisiting: 'Then Joseph said to his brothers, "I am about to die; but God will surely come to you, and bring you up out of this land to the land that he swore to Abraham, to Isaac, and to Jacob." So Joseph made the Israelites swear, saying, "When God comes to you, you shall carry up my bones from here." And Joseph died, being one hundred and ten years old; he was embalmed and placed in a coffin in Egypt.' Thus, the narrator's report about Joseph's burial says, 'Israel is back in the land and now possesses it!' What had been anticipated has now become reality.

Eleazar's death and burial

Finally, the narrator closes the book with a brief report of Eleazar's death and burial (v. 33). Eleazar, the son of Aaron, was the high priest who had helped Joshua with the distribution of land by casting lots (14:1; 17:4; 19:51; 21:1) and who handled the altar controversy (ch. 22). The report of his death and burial highlights the passing of Joshua's generation from the scene. Through Joshua and Eleazar, Israel conquered and divided the land.

Message for today

The book's satisfying, fulfilling ending underscores its message: it makes sense to trust and obey Yahweh when he leads you into new challenges because Yahweh keeps his promises. Like the ancient Israelites, we have to choose how we will spend our lives. As the end of the book of Joshua shows, the only choice that makes sense is the choice to serve God. Nothing compares with the inheritance that God's people have in Jesus Christ (1 Peter 1:3–5).

PRAYER

O God of Promise,
you alone are worthy of my trust and praise.
Help me to find joy and satisfaction
in the inheritance you have given to me through Jesus Christ.
Help me to live a life that honours
your glory as a keeper of promises. Amen.

The BOOK *of* JUDGES

The book of Judges covers a period in Israel's history between Joshua's death and the establishment of the monarchy, when Israel was ruled by kings (see Ruth 1:1). As a former prophet (see Introduction, p. 13), Judges uses the medium of historical narrative to offer a prophetic message to a later generation of God's people.

Title and authorship

The English title of the book reflects the Hebrew title *shopetim*, which means 'judges'. Thus, the title stems from the central characters of the book (see 2:16–19). The judges, however, do not fulfil a judicial role (except for Deborah in 4:5) but function as deliverers. God raised up these deliverers to deal with external enemies, not internal disputes. While Jewish tradition recognizes the prophet Samuel as the author of the book, Judges is anonymous. It is apparent that the author worked from the same theological tradition shaped by the book of Deuteronomy. The concern that the Israelites 'did what was evil in the sight of the Lord' (Judges 2:11; 3:7, 12; 4:1; 6:1; 10:6; 13:1) finds its roots in Deuteronomy (Deuteronomy 4:25; 9:18; 17:2; 31:29). The recurring statement, 'In those days there was no king in Israel' (Judges 17:6; 18:1; 19:1; 21:25) indicates that the book was completed sometime during the monarchy in Israel. The reference in 18:30 to 'the time the land went into captivity' places its completion after Dan and the other northern tribes fell to Assyria between 734 and 722BC.

Purpose and message

The author selected and arranged stories from the pre-monarchy period of the judges to challenge God's people living during the monarchy. Specifically, he shaped his material to issue a call to return to Yahweh, Israel's God, and to abandon the pagan religion of Israel's neighbours.

The message of the book is in line with this purpose. Many scholars take their cue from the refrain, 'In those days there was no king in Israel' and conclude that Judges defends the establishment of the monarchy in order to bring order to the chaos in Israel. However, the writer includes material that seems to criticize the monarchy (Judges 8:22–32; 9:7–16). Furthermore, as a prophetic work, the book's mission is not to defend an institution (the monarchy) but to challenge people's beliefs and behaviour. The message of the book is that God's people in pre-monarchy days disintegrated when they became like their Canaanite neighbours. The implication is that God's people living during the monarchy will disintegrate too if they live like their pagan neighbours instead of following God's law as it was given through Moses. The prophet directed this message to the southern kingdom of Judah because, according to 18:30, the fall of the northern kingdom of Israel had already taken place (in 734–722BC).

Structure

The writer arranged the book of Judges in three distinct sections. A prologue (1:1—3:6) provides a summary overview of Israel's failure to conquer the Canaanites (1:1—2:5) and then attributes this failure to Israel's tendency to serve the gods of the Canaanites instead of Yahweh (2:6—3:6). The main body of the book (3:7—16:31) tells the actual stories of the deliverers in Israel. The writer reviews thirteen deliverers but singles out seven to cover in detail. Together, these stories portray a downward spiral as the quality of the deliverers and their leadership deteriorates. The epilogue (chs. 17—21) contains two stories that emphasize the extent to which Israel adopted the religion and morals of its Canaanite neighbours.

Relevance for today

Hebrews 11:32 cites Gideon, Barak, Samson, and Jephthah as models of faith. This might tempt us to read Judges as a book of stories of heroes whom we should emulate. However, each of these leaders had major shortcomings. Judges offers the 21st-century reader a warning and encouragement. The warning is that God's people will self-destruct when they are conformed to popular culture instead of following God's word. The encouragement is that God graciously intervenes to bring peace to those who turn back to him.

PRAYER

Father, as I read Judges, turn my heart to your laws
and to your ways.

A MISSION *to* FINISH

Verse 1 reminds us of Joshua 1:1. At the beginning of Joshua, Moses had died. Yet the people faced the challenge of conquering the rest of Canaan and then settling in it. Joshua rose to the occasion to lead God's people. Now, in Judges 1:1, Joshua has died. Yet the people of Israel are poised to finish the mission—occupying the promised land.

Inquiring of Yahweh

The first step the people took was to inquire of Yahweh. This stands in contrast to a previous failure to inquire of Yahweh before taking action (see Joshua 9:14, where the same Hebrew term for 'inquire' is used). As in the rest of the Old Testament, the term 'LORD' in all capital letters signals to the reader that the Hebrew name for God here is 'Yahweh'. This name reflects the intimate relationship that God has with his people. Obviously, the Israelites were prepared to obey God's will, and they understood that God wanted them to wipe out the Canaanites (Deuteronomy 20:16–17). The reason for this was to preserve the purity of the Israelites. God did not want Israel to become evil like the Canaanites (Deuteronomy 20:18).

Yahweh's response

Yahweh responded first by giving direction. He selected Judah to go up against the Canaanites, and he offered a promise of victory. Yahweh also responded by giving success. The narrator makes it clear that Yahweh was responsible for the victory. Yahweh 'gave the Canaanites and the Perizzites into their [Judah's] hand' (v. 4).

An alert reader will also notice the tribes of Israel working together. Judah asks Simeon for assistance, and Simeon responds favourably. The alliance was natural since the founders of these tribes, Judah and Simeon, were full brothers. Both were sons of Jacob and Leah (Genesis 29:33, 35). Furthermore, Simeon's land grant was located within Judah's territory (Joshua 19:1, 9).

Amputating thumbs and big toes

The narrator then takes time to relate a strange detail about the battle at Bezek. While the location of this city is presently unknown, it must have been near Jerusalem. Anyway, Judah's warriors pursue, capture, and then torture the 'lord of Bezek'—the meaning of the Hebrew expression, 'Adoni-Bezek'. They cut off his thumbs and big toes. Though horrifying to our sensibilities as modern readers, such an act of mutilation was common in ancient warfare. While the narrator does not comment on this act of mutilation, he allows Adoni-Bezek to interpret its significance. Ironically, Adoni-Bezek accepts it as God's way of paying him back for his own similar acts of cruelty. Adoni-Bezek, in fact, had humiliated seventy other kings by cutting off their thumbs and big toes and then reducing them to the status of beggars. They had to scavenge scraps from his table in order to subsist. If the number seventy seems a bit large to us, we must remember that these kings are rulers of city-states, not of entire countries.

A noble beginning

So, in the opening scene of Judges, the people of Israel offer a model for beginning a successful campaign. Prepared to do God's will, they inquire of him before proceeding. Then, they work together. God responds by giving the victory he promised. This scene raises our expectations as readers. The people of Israel show so much promise. Will they continue to follow Yahweh and revel in the success he gives?

An alert reader may detect an ominous note in this opening scene. The narrative subtly hints that the newly arrived Israelites are acting like the Canaanites. On the one hand, the warriors of Judah obey God once they reach Jerusalem by completely destroying the city (v. 8; Deuteronomy 20:16–18). But instead of executing Adoni-Bezek along with the rest of the residents of Bezek, the warriors mutilate him and bring him to Jerusalem as a trophy of war. He dies at Jerusalem, possibly from loss of blood or from infection.

PRAYER

Yahweh God, I need to ask you before I act for you.
Help me to inquire of you before I proceed to do your will. Help me
to co-operate with other servants who are also
working for your kingdom.

52

An IMPRESSIVE FAMILY

In verse 9, the time reference ('Afterward') and the verb form work together to signal the start of a new episode. This episode documents the progress that the Israelite tribes made towards driving the Canaanites out of the hill country south of Jerusalem, out of the Negeb (the desert region further south), and out of the lowland (the western foothills between the Judean hills and the Mediterranean coast).

Why all the details?

As we read the narrative, we may find the details tedious. Why does it matter that 'the name of Hebron was formerly Kiriath-arba' (v. 10)? Why does the narrator need to mention the names of the defeated leaders—Sheshai, Ahiman and Talmai (v. 10)? While boring to modern readers, these details validate the narrator's claim: the mention of actual places and specific leaders verifies that this conquest actually happened.

Caleb's challenge

In verses 11–15, the narrator includes an account of the attack against Debir, involving Caleb (see Joshua 14:6–15) and his daughter, Achsah. This account has already appeared in Joshua 15:14–19, so why does the narrator of Judges duplicate it here? The answer is that the account contributes to the narrator's argument. Before exploring this argument, let's consider the details of the story. Caleb promises his daughter, Achsah, as a wife to anyone who attacks Kiriath-sepher, the former name of the city of Debir (v. 11). Apparently, this city existed within his allotment of land. Othniel, Caleb's nephew and a member of the next generation, accepts the challenge. Caleb then gives his daughter, Achsah, to Othniel as a wife.

Achsah's initiative

Far from being a pawn, however, Achsah takes action herself. She urges her husband to ask her father for more land. The Hebrew verb translated 'urged' in verse 14 means 'to incite, prompt, instigate'. When her father questions her about her wish, she asks for a field with water resources. She needs this because of her land's location in the Negeb—a desert region. Curiously, the NRSV does not translate some key Hebrew expressions but puts them into English characters. Achsah asks for 'Gulloth-mayim', which means 'bowls (reservoirs) of water' (v. 15). Caleb grants her request, giving her 'Upper Gulloth and Lower Gulloth', meaning 'upper and lower bowls (or reservoirs)' (v. 15).

Making sense of this scene

How do we understand this scene? The narrator shapes his account to draw attention to Othniel and Achsah. Hebrew narrative generally shows us rather than tells us about a character's traits, and this story is no exception. Othniel's actions reveal his courage and his willingness to tackle a challenge. Achsah's actions portray her as a shrewd, resourceful person. She understands the challenge of living in an arid land, so she pursues a source of water.

What, then, does this scene contribute to the narrator's argument? Again, Hebrew narrative communicates indirectly. Through this anecdote, the narrator informs us that Caleb's son-in-law possesses the same courage and initiative that marked out his father-in-law. Likewise, Caleb's daughter possesses the same spirit of determination as her father. Both Othniel and Achsah model the courage and determination needed by the people of Israel to experience the blessings that God had promised. Israel will succeed in her mission if her sons and daughters resemble Caleb and act faithfully to fulfil the charge that God gave through Joshua (Joshua 1:6, 10–11).

The theology communicated by this principle still holds true today: God honours those who take proactive, intentional steps to pursue what he has asked them to do.

PRAYER

Father, give me the courage and the strength to act on your promises. Help me to pursue your commands with determination, with shrewdness, and with intensity. 'Oh that you would bless me and enlarge my border' (1 Chronicles 4:10).

The CAMPAIGN of COMPROMISE

The account of the Israelite tribes' conquest of Canaan continues in verse 16, with a shift in topic. Beginning with the descendants of Moses' father-in-law and with the men of Judah, the remainder of Judges 1 describes the various tribes' level of success in displacing the Canaanites from the land. An alert reader will detect a problem. Israel is struggling to drive the Canaanites completely out of the land.

Failure to drive out the Canaanites

Compromise taints the campaign. First, the descendants of Moses' father-in-law settle with the Amalekites rather than driving them out of the land (v. 16). Then, while Yahweh's presence enabled Judah to take possession of the hill country, Judah could not drive out the inhabitants of the plain (v. 19). The narrator attributes this failure to the iron chariots possessed by the inhabitants of the plain, yet the reader must wonder why Yahweh's presence does not enable Judah to overcome superior military technology. Then, in contrast to Caleb's success at Hebron (v. 20), the Benjaminites fail to dislodge the Jebusites living in Jerusalem (v. 21).

In verses 22–26, the narrator offers a brief account of the house of Joseph's campaign against the city of Bethel. At first, the capture of Bethel seems to present itself as a parallel to the capture of Jericho (Joshua 2; 6). Yahweh is with the house of Joseph (v. 22). They send spies to Bethel (v. 22), and these spies end up making a deal with a resident of the city (v. 24). Once the house of Joseph captures the city, they destroy all its inhabitants except for the man and his family (v. 25). Upon further reflection, however, the narrator has related the story in a way that invites readers to see the *contrast* between this event and the capture of Jericho. In the Jericho story, the spies make their agreement with Rahab after testimony concerning Yahweh (Joshua 2:8–14). In our present story, the man who helps the spies is silent concerning Yahweh. Most significantly, he does not identify himself with the Israelites and their God, Yahweh. Rather, the Israelites release him, and he builds another Canaanite city of his own.

Throughout the remainder of Judges 1, the report of failure picks up momentum as the narrator looks to the tribes in the north. The tribes of Manasseh (vv. 27–28), Ephraim (v. 29), Zebulun (v. 30), Asher (vv. 31–32), and Naphtali (v. 33) failed to drive out the Canaanites in their respective regions. Nor could the tribe of Dan overcome the Amorites who controlled the plain and confined the Danites to the hills (v. 34–36).

A disheartening assembly

What conclusion should we draw from Israel's failure to achieve complete conquest? Who is at fault? The scene in Judges 2:1–5 answers our questions. Once again, the people of Israel are assembled. Unlike the positive atmosphere of the first assembly when Yahweh promised success (Judges 1:1–2), this second assembly deteriorates into weeping.

The reason for the weeping is the heavy word of judgment communicated by the angel of Yahweh. This message contains a formal charge (vv. 1–2) followed by pronouncement of sentence (v. 3). Both reflect God's clear instructions in Exodus 23:20–33. As a result of Israel's disobedience, the angel of Yahweh announces that Yahweh will not drive out the people of the land. Instead, he will allow the Canaanites to cause trouble for Israel. Specifically, the Canaanite gods will trap Israel. The people of Israel will not find the fertility, prosperity or security supposedly found in the Canaanite gods. Rather, they will find emptiness, misery and slavery.

In response to the angel of Yahweh's word of judgment, the people wail and weep. This event was so significant that they named the place 'Bochim'—a Hebrew word which means 'weepers'. Their sacrifice seems to indicate repentance, but the repentance is too late and turns out to be short-lived.

MEDITATION

Identify some areas in your life where you find it difficult to obey God's word completely. Ask God to help you to pursue complete obedience rather than compromise.

ISRAEL'S DOWNWARD SPIRAL

After narrating the events that followed Joshua's death (Judges 1:1 to 2:5), the narrator returns in verse 6 to a time prior to Joshua's death. The narrator wants to trace Israel's spiritual decline. This decline follows a recurring pattern. Some have described it as a series of cycles. However, these cycles form a downward spiral as Israel's spiritual condition continues to deteriorate throughout the book of Judges.

Before describing the recurring pattern of spiritual decline, the narrator explores the cause of rebellion. How could a people whose ancestors worshipped Yahweh all the days of Joshua (v. 7) rebel against Yahweh? How could people do evil in Yahweh's sight when their ancestral leaders after Joshua saw all of Yahweh's great work on behalf of them (v. 7)? The answer is that they failed to keep alive the memory of Yahweh's acts on their behalf (v. 10). The memorial that they set up after crossing into Canaan (Joshua 4) did not work. Somehow, the awareness of God's deliverance did not get passed down from one generation to the next. When God's people forget his goodness to them, rebellion is sure to follow. Forgetting Yahweh's work on their behalf thrust the people into a downward spiral. This downward spiral will be played out in the narratives that make up the main body of the book of Judges. In verses 11–19, the narrator describes it.

Israel's rebellion

The formula at the beginning of verse 11—'the Israelites did what was evil in the sight of the Lord'—echoes language from the book of Deuteronomy (Deuteronomy 4:25; 9:18; 17:2; 31:29). This act of rebellion consists of abandoning Yahweh, who had delivered their ancestors from Egypt, and worshipping the Baals and Astartes (vv. 11, 13).

When Israel entered the promised land, the Canaanites who lived there believed in an assortment of gods and goddesses. These deities resembled the people who invented them. They got drunk, they murdered, they lied, they cheated, and they even got involved in incest. One of the chief Canaanite gods was called Baal. Supposedly, he was one of seventy sons of El, the father of all the gods. Canaanites believed that Baal controlled the rain, caused crops to grow, controlled fire and lightning, and exercised power over life, birth, sickness and death. Baal was represented by an upright stone. Astarte, Baal's spouse, was the goddess of fertility, love and war. She was represented by carved female figurines with exaggerated breasts and prominent genitals. The Israelites rebelled against Yahweh by abandoning exclusive allegiance to him and paying homage to these local deities.

Yahweh's response

In his anger over Israel's rebellion, Yahweh sells them out to their enemies, even as they have sold him out in exchange for false gods (vv. 14–15). As a result, the people of Israel find themselves in 'great distress' (v. 15)—an expression that refers to a tight, narrow spot. Yahweh responds, though, to this distress by raising up judges who deliver the Israelites from their oppressors (v. 16). As noted previously, these judges function as deliverers rather than judicial leaders. Unfortunately, Israel did not listen to these judges but instead turned to the worship of false gods (v. 17).

In the Hebrew text, the grammar of verses 18–19 indicates that the narrator has stopped the action to add some further details. Two major details emerge. First, we are informed that Yahweh's deliverance of the people stemmed from his compassion for them. Second, we learn that each time a judge died, the people returned to ways even more corrupt than before.

MEDITATION

Identify some examples of how evil in our society has progressively worsened. Where do you see this downward spiral happening in our communities of faith?

TESTING & FAILURE

The discussion begun in Judges 2:6 continues. Now the narrator introduces a new dimension: instead of removing the peoples that Israel failed to remove, Yahweh will leave them for testing purposes.

Yahweh's statement

After a reference to Yahweh's anger, the narrator quotes Yahweh's statement about his future relations with his people (vv. 20–21). Yahweh's reference to Israel as 'this people' instead of 'my people' expresses the distance that Israel's disobedience has created. As a result of this failure to obey, Yahweh announces that he will no longer drive the evil nations out of the promised land.

The narrator's assessment

The narrator assesses Yahweh's purpose behind his decision, concluding that Yahweh is leaving evil nations in Canaan in order to test Israel (v. 22). The term 'test' must have reminded the original readers of God's test of Abraham's faith (Genesis 22:1). Once again, God is testing the faith of his people. He will see whether or not they care to walk in the 'way of Yahweh'.

A catalogue of nations

Next, the narrator elaborates on the nations that Yahweh left to test Israel. Readers must not surmise from the chapter break that a new discussion has begun. Judges 3:1–6 simply continues the discussion begun in 2:6.

According to verses 1–2, the test will involve war. The phrases in verse 2 are critical—'that successive generations of Israelites might know war, to teach those who had no experience of it before'. Some scholars suggest that the concern is for the Israelites to learn how to fight so that they will be ready for confrontations with major powers. The real concern, however, is for Israel to learn the nature of holy war—the challenge of wiping out the evil nations under the command of Yahweh.

In verse 3, the writer provides a catalogue of the 'nations of testing'. The Philistines were sea peoples who migrated from Crete and the area of the Aegean Sea. After defeat by the Egyptians in 1190BC, the Philistines settled in five cities along the Mediterranean coast of southern Canaan. This explains the reference to the 'five lords of the Philistines'. The mention of 'all the Canaanites' apparently includes all the residents of Canaan, including people groups mentioned in verse 5. The Sidonians represent the Phoenicians, whose leading port city was Sidon. Based on the accompanying geographical descriptions, the Hivites lived north of the Sea of Galilee. Referring to these four groups provided a means of referring to the entire region of Canaan: south-west (Philistines), south-east (Canaanites), north-west (Sidonians), and north-east (Hivites).

Verse 4 functions as a reminder, stressing what the narrator concluded earlier in the discussion (2:22): Yahweh's purpose in leaving these nations is to test Israel's obedience to his commands given through Moses.

Failing the tests

So how did Israel handle these tests? Sadly, the narrator reports that Yahweh's people failed his tests. He cites two pieces of evidence in verse 6. First, they practised intermarriage with the pagan people of the land, violating Deuteronomy 7:1–4. Second, they worshipped the gods of these pagans, violating Deuteronomy 7:5. Even Yahweh's gracious interventions did not keep Israel from becoming like her pagan neighbours. Clearly, something more was needed. The sombre message of Judges prepares us for the later promise of a new covenant which will provide a measure of forgiveness and spiritual power needed for obeying God's commands (Jeremiah 31:31–34; see also Ezekiel 36; Joel 2).

PRAYER

Holy Father, help me through the power of your Spirit to pass the tests that you place in my life. I want to honour you, not fail you.

The OTHNIEL STORY

In the main body of Judges, which runs from 3:7 to 16:31, the narrator reviews thirteen deliverers. However, he singles out seven of them to cover in detail: Othniel (3:7–11), Ehud (3:12–30), Deborah (4:1—5:31), Gideon (6:1—8:32), Abimelech (8:33—9:57), Jephthah (10:6—12:7), and Samson (13:1—16:31). These stories form a downward spiral, reflecting the deterioration of Israel's spiritual condition.

The initial story of Othniel functions as a sort of template. The story is rather lean, but it establishes a recurring pattern. In each of the later stories, the narrator elaborates on particular elements of the pattern and leaves out others. By the time the reader arrives at the Samson account, the elements are barely visible. Perhaps this breakdown of the literary template established in 3:7–11 reflects the breakdown of the moral condition in Israel.

Rebellion

The pattern begins with Israel doing evil in the sight of Yahweh (v. 7). This evil consists of forgetting their God, Yahweh, and serving 'the Baals and the Asherahs'. Most references to the Asherahs in the Old Testament refer to wooden idols, or even idols carved into trees.

Retribution

As a result of this evil, Yahweh's anger burned against Israel, and he sold them into the hand of a king identified as Cushan-rishathaim of Aram Naharaim. The term 'Naharaim' is a Hebrew expression meaning 'of the two rivers'—most likely the Euphrates and Tigris rivers. The region is modern-day eastern Syria and northern Iraq. After the name Cushan, the designation 'rishathaim' means 'of double evil'. This designation provides intimidation and testifies to Yahweh's resolve to bring judgment on his wayward people.

The narrator makes an interesting connection which gets lost in the NRSV's translation. The same Hebrew term (*abad*) appears in verse 7 (translated 'worshipping') and in verse 8 (translated 'served'). The point is that when the Israelites served false gods, they ended up serving enemy nations. Thus, they reversed Yahweh's wonderful act of deliverance of their ancestors out of Egypt. Formerly, the Israelites had experienced agony when they served Egypt (see Exodus 1:11 and 2:23 where forms of the same Hebrew term *abad* are used). But then, they were delivered to serve God. Several statements in Exodus which call for the Egyptian Pharaoh to release God's people so that they can 'worship' him use the Hebrew term *abad* (Exodus 3:12; 7:16; 8:1). In effect, then, Yahweh allowed his rebellious people, during the time of the judges, to return to the bondage that they had previously escaped. They ended up serving King Cushan-rishathaim for eight years.

Repentance leads to restoration

Verse 9 reports that the Israelites cried out to Yahweh. The term 'cried out' is used in the Old Testament to refer to a cry of distress by a person in trouble.

In response to his people's cry of distress, Yahweh raised up a deliverer who delivered them (v. 10b). The deliverer is Othniel, Caleb's nephew, who has already distinguished himself as a man of courage and initiative (1:9–15). This is the first of seven times in Judges when the narrator refers to the 'spirit of Yahweh' coming upon, stirring, or taking possession of a deliverer (see also 6:34; 11:29; 13:25; 14:6, 19; 15:14). As a result, Othniel 'judged Israel'. The context confirms that the term 'judge' refers to acts of military leadership and deliverance rather than to judicial acts. Because of Yahweh's help, Othniel exercised power over the enemy.

Rest

As a result of Othniel's victory, the land had rest for forty years. This round number signifies a generation. The ratio of eight years' oppression to forty years' rest resembles the ratio of God's judgment on the third and fourth generations compared to his love to thousands (see Exodus 20:5; 34:7). While God's character obligates him to judge sin, his outstanding character quality is love and mercy.

PRAYER

Father God, draw me close to you. Serving other masters results only in terrible bondage. Help me to cling to you and serve you with my whole heart.

The LEFT-HANDED WARRIOR *from the* RIGHT-HANDED TRIBE

Few stories in the Old Testament appear as bizarre or crude as the Ehud story (Judges 3:12–30). But besides offering a literary master-piece—full of plot twists, foreshadowing, plays on characters' names, satire (the exposure of a character flaw through ridicule), and even humour—the narrator has provided a subtle yet profound answer to a question about God. In essence, the story functions as a literary cartoon which pokes fun at the Moabites and exalts Yahweh.

Verses 12–14 set up the story. Israel has fallen back into a cycle of rebellion against Yahweh, so Yahweh responds by raising up King Eglon of Moab to go on the attack against Israel. The Moabites were relatives of Israel. They had descended from Lot, Abraham's nephew (Genesis 19:36–37), and had settled east of the southern half of the Dead Sea. When the Israelites prepared to enter Canaan, God instructed Moses, Israel's leader at the time, not to harass or fight the Moabites (Deuteronomy 2:9). The Moabites eventually allowed Israel to pass through Moabite territory (Deuteronomy 2:29), but only after a failed attempt to curse Israel (Numbers 22—24). God turned this curse into a blessing (Deuteronomy 23:4–5). But now, Yahweh strengthens the Moabite king, Eglon, against Israel. Ironically, Eglon ends up controlling Jericho ('the city of palms')—the very first city that Joshua and the people conquered when they entered Canaan.

Where is the splendour?

In response to the cry of Israel, Yahweh raised up a deliverer named Ehud. 'Ehud' is the Hebrew expression, 'Where is the splendour?' Ehud's name raises the question which Israel had been asking for the eighteen years of Eglon's oppression: 'Where is the splendour?' 'God, where is your majesty?' The story will answer this question.

Left-handed warrior and fattened calf

At the end of verse 15, the narrator supplies a key detail about Ehud: he was left-handed. Unlike storytellers such as Charles Dickens or Sir Arthur Conan Doyle, Hebrew storytellers rarely offer any physical description of their characters. When such details appear, they always serve the storyline. Ehud's left-handedness is even more ironic and humorous in the light of his tribe of origin—the tribe of Benjamin. Benjamin is a Hebrew expression meaning 'son of the right hand'. So what should we make of Ehud's left-handedness? Verse 16 hints at the answer. Ordinarily, a right-handed warrior strapped his sword on to his left hip. When a man arrived to present tribute to a king like Eglon, the king's bodyguards would normally make a visual check or frisk the visitor's left hip for a weapon. According to verse 16, though, Ehud made a shorter-than-usual sword (18 inches) with a double-edged blade. This made it suitable for a quick stab rather than a forceful hack. He then concealed the weapon under his clothes on his right thigh—a location not normally frisked. This action raises suspense and foreshadows Ehud's intention.

In verse 17, the narrator describes King Eglon, to whom Ehud presented the tribute, as a 'very fat man'. Once again, commenting on a character's physique is rare, and this comment seems downright offensive. However, given the fact that the name Eglon means 'calf', the narrator uses a touch of humour to foreshadow Eglon's fate. King Eglon is a fattened calf headed for slaughter! He has fattened himself by practising extortion. As conquering king, Eglon would have extracted a hefty tax from the defeated Israelites. This is confirmed by the need for Ehud to enlist people to help him transport the tribute (3:18).

By this point in the story, the narrator holds us in suspense. Ehud has paid the tribute. Is he going to use his concealed weapon? After all, Yahweh has raised him up as a deliverer (v. 15). What will happen to Eglon, the fattened calf? Most of all, we wonder about the question contained in Ehud's name: 'Where is the splendour?' The Israelites have suffered under the hand of Eglon for eighteen years. They have turned from their rebellion to cry out to Yahweh. When will Yahweh intervene and show his splendour and majesty?

MEDITATION

Identify some situations in your life—including the consequences you face for your own rebellion—which prompt you to ask, 'God, where is your majesty?'

EHUD'S SECRET MESSAGE *for* EGLON

The story continues in verse 18 with Ehud presenting tribute to King Eglon of Moab. Is Ehud going to use his concealed weapon? Not for the moment. The presentation of the tribute goes off without incident, and Ehud and his assistants head for home.

Turning back to Moab

But Ehud turns back when he reaches the sculptured stones at Gilgal. Apparently, he had planned all along to do so, perhaps after gaining the king's trust by paying the tribute. The crossing at Gilgal simply represented the boundary between Israel and Moab. What was once a place of memorial of Yahweh's deliverance (Joshua 4) had become a place of idol worship.

The secret message

When Ehud arrives back at the palace, he announces that he has a secret message for the king (v. 19). The Hebrew term translated 'message' in verse 19 means 'a word, a matter, or a thing'. It resembles our English term 'something', which can refer to just about anything. The promise of 'something' for Eglon grabs his interest, so he silences and dismisses his attendants. He may have expected an additional gift or a report about a traitor in one of the Israelite tribes.

Once alone with the king, Ehud approaches. King Eglon is now sitting alone in his throne room—probably an upper room in his summer palace. This time, Ehud changes his words ever so slightly. 'I have something from God for you.' Eglon rises from his seat in anticipation, although his obesity must have made it a chore. A flurry of verbs describes Ehud's quick action. 'He *reached* with his left hand, *took* the sword from his right thigh, and *thrust* it into Elgon's belly' (v. 21). Eglon, the king God had strengthened (3:12), was now reduced to a mound of fat which oozed excrement (v. 22).

Ehud's escape

The term 'vestibule' in verse 23 occurs only here in the Old Testament, and it appears to refer to an opening of some kind. This opening, perhaps a toilet drain, must have led to a room below the king's throne room. Before escaping through this opening, Ehud locked the doors, apparently from the inside. The Hebrew verb form suggests that his act of locking the doors was a significant event in the story-line. After Ehud's departure, the king's servants waited to the point of embarrassment. The smell of human waste must have suggested that he was seated on his other 'throne', since his servants concluded, 'He must be relieving himself in the cool chamber' (v. 24). Eventually, when they could wait no longer, they took the key and opened the doors to the throne room. 'There was their lord lying dead on the floor' (v. 25).

A lengthy delay gave Ehud ample time to escape. It probably took the servants a while to realize the cause of Eglon's death, since the fat covered the dagger. When he arrived home, Ehud sounded the trumpet to summon troops (v. 27). He announced that Yahweh had given the Moabites into the hands of Israel (v. 28). Then the Israelites delivered a crushing blow to Moab, and lived at rest for the next eighty years (v. 30).

An unexpected deliverance

The resolution to the story has silenced the question posed by Ehud's name. There is no more need to ask, 'Where is the splendour?' As Ehud himself admits in verse 28, Yahweh is responsible for delivering Israel from the hands of the Moabites. But Yahweh did it in a rather unexpected way—a left-handed warrior from a right-handed tribe, a fat king tantalized by a secret message, and an escape made possible when the king's servants mistook the smell of death for the smell of a king presumably going to the toilet. Just when God's people think there is no way out of their problem, God comes through in a surprising, unexpected way!

PRAYER

Almighty God, I praise you for delivering your people in the most unique, unexpected ways.

The VICTORY of SHAMGAR

While the Shamgar story is brief, it possesses mystery and intrigue. In its brevity, it lacks the features that regularly appear in the other deliverance stories—statements about Israel's evil, Yahweh's selling them into enemy hands, Israel's distress-cry to Yahweh, Yahweh's provision of a deliverer, the land's subsequent rest, and the deliverer's death. As a result, some Bible scholars dismiss the Shamgar story as a late insertion. To be sure, the account definitely breaks up the narrative flow in this section of Judges. But readers must remain open to the possibility that the narrator intentionally inserted this story to advance the argument of the book.

Deliverance by a foreigner

Several details provide mystery and intrigue. Scholars note that the name 'Shamgar' reflects foreign origin. Hebrew names are usually built on three consonants, but this one builds on four: sh-m-g-r. In fact, the name Shamgar is repeatedly attested in texts from Nuzi, a town in northern Syria, when it was occupied by the Hurrians shortly before the period of the judges. According to ancient Egyptian texts, Hurrian rulers occupied several city-states in Canaan by the time the events in Judges took place.

Also intriguing is the designation 'son of Anath'. In Canaanite mythology, Anath was the goddess of war, as well as a wife of Baal. Thus, the designation 'son of Anath' either identifies Shamgar simply as a man or war or, more likely, as one devoted to the service of Anath. It may even identify Shamgar as a member of a group of mercenaries who fought for the Egyptians against the Philistines and were named after this Canaanite goddess of war. One ancient Egyptian inscription recognizes such a group of warriors. Besides, Anath was recognized by the Egyptians as the goddess of war. Whatever the case, Shamgar appears to be a foreign warrior identified as a servant of the Canaanite war goddess. Shamgar may not even have fought on behalf of Israelite interests, but his slaughter of six hundred Philistines (see Judges 3:3) still provided deliverance for Israel.

An unusual weapon

The narrator reveals that Shamgar accomplished his slaughter of the Philistines with an oxgoad. Judges 3:31 is the only occurrence of this term in the Old Testament. This instrument consisted of a stout stick with a bronze or iron tip, ordinarily used to prod livestock. Shamgar's choice of weaponry reflects a circumstance described by Deborah's song in Judges 5:6–8: the lack of weapons in Israel. Either the Philistines had disarmed the Israelites and their neighbours, or else the Israelites and their neighbours were too poor to craft or acquire weapons. Shamgar uses what is available and is still able to slaughter six hundred Philistines. In the end, despite Shamgar's status as a foreigner—who was, perhaps, not even fighting for Israel—and his lack of weaponry, he achieved deliverance for Israel.

Making sense of the story

What does this rather brief account contribute to the theology of the book of Judges? Like the previous story of Ehud, the story showcases God's unexpected, surprising means of deliverance. Yahweh, the real hero of Judges, shows his resourcefulness by using a foreign deliverer who lacks an instrument of warfare. Yahweh is not mentioned in this brief story, but his power and his grace are evident by the way he intervenes for Israel.

MEDITATION

Think of some difficult situations you created for yourself because of your failure to obey God. How did God show his grace and mercy by intervening on your behalf in a surprising way?

BARAK, *the* RELUCTANT GENERAL

The narrator of Judges communicates the next deliverance cycle in both a story and a song. Judges 4 offers the prose account of the events, while Judges 5 celebrates the same events in poetry. The story in Judges 4 breaks down into two episodes. The first episode runs from verses 1–10. Then, the narrator inserts a piece of information in verse 11 before moving on to the second episode.

Once again, Israel lapsed into a cycle of rebellion against Yahweh (v. 1). As a result, Yahweh sold his people into the hands of Jabin (v. 2). Jabin was king of the Canaanite city-state at Hazor, located a few miles north of the Sea of Galilee. Jabin's army general was Sisera. The reference to nine hundred chariots of iron (v. 3) indicates that Sisera's army possessed state-of-the-art military equipment.

God's command to Barak

Yahweh, through a prophetess named Deborah, issued a command to Barak to take charge of Israel's army and engage in battle with Sisera and his Canaanite army. Deborah explained that Yahweh promised to lure Sisera into battle and deliver him into Barak's hands. Yahweh's instructions for Barak to take position at Mount Tabor (v. 6) provided a distinct advantage for the Israelite army. Any Israelites who read or heard this story would have recognized that the steep, wooded slopes of Mount Tabor made chariot attack difficult. Furthermore, they would have recognized that Mount Tabor's high summit, about 1300 feet above the plain, offered a commanding view of the surrounding terrain. Israel could rush down and attack Jabin's army in the valley below, near the Wadi (a term for 'river') Kishon.

Barak's reluctance

The plot thickens when Barak balks at the assignment. He consents to go only if Deborah will go with him (v. 8). Deborah agrees to go, but adds that the way Barak is handling the situation will not lead to his glory. Rather, Yahweh will deliver Sisera into the hand of a woman (v. 9).

One option is to view Barak's reluctance as commendable. He recognized Deborah as a prophetess, and thus his desire for her to accompany him amounts to a desire for the presence of God. The assurance that Yahweh would deliver Sisera into the hand of a woman functions, then, as an authenticating sign. However, this interpretation does not account for Deborah's insistence to Barak that 'the road on which you are going will not lead to your glory' (v. 9). This amounts to a negative assessment of Barak's reluctance.

Furthermore, Deborah's promise that Yahweh would sell Sisera into a woman's hands seems unlikely as an authenticating sign. For the honour to go to a woman in a military victory would have been a shameful, embarrassing situation for a warrior. It is like a young mother rescuing an elderly man from a burning house while a veteran fireman looks on from outside, reluctant to enter. Therefore, Barak's reluctance appears to reflect a lack of faith in Yahweh rather than a desire for Yahweh's presence. This should be General Barak's finest hour. Instead, Yahweh will raise up an unlikely hero who will steal Barak's glory.

An important comment

For a moment, the narrator interrupts the story line with a comment that seems out of place (v. 11), but there are no throwaway lines in Hebrew narrative. This information about Heber the Kenite not only heightens the tension by delaying the story, but it also provides the reader with a crucial bit of information which will come into play later. A defection has taken place. Heber the Kenite, whose ancestors came from the family of Moses' in-laws, has switched his loyalties. The Kenites had been with Israel since the days of Moses, so the defection is startling. The Kenites happened to be smiths (that is, metal workers), so Heber would be useful to an army with nine hundred chariots.

The tension level is high. How will Heber the Kenite play into the drama? Who is the woman who will emerge and defeat Sisera, the Canaanite army general?

MEDITATION

Name some situations in life in which you feel a reluctance to move ahead, even though God promises victory. How will you miss out on the glory or joy of victory if you shrink back from the challenge?

JAEL, *an* UNLIKELY HERO

The second episode of the Deborah story begins with the Canaanite general, Sisera, finding out that Barak, the Israelite army general, had gone up to Mount Tabor (v. 12). The narrator does not explain how Sisera received this information but, as readers, we wonder if Heber the Kenite was the informer. After all, his defection was reported in verse 11.

Yahweh goes ahead of Israel's army

Sisera responds to this information by going on the attack. His actions are ironic. Although he seems to take charge by going on the offensive, the reader knows that Sisera is heading into a trap laid by Yahweh. Deborah, the prophetess, challenges Barak to rise and then offers two assurances of victory (v. 14). First, she announces that Yahweh has given Sisera into Barak's hands on this day. Second, she insists that Yahweh has gone out before him. The NRSV translates this second assurance as a statement, but it is actually a question. Literally, she says, 'Has not Yahweh gone out before you?' Once again, it appears as if Barak is hesitant to go into battle.

Barak responds to Deborah's charge and leads his ten thousand warriors into battle. Verse 15 credits Yahweh with the victory, revealing that he threw the enemy army into a panic. The narrator is careful to specify the objects of Yahweh's action as 'Sisera and all his chariots and all his army' (v. 15). The mention of the chariots is a subtle reminder that the technological edge held by the Canaanite army over the Israelites is no obstacle for Yahweh. In fact, General Sisera leaps from his chariot and flees on foot! Meanwhile, Barak and his soldiers completely destroy the Canaanite army. Barak has his glory, for a moment. The great battle is over, but Barak has missed his quarry— Sisera. The tension rises. How will God deliver Sisera into a woman's hand?

Jael and Sisera

Sisera flees to the tent of Jael, the wife of Heber the Kenite. Verse 17 reminds the reader of the alliance between the Canaanite king Jabin and Heber. In Jael's culture, she had no choice but to comply with her husband's loyalties. She pretends to do so by offering Sisera protection, including a nourishing drink of milk when he asked for water, as well as a covering when he lay down to take a nap. The last recorded words of Sisera's life drip with irony. In the Hebrew text, his command to Jael (v. 20) reads, 'If anyone comes by and asks, "Is there a man here?" you are to say, "There is not."'

While General Sisera was sleeping, Jael killed him. She had no sword, only the implements with which a woman secured a tent. There is delightful irony here. The commander of iron chariots ends up pinned to the ground by a wooden tent peg, driven home by a mallet in a woman's hand.

Narratives communicate theology, and this one is no exception. This story shows that Yahweh, the hero of the battle, makes heroes out of people who have the loyalty and courage to act on his promises. Barak and Jael provide a sharp contrast. General Barak lacked the courage to act on a specific promise issued by Yahweh. Jael possessed such a fierce loyalty to Yahweh and his people that she acted even without a specific word of promise from Yahweh.

The narrative closes in verse 23 with an important reminder. God is the hero. The actions of the two remarkable women, Deborah and Jael, are successful because of God's power.

What's in a name?

In this story, the names of the main characters cement the meaning and provide a dash of irony. In Hebrew, Barak means 'lightning', Deborah means 'bee', while Jael means 'mountain goat'. In the story line, 'Lightning' didn't flash. He remained passive. Meanwhile, 'Bee' is situated under a honey tree, dispensing the sweetness of justice. She also stings 'Lightning' with her words of rebuke. 'Mountain Goat' provides nourishing milk to charm the enemy into a fatal nap. Through two faithful women, 'Bee' and 'Mountain Goat', Yahweh delivers his people and restores peace to the land which flows with milk and honey.

PRAYER

Almighty God, you are the hero whose power wins battles.
May your Spirit strengthen my courage to use whatever resources
I possess to confront whatever challenges I face.

VICTORY REFLECTIONS

Judges 5 consists of a victory song of praise to Yahweh for Israel's defeat of the Canaanites in chapter 4. The song resembles the song in Exodus 15 sung by Moses and the Israelites to Yahweh after deliverance from Egypt.

As poetry, this song helps the reader to feel the rush of emotions felt by the characters involved in the battle: joy before Yahweh (vv. 2–3), the awe of Yahweh's power (vv. 4–5), the feeling of helplessness before Deborah took charge (vv. 6–8), the pride over willing volunteers (vv. 9–11), the resolve of the participating tribes (vv. 12–15a), the regret over the tribes who refused to participate (vv. 15b–17), the admiration of two particular tribes (v. 18), the swell of confidence created by such a decisive victory (vv. 19–22), the bitterness against another town that failed to help (v. 23), the admiration of Jael for her heroics (vv. 24–27), the anxiety of the fallen enemy general's mother (vv. 28–30), and the zeal for Yahweh to destroy his enemies and bless his friends (v. 31).

The narrator's introduction

The narrator declares that Deborah and Barak sang this song (v. 1). The expression 'on that day' suggests that it was a spontaneous, immediate response to the victory. Traditionally, Deborah gets credit for composing it. While this is uncertain, it certainly fits with the frequent first-person perspective and the prophetic voice of the song.

Joy before Yahweh

The song opens with a call to praise Yahweh for his people's response to the Canaanite challenge (vv. 2–3). The first line in the NRSV's translation of verse 2 is curious: 'When the locks are long in Israel'. Other English translations render it something like, 'When leaders lead in Israel'. Two occurrences of the same Hebrew root word cause the confusion. The root word may mean either 'lead' or 'grow long'. The NRSV takes its cue from Numbers 6:5 in which the root word is used to describe the practice of allowing the hair to grow long in order to fulfil a vow. If the NRSV translation of Judges 5:2 is correct, then it refers to an act of dedication in preparation for holy war. The song moves quickly, though, from recognition of human participants to the praise of Yahweh. This sets the tone for the entire song.

Power and helplessness

Verses 4–5 picture Yahweh as the supreme ruler before whom all the forces of nature tremble as he moves into battle. From Sinai, the place where he entered into covenant relationship with Israel (Exodus 19—20), he marches through Seir and Edom. This establishes his dominance over Baal and other Canaanite gods of the region.

The mood shifts in verses 6–8 as the song describes the feeling of helplessness that dominated Israel in the days before Deborah emerged to lead the people. Canaanite raiders disrupted travel, commerce and village life. Weapons of war were scarce, probably because of economic hardship.

Pride over willing volunteers

Yet despite the bleak conditions, leaders and people offered themselves to face the enemy. Verses 9–11 swell with pride and praise because of these willing volunteers. The response is so phenomenal that the song calls on all kinds of travellers to proclaim and hear it. This includes the Canaanite merchants, who are portrayed as riders of light-coloured donkeys with luxurious saddle blankets—the ancient equivalent of modern people who drive a Mercedes-Benz or a Porsche. It includes travellers who stop at watering-places and hear the gossip and news. The final line in verse 11 provides closure to the stanza by matching the opening lines in verse 9. The people who willingly offered themselves are heading to war.

MEDITATION

Think about a time when God delivered you—from danger, from a troubled spirit, from rebellion, or from an unhealthy relationship. Now, express your gratitude and joy to God for his work on your behalf.

FURTHER REFLECTIONS

As the 'Song of Deborah' continues, the dominant mood is celebration. Still, the song expresses a variety of emotions experienced during and after the defeat of the Canaanites (Judges 4).

Participants and non-participants

After offering a rousing call to Deborah and Barak (v. 12), the song describes the resolve of the tribes who accepted the summons to battle. The reference to 'the remnant' in verse 13 reminds us of the oppression that has decimated Israel. Still, though battered and beaten, several tribes rise to the occasion (vv. 14–15a).

But unexpectedly, the song begins expressing lament and regret over the tribes who refused to answer the call to arms. Reuben at least wrestled with the decision (v. 15b), but in the end its potential warriors refused to leave their comfort zone. Instead, they hung around their sheep pens and enjoyed entertainment—listening to the music played on shepherds' pipes (v. 16). Three other tribes also failed to participate (v. 17). Gad, referred to as Gilead, would not come across the Jordan. Dan was apparently preoccupied with its shipping industry. Asher was unwilling to come inland to join the battle.

Admiration and more bitterness

The mood quickly shifts from lament to praise in verse 18. The tribes of Zebulun and Naphtali receive admiration for risking their lives. Then, the emotional intensity swells in verses 19–22 as the song rehearses the actual battle. Verse 19 starts with a poetic flourish, announcing the Canaanite attack with two lines of reversed elements: 'kings–fought / fought–kings'. The observation that these kings 'got no spoils of silver' adds a touch of sarcasm. These Canaanite kings, who were used to victory, were now destined for defeat.

In verse 20, the stars are personified as warriors. This is a poetic way of referring to Yahweh's intervention. Two features—the role of cosmic forces and the flooding of the Kishon River which sweeps away the charioteers—remind the reader of Yahweh's Red Sea deliverance (see Exodus 14:19–28). This victory over the Canaanites, then, is another Red Sea-type miracle. No wonder there is a surge of confidence at the end of verse 21: 'March on, my soul, with might!' The vivid language in verse 22 signals either retreat or, perhaps, the useless flailing of the horses' front hooves as they rear up in the chaos of flooding and battle.

Once more, the mood shifts quickly in verse 23 from a rush of enthusiasm to bitterness. The angel of Yahweh announces a curse against Meroz, apparently a town in the region. The poetic language is particularly stunning. The double statement of cursing is matched by a double statement of the town's sin. Twice, the angel of Yahweh mentions their failure to come to the help of Yahweh.

Jael's heroics and Sisera's mother

In verses 24–27, the song celebrates the heroics of Jael. It lingers on the death-blow she administered by taking three lines to describe it: 'she struck... she crushed... she shattered and pierced'. The repetition of 'sank... fell' in verse 27 provides an graphic picture of Sisera's defeat. As the song crescendos towards its finale, it dramatizes the anxiety of Sisera's mother as she waits for the return of her son (vv. 28–30). She surmises that the delay in his return is due to his engagement in looting. In verse 30, the expression translated 'a girl or two' is literally 'a womb, two wombs'. This language reflects the fate of women who lived in a defeated country. They were taken as objects for sexual pleasure. The reader knows, however, that the delay in Sisera's return stems from his death at the hands of a woman.

The song closes with a zealous prayer, requesting defeat for Yahweh's enemies and success for his friends (v. 31).

PRAYER

Yahweh, you are my help, yet you call me to help you. You do not need my help, but you display your power through it. Give me courage and sun-like strength when I rise to serve you.

A DELIVERER IN HIDING

The next cycle in Israel's downward spiral centres around Gideon. Judges 6:1—8:35 contains Gideon's complex, sometimes puzzling story. The Gideon cycle reflects the larger story in Judges by starting out well but ending in disaster.

Rebellion, retribution and accusation

The story begins with the familiar report of rebellion: Israel did what was evil in Yahweh's sight, so Yahweh gave them into the hands of an oppressor (v. 1). This time, the oppressor is Midian. The Midianites lived in the dry, desolate desert region of south-eastern Sinai—far south of the Dead Sea. They were distant relatives of the Israelites, having descended from Abraham through his second wife, Keturah (Genesis 25:1–4). Typically, they invaded with the Amalekites and people of the East when the Israelites had planted crops. Pictured 'as thick as locusts' (v. 5), these invaders set up camp in Israelite territory and ravaged the produce. The Israelites' flight to the mountains, caves and strongholds suggests that the Midianites were brutal invaders. As a result of being brought low ('impoverished'), the Israelites cry out to Yahweh for help (v. 6).

Yahweh responds by reminding the Israelites of his past deliverance of them out of Egypt and his command prohibiting them from showing reverence to the gods popular in Canaan. His statement 'I am Yahweh your God' (v. 10a) signifies the special relationship he has with them. This leads to his accusation that Israel had not obeyed his voice (v. 10b).

A mighty warrior in hiding

Following his accusation, Yahweh raises up a deliverer. The angel of Yahweh appears to Gideon, son of Joash. Joash, a shortened form of Jehoash, means 'Yahweh is strong'. The name Gideon means 'hacker'. This foreshadows a function that he will soon fulfil. There is a touch of humour as the angel finds the 'mighty warrior' (v. 12) threshing wheat in a wine-press to avoid detection by the Midianites. Normally, farmers would separate the grain from the chaff in an exposed area where the wind could blow away the chaff. By contrast, a wine-press was essentially a sheltered vat—a pit in the ground.

The dialogue is interesting. Gideon questions the angel's declaration that 'Yahweh is with you' (v. 12). He asks where the wonders are, that his ancestors told about when describing the exodus event. He concludes that Yahweh has abandoned the people of Israel. But the angel of Yahweh replies by commissioning Gideon to deliver Israel (v. 14). Gideon objects, citing the weakness of his clan and his stature as the least in his father's house. Gideon's excuses call to mind Moses' excuses when Yahweh commissioned him to deliver Israel from Egypt (see Exodus 3:11). Yahweh's reply to Gideon resembles his earlier reply to Moses as he promises his presence (Exodus 3:12). Despite the promise of Yahweh's presence, Gideon harbours reluctance and asks for a confirming sign.

Yahweh's dramatic sign

The angel of Yahweh grants Gideon's request. When Gideon returns with an offering, the angel of Yahweh torches it (v. 21). Fire shoots out from the rock and literally eats the food. Then, the angel of Yahweh vanishes from sight. Instead of accepting this as a sign of favour, Gideon expresses fear for his life, but Yahweh offers reassurance. The narrator does not tell us how Yahweh communicated to Gideon, but he does relate the content of the message: 'Peace be to you; do not fear, you shall not die' (v. 23). Gideon confirms his acceptance of this message by building an altar which he names 'Yahweh is peace' (v. 24). The term 'peace' in the Old Testament refers to wholeness and well-being, not just the absence of war.

These first episodes in the Gideon cycle picture Yahweh as a gracious God who responds to his people's cry for help, who promises his presence, and who seeks peace—even though he has the power to destroy them for disobedience.

MEDITATION

God of peace, I confess that I am far too easily pleased.
I get infatuated with the false gods of our culture instead of loving
you, the true and living God. Thank you for your grace which
restores me, for your presence, and for your gift of peace.

The EXPLOITS of JERUBBAAL

Gideon had already faced a remarkable day of encounters with Yahweh. By the end of the day, this timid farmer had received a commission from Yahweh to deliver Israel from the Midianites (6:14, 16). But that same night, Yahweh called him to action. The time reference 'that night' in verse 25 signals the start of a new episode as well as the continuity of this episode with the events that took place earlier in the day. Yahweh's call to action, though, is not a call to battle the Midianites. Before striking down the Midianites, Gideon must strike down the cause of Midianite oppression—Israel's idol-worship. Yahweh had called Israel to serve him and him alone (Exodus 20:1–7; Deuteronomy 6:4), but Israel had rebelled against this command.

Demolishing the idols

The episode begins with Yahweh instructing Gideon to demolish his father's pagan worship centre. First, Gideon must take his father's 'second bull' (or 'prized bull') and pull down the altar of Baal (v. 25). Then, Gideon receives instruction to cut down the sacred pole—that is, the Asherah pole—and replace this complex with an altar to 'Yahweh your God' (v. 26). Finally, Gideon must commit the ultimate disgrace against Baal worship by offering to Yahweh the bull used to destroy the altar of Baal. In fact, Gideon is instructed to use the wood of the sacred pole for fuel. Gideon enlisted ten of his servants and complied with Yahweh's command, thus exhibiting the meaning of his name, 'hacker'. At this point in the story, the narrator offers a rare insight into a character's motive. It turns out that fear of his family and the townspeople motivated Gideon to act at night (v. 27).

An angry response

In the next scene, the townspeople rise to an unexpected sight. What they discover is a destroyed shrine and the ashes of Joash's bull on a new altar at the site (v. 28). Their speech betrays their attitude: 'Who has done this?' Instead of reflecting on Baal's inability to protect his own shrine, they show concern only for finding the person responsible for this destruction. Heresy has displaced true religion.

When the townspeople discover that Gideon is responsible, they pronounce a death sentence upon him. There is definite irony here. The townspeople pronounce the sentence they deserve for idolatry on the one who destroyed their idol.

Jerubbaal

The episode closes with Joash defending his son, Gideon, and sparing his life. For a man entrenched in idol worship, Joash shows uncommon wisdom. The point of his speech in verse 32 is that if Baal is really a god, then he can fight for himself. He can plead for himself and pass sentence in his own court of law. Thus, Joash warns that anyone who tries to interfere by doing what Baal should do (killing Gideon) will face death—presumably at the hands of Joash.

As a result of this incident, Gideon was called 'Jerubbaal'. This compound Hebrew word means 'let Baal contend'. The Hebrew grammar in verse 32 suggests that Gideon's father, Joash, gave this name to Gideon. The narrator explains the emphasis of the name, indicating that when Gideon's father called him by it, he was saying, 'Let Baal contend against him' (v. 32). Does this reflect a change of heart on the part of Joash? Does he now realize the foolishness of his pagan ways? Or does the name reflect a conviction—certainly held by the townspeople—that Baal will in fact contend against Gideon? The narrator does not make this clear. But as the story continues to develop and no harm comes to Gideon, the name will serve as a reminder of Gideon's victory over Baal.

This episode is both disturbing and encouraging. The people of Israel are becoming more and more like their pagan neighbours. They keep violating Yahweh's demand of exclusive allegiance. Yet Yahweh in his grace is still fighting for his people.

PRAYER

Father in heaven, help me to identify and demolish the idols
in my life that steal the attention you deserve. You are the lover
of my heart, and I owe you my exclusive allegiance.

OVERCOMING WEAK FAITH

A major battle is taking shape. The Midianites and their allies have assembled, crossed the Jordan River, and camped in the Valley of Jezreel (v. 33). But Israel is ready, too.

Clothed by the spirit of Yahweh

The spirit of Yahweh has taken possession of Gideon (v. 34). This is the second of seven times in Judges when the spirit of Yahweh empowers a deliverer (see also 3:10; 11:29; 13:25; 14:6; 14:19; 15:14).

The verb 'took possession' in verse 34 does not occur in any of the other six 'spirit of Yahweh' statements in Judges. Literally, the Hebrew text reads, 'And the spirit of Yahweh clothed Gideon.' In the ancient Near East, the imagery of clothing someone was used to refer to a divine or demonic force overpowering that person. Therefore, verse 34 emphasizes that the spirit of Yahweh overpowered Gideon. As a result, Gideon issued a trumpet call to arms, and his clan, as well as the rest of the tribe of Manasseh and other northern tribes, followed him.

A surprising request for confirmation

Although the reader expects to read about Israel's forces setting up camp and proceeding into battle, verse 36 offers a surprise. Gideon requests further confirmation from God. Once again, Gideon proves to be a hesitant, reluctant hero. The account of the battle will not resume until chapter 7.

Gideon asks God for a sign of confirmation and sets up the terms. He will place a fleece of wool on the threshing floor. If the fleece ends up wet with dew, though the ground is dry, then Gideon will know that God wants him to deliver Israel. Threshing floors were hard, flat surfaces free from grass or vegetation—dew-collecting agents! Thus, the result Gideon wanted could happen only if God intervened. Verse 38 indicates that 'it was so'.

But Gideon needs more confirmation. He has the audacity to ask God for another sign, even though he seems aware that his second request borders on the unreasonable. After requesting that God's anger might not burn against him, Gideon admits that he is testing

God. Gideon's expression 'make trial' in verse 39 is actually the Hebrew word 'test'—the very word that appears in Exodus 17:2 and 17:7, when Israel's response to God was clearly inappropriate. This time, Gideon asks for the fleece to be dry and the ground to be wet. Verse 40 makes it clear that God complied with this request. Gideon has now received two signs of confirmation.

Applying the event

Some modern Christians have used this episode as a model for determining God's will. They speak of 'putting out a fleece'. The procedure works like this. A believer will pray, 'Lord, if you want me to go and do missions work, please give me a sign.' Four days later, the person gets a travel agency advertisement in the mail with pictures of the Eiffel Tower and the Louvre. So the person concludes that God is directing him or her to go to France. Or a believer might say, 'Lord, if you want us to sell our home, have someone inquire about it next week even though we haven't put it on the market yet.' If someone asks about the home, the believer assumes that this is a sign from God to sell the house.

This approach is misguided, even though it is popular. In the first place, Gideon asked for a miraculous sign, not just a coincidence. Christians today who 'put out the fleece' rarely ask for something miraculous, like receiving a cheque in the mail from the Queen— someone unfamiliar with them and their needs. Second, and most important, Gideon already knew God's will. He did not 'put out a fleece' to determine God's will but to strengthen his weak faith to do what he already knew God wanted him to do.

What this story teaches us is that God, in his mercy, is patient with his people's weak faith. While unbelief shuts down God's power (see Mark 6:1–6 and James 1:6–7), God also allows weak faith time to grow.

PRAYER

Lord, help my unbelief. In your mercy, overpower my lack of faith. Give me grace to trust you more.

67

TOO MANY TROOPS

Gideon is finally ready to lead his troops into battle. As the narrator
sets the scene in verse 1, he includes two interesting features which
raise tension. First, he refers to Gideon as Jerubbaal. This reference
revisits an earlier controversy (see 6:31–32). Will Baal contend against
Gideon for tearing down Baal's worship shrine, or will Gideon be
vindicated for his devotion to Yahweh? Second, the narrator locates
the Israelite army camp beside the spring of Harod. The term 'Harod'
is a form of the Hebrew term 'trembling'. An alert reader, then, will
wonder what this designation foreshadows. What happens in the
battle to leave this site with the name 'spring of trembling?'

The first reduction of troops

Yahweh emerges in verse 2 and announces a problem with the
number of troops. His words contain irony. Instead of claiming that
Israel has too few troops, Yahweh contends that Israel has too many.
This is surprising because the Midianites have 135,000 soldiers (see
8:10) while the Israelites have only 32,000 soldiers (v. 3). Thus, the
Midianites outnumber the Israelites four to one.

Yahweh then shares the reason for his surprising assessment. With
the present number of Israelite soldiers, the Israelites would take the
credit for winning the battle instead of attributing their victory to
him. The nation would brag about its power, as indicated by the
claim, 'My own hand has delivered me' (v. 2).

Therefore, Yahweh calls on Gideon to give 'fearful and trembling'
troops the opportunity to go home (v. 3). The Hebrew language is
short on adverbs like 'very' or 'extremely'. So by putting 'fearful' and
'trembling' side-by-side, the narrator describes soldiers who are, as
we say in English, extremely afraid. Now the tension raised in verse 1
has been solved. The 'spring of trembling' received its name from
the soldiers who returned home because they trembled with fear.
Interestingly, Yahweh's command reflects his instructions in Deuteronomy 20:8. There, Israelite officials are instructed to release any
troops who are afraid or disheartened in case their fear might prove
contagious and diminish the courage of the other warriors.

As a result of Gideon's offer, 22,000 soldiers depart, leaving only 10,000 troops. Now Israel is outnumbered by about thirteen to one!

The second reduction of troops

But Yahweh is not finished reducing the troops. He says that there are still too many (v. 4). So he sets up another test designed to pare down the army. While the first test dealt with courage, the second test seems to deal with alertness. Yahweh instructs Gideon to separate the men into two groups. The Hebrew text in verses 5 and 6 is difficult. The NRSV follows the other major English translations in distinguishing between two groups of warriors. One group includes warriors who lap water as a dog laps water with its tongue. A second group includes warriors who kneel to drink. The NRSV has rearranged the order of some of the clauses and has described the 'kneelers' in verse 5 as those who are 'putting their hands to their mouths'. However, in the Hebrew text, this clause actually appears in verse 6 and describes the 'lappers'. Thus, the lappers are really pictured as scooping water with their hands like a dog uses its tongue. The kneelers simply slurp water directly from the spring. The kneelers are sent home, while the lappers are retained. It is possible that the kneelers fail the test of alertness since they could not watch for the enemy while kneeling to drink.

At any rate, 9,700 soldiers fail the test! Gideon sends them home, but their provisions and trumpets stay with the remaining three hundred. Now the odds are ridiculous: the Midianite army outnumbers the Israelite army by 450 to one. Still, Yahweh assures Gideon of victory with this pathetically small group of three hundred soldiers (v. 7). Any victory by the Israelites must now surely be attributed to the power of Yahweh.

PRAYER

Almighty God, help me to remember that you build weakness into my life to teach me that battles are won in your strength, not mine. When I face physical, emotional or intellectual weakness, show me your power.

VICTORY AT LAST!

The next episode in the Gideon story takes place 'that same night' (v. 9)—that is, immediately following the dismissal of all but three hundred soldiers in Israel's army.

A fact-finding mission

Earlier in the day, Yahweh dealt with the problem of pride. Now, he deals with the opposite problem—the presence of fear. Yahweh offers Gideon the opportunity to sneak down to the enemy camp with his servant, Purah, and overhear what the enemy is really saying. Yahweh has provided this opportunity in order to strengthen Gideon's hands —that is, to provide encouragement (v. 11). Gideon's fear stems from the enemy's strength.

The barley bread dream

Verses 13–14 record the conversation that Gideon heard when he arrived at the outskirts of the Midianite camp. One soldier tells another about his dream. In the dream, a cake of barley bread tumbled into the Midianite camp and completely knocked down the tent—that is, the entire camp. The soldier listening to this provides the interpretation, identifying both the main character and what he accomplishes. The main character is Gideon. The mention of 'the sword of Gideon' is a reference to his leadership role and his might. As to Gideon's accomplishment, the interpreter cites God's deliverance of the Midianites into Gideon's hand.

What is the significance of Gideon being portrayed in this dream as a loaf of barley bread? The narrator does not explain. However, this detail may signify Gideon's ordinariness. After all, the Jewish historian Josephus described barley bread as a tasteless, teeth-bending biscuit!

Heading into battle

Once Gideon heard the report of the dream and its interpretation, he worshipped (v. 15). The Hebrew term used here for 'worshipped' means 'to prostrate oneself on the ground before a superior'. This is the only place in Judges where the term is used to describe an Israelite's response to Yahweh. In Judges 2:12, 17, this same term describes the Israelites' sin of bowing down before pagan gods—a violation of the second commandment (see Exodus 20:5, where the same term 'bow down' is used).

After worshipping, Gideon returns to the camp of Israel and issues a call to battle which resembles the one Yahweh had issued to him earlier (v. 9). Gideon's call to battle reveals that he finally believes that Yahweh has given the Midianite army into the hand of Israel. Next, he divides the men into three companies and then distributes weapons —but the weapons turn out to be trumpets, and jars containing torches. Gideon instructs the warriors to 'do as I do' and specifically mentions blowing the trumpet. But the reader must wonder how three hundred soldiers armed with trumpets and torches will overtake a huge army.

Mass confusion

The 'middle watch' referred to in verse 19 must have been at about midnight. At this dark hour, just when the Midianites changed guards, the Israelites attacked. The attack consisted of blowing trumpets, smashing the clay jars to reveal lit torches, and crying out, 'A sword for the Lord and for Gideon!' Their cry is ironic because the Israelite warriors had no swords!

However, Israel's actions threw the Midianite army into confusion. Ordinarily, only army officers used trumpets, to give orders. So the sound of three hundred trumpets must have suggested a great number of leaders with soldiers behind them. The Midianites thought they were surrounded, so they fled and ended up using their swords on each other. Ironically, again, these swords were the only ones used in the battle. The narrator makes it clear that Yahweh gets the credit for this self-destructive sword-play (v. 22). Yahweh has demonstrated that battles are won in his strength, even when the humans involved have to operate from weakness.

MEDITATION

Hebrews 11:32–34 mentions Gideon as one who 'won strength out of weakness'. How has God forced you to operate from a position of weakness? Through your weakness, how have you experienced God's power?

HANDLING RESENTMENT

To a Hebrew reader or hearer, the grammar of the opening clause in verse 24 would have signalled a new episode. With the survivors of the Midianite army in retreat, Gideon finally calls upon the Ephraimites for help.

Heroics by the Ephraimites

When Gideon called the Ephraimites to 'seize the waters' against the Midianites (v. 24), he was asking them to prevent the Midianites from crossing the Jordan River at natural points of crossing. The location of Beth-barah is unknown to us, but it was apparently a significant crossing point on the Jordan River.

In the last half of verse 24, the narrator makes it clear that the Ephraimites accomplished their mission. In the process, they captured and executed a couple of key Midianite leaders—Oreb and Zeeb. These Hebrew names mean 'raven' and 'wolf' respectively. The fact that the Israelites named the sites after the men who were executed there reflects the significance of what the Israelites accomplished. These fierce military leaders, 'raven' and 'wolf', have been reduced to nothing. This fact is underscored by the delivery of their heads to Gideon as trophies of war (v. 25).

Was Gideon wrong to get help?

Did Gideon make a mistake by calling the Ephraimites to help, or by previously calling out men from the tribes of Naphtali, Asher and Manasseh to join the pursuit (see 7:23)? Probably not. After all, Ehud's call for additional troops to go after a retreating army seems to establish a precedent (see 3:27–28). So Gideon was not necessarily shifting from dependence on God's power to a reliance on human strength.

The Ephraimites' complaint

The chapter break here is misleading. The narrator simply presents the Ephraimites' speech to Gideon in 8:1 as the next event in the episode. The Ephraimites' words to Gideon form a bitter complaint for his failure to summon them to help fight against the Midianites.

They are referring either to his summons of men from Naphtali, Asher and Manasseh in 7:23 or even back to the initial attack (7:16–22). In case the reader misses the hostile tone behind the Ephraimites' speech, the narrator follows their words with an interpretive insight: 'And they upbraided him violently' (8:1).

Gideon offers a well-crafted diplomatic reply which diffuses the Ephraimites' anger. He states his main idea at the beginning of his speech and then restates it at the speech's end: 'What have I done now in comparison with you?' (8:2) and 'What have I been able to do in comparison with you?' (8:3). Each question is rhetorical in nature and expects the answer 'nothing'. A question is rhetorical when it intends to make a statement rather than to gain information. In between these questions, he adds yet another rhetorical question and then follows it with a declaration. The rhetorical question—'Is not the gleaning of the grapes of Ephraim better than the vintage of Abiezer?'—anticipates the answer 'yes'. The contrast is striking. The leftover grapes of Ephraim, picked when a harvester goes through the vineyard a second time, exceed the first crop of grapes of Abiezer, the clan to which Gideon belonged. Gideon's point is that the Ephraimites accomplished more than he did. His declaration, following his rhetorical question, confirms the point. God gave the Ephraimites tangible trophies of war. In ancient warfare, the ultimate triumph consisted of capturing the enemy commanders. Gideon's reply works. The anger of the Ephraimites fades.

After reading this story, readers will wonder what it contributes to the message of Judges. Basically, this story shows a breakdown of unity in Israel. Even in victory, resentment and jealousy surface. Communities of faith break down when selfish concerns overshadow the mission. It takes a brilliant, astute reply by Gideon to preserve the fragile cooperation between the tribes.

PRAYER

O Lord, keep me from the resentment and jealousy which undermine the bond of love and peace that you want your people to experience. Help me to set aside my pride and diffuse any resentment and jealousy that may be harboured by my brothers and sisters in the family of God.

INTERNAL VIOLENCE

The Gideon story takes a sad twist as Gideon, the leader who had just diffused the anger of the Ephraimites, lashes out in anger against some uncooperative Israelite cities.

Trouble at Succoth

The episode begins with Gideon crossing over the Jordan River (v. 4). At this point, he and his men are exhausted and famished, so Gideon offers a polite request to the leaders of Succoth for food since he and his men are pursuing two Midianite kings (v. 5). Succoth had been allotted to members of the tribe of Gad (see Joshua 13:24–27), so its citizens were now fellow Israelites.

Surprisingly, the officials of Succoth reject this request with a sarcastic question (v. 6). The language of their question reflects the custom in which warriors cut off the hands of their slain enemies, to provide gruesome confirmation of the warriors' accomplishment. Even more surprising, though, is Gideon's vicious reply. Instead of answering diplomatically as he had done in the previous episode (8:2), he promises to 'trample your flesh on the thorns of the wilderness and on briers' once Yahweh provides victory (v. 7). The verb 'trample' pictures someone beating grain on the threshing floor. The whole picture is savage!

Trouble at Penuel

From Succoth, Gideon heads about six miles east to Penuel, the place where Jacob had encountered God and had his name changed to 'Israel' (Genesis 32:28–30). Sadly, Gideon does not encounter 'the face of God'—the Hebrew meaning of 'Penuel'. Rather, he meets the same kind of rejection that he encountered in Succoth (v. 8). Once again, Gideon promises retaliation. Once he achieves victory over the Midianite kings, he will return and tear down the guard tower that allowed the city to protect its gate (v. 9).

Victory and retaliation

In verse 10, the narrator stops the action long enough to locate the two Midianite kings and to remind the reader that only 15,000

Midianite warriors were left after 120,000 had died in battle. Then, he resumes the action in verses 11–12, reporting Gideon's attack and subsequent capture of the fleeing kings. A comment at the end of verse 11 explains the reason for his success: the Midianite army felt safe and was not expecting attack.

The narrator adds a nice touch at the end of verse 12 when he observes that the army was in a state of panic. The term 'panic' is the same Hebrew root word translated 'trembling' in Judges 7:3. The battle began with Gideon sending home 'trembling' Israelite warriors. Now, the battle ends with Midianite warriors 'trembling' after Gideon has finished with them. Despite the narrator's skill in making this connection, he does not show an interest in the details of how Gideon captured the Midianite kings. Rather, he moves quickly to Gideon's return to Succoth and Penuel.

In verses 13–16, the narrator describes how Gideon acquired a list of the officials and elders of Succoth and then fulfilled his earlier promise to beat them with thorns and briers. According to verse 17, Gideon also followed through on his threat to the people of Penuel. He went beyond it, though, by killing the men of the city in addition to tearing down the tower.

Finally, Gideon executes the two Midianite kings, but first he hears them confess the killing of his own brothers at Tabor. Their statement about Gideon and his brothers resembling 'the sons of a king' anticipates the next episode in 8:22–27.

Narrative strategy

This episode amounts to a turning point in the book of Judges and confirms the narrator's message that Israel has become Canaanized. Gideon has turned from humility to brutality. Tragically, he has taken vengeance on his own people. Gideon's young son, Jether, in verse 20 serves as a foil to his father. Unlike his father, he shies away from violence. The ominous note at the end of verse 21 stimulates the reader's interest. What is Gideon going to do with the crescents that hung on the camels' necks? Will he succumb to idolatry as well as to brutality?

PRAYER

Father in heaven, keep me from brutality and revenge.

The OFFER *of a* DYNASTY

Israel's spiritual decline gains momentum in this episode as the people offer Gideon the kingship of Israel. The reader is left wondering whether or not Gideon actually refused the offer. His words and his actions seem to contradict each other. Whatever the case, Gideon continues to undermine what he had previously accomplished for Yahweh's people.

Does Gideon become king?

In return for Gideon's deliverance of Israel, the Israelites offer Gideon a dynasty. That is, they offer to establish his family as the ruling family in Israel (v. 22). Gideon appears to reject the offer. He is emphatic, stating that neither he nor his son will rule over them. Instead, he cites Yahweh as the legitimate ruler in Israel (v. 23).

However, Gideon's subsequent request (v. 24) and actions (vv. 25–27) cast doubt on the sincerity of his answer. First, although Gideon has refused to rule over them, he requests an act of submission when he asks the warriors each to give him an earring from the goods they recovered from the fallen enemy (v. 24). The warriors willingly comply with this request (v. 25). Second, the huge amount of gold received by Gideon, 1700 shekels, looks suspiciously like the creation of royal treasure. Third, Gideon possesses symbols of royalty —the crescents, the pendants, and the purple garments worn by the Midianite kings (v. 26). Fourth, he sets up his town as the religious centre of the nation (v. 27).

Gideon's ephod

The mention of Gideon making an ephod and putting it in his town (v. 27) arouses our curiosity as readers. Ordinarily, an ephod was a garment worn by Israel's high priest. Resembling an apron, it consisted of gold, blue, purple and crimson yarns, of fine twisted linen, and of onyx stones mounted on the shoulder straps. An elaborate breastpiece with twelve stones and the engraved names of each of the twelve tribes was attached to the ephod (see Exodus 28:6–30). Since the people of Israel prostituted themselves to Gideon's ephod, it must have been displayed prominently. Did Gideon make a gold replica of an ephod? Did he make a garment to drape over an image or a statue, or even to wear himself?

Gideon, raised up by Yahweh to deliver Israel from the Canaanites, is himself acting more like a Canaanite than a follower of Yahweh. While acknowledging Yahweh as Israel's true ruler, he acts as if he is accepting the offer that he verbally rejected. If so, he certainly does not fulfil the qualifications for Israel's kings as specified by Yahweh (see Deuteronomy. 17:14–20). Making the ephod is the climax of his actions. While he was previously 'clothed' by the spirit of God (see 6:34), he now clothes himself with a self-made ephod which leads the people astray!

A return to idolatry

The tragedy of Gideon's actions becomes clear in the last two clauses of verse 27. First, Israel 'prostituted' themselves to Gideon's ephod. This language, used previously in 2:17, pictures Israel as a spouse unfaithful to Yahweh. Second, Gideon's ephod became a 'snare' to him and his family. This picture, which first appeared in 2:3, portrays Gideon as a hunter who gets caught in his own trap. Ironically, the man commissioned to deliver his people from idolatry and bondage, the consequence of idolatry (6:25–27), leads them right back into what caused their bondage in the first place. How long will Israel experience peace before Yahweh has to send enemy raiders once again to get the people's attention?

MEDITATION

Proverbs 26:11 says, 'Like a dog that returns to its vomit is a fool who reverts to his folly.' Where do you see this tendency in yourself to return to the life from which God delivered you? Take a moment and ask God to deliver you from this temptation.

GIDEON'S LEGACY

True to the pattern of other deliverance stories, the Gideon story ends with a formal statement of resolution, announcing that the enemy had been subdued and the land had rest (v. 28). Before moving on to the next deliverance cycle, however, the narrator adds a denouement or conclusion which reflects on the legacy of Gideon.

Mixed reviews for Gideon

Gideon's legacy is mixed. On one hand, his leadership provided forty years of peace (v. 28). The use of Gideon's alternate name Jerubbaal ('let Baal contend') reminds us that Baal did not contend with him, at least not on the battlefield (v. 29). Furthermore, Gideon lived until 'a good old age' (v. 32).

Other details, however, add more fuel to the speculation that Gideon accepted the offer to rule Israel. The mention of Jerubbaal (Gideon) returning to 'live in his own house' is unique. The narrator does not use this language to describe any other deliverer in the book of Judges. Does it serve as a veiled reference to a dynasty in the same way that later Scripture refers to the 'house of David' (see 2 Samuel 7:11, 16)? Furthermore, Gideon's possession of a large harem of wives (v. 30) reflects the practice of ancient kings. In such a case, it clearly violates Yahweh's plans for Israelite kings (see Deuteronomy 17:17). Likewise, with seventy sons, Gideon had a king-sized number of offspring (see 2 Kings 10:1; see also Genesis 46:27 and Judges 1:7). Few private citizens had families this large.

The name of one of Gideon's sons, Abimelech (v. 31), teases the reader. Abimelech is the Hebrew expression 'my father is king'. Does this name refer to Abimelech's earthly father, Gideon, or his heavenly father, God? Perhaps the narrator's reticence to make a clear case one way or another reflects the times. Nothing is clear. At times, Gideon appears devoted to Yahweh. At other times, he resembles the Canaanite culture around him. In addition to his brutality (see 8:4–21), he has taken a concubine—a second-class or low-ranking wife obtained primarily for sexual fulfilment. Even more troubling, though, is the woman's background. As a Shechemite, she is a Canaanite woman. Yet the law of Moses had specifically prohibited marriage to the daughters of the land—not because of differences in nationality but differences in religion (Exodus 34:16; Deuteronomy 7:1–4).

Israel's relapse

After Gideon's death, the people of Israel turned (the meaning of 'relapsed' in v. 33) back to their evil practices. The people's return to evil worked itself out in three ways. First, as an unfaithful spouse, the nation pursued Baal worship. Specifically, they made Baal-berith their god. The term *berith* is the Hebrew word for 'covenant'. Forsaking their covenant with Yahweh (see Exodus 19—20), they opted to pursue a covenant relationship with a Canaanite god. Second, the people of Israel did not remember Yahweh their God who had provided deliverance for them. In the Hebrew language, a failure to 'remember' is not so much a lapse in memory (simply forgetting) as a failure to acknowledge or respond to reality. Third, the Israelites failed to show loyalty to the house of Gideon for the good he had done for them. The term 'loyalty' translates the Hebrew term *hesed*—a term signifying 'covenant love' or 'covenant loyalty'. Again, the language sounds suspiciously 'royal'. Apparently, Israel had formalized some kind of agreement with Gideon and his house.

On the decline

In the overall flow of the book of Judges, Gideon serves as a turning point. He is the fourth of seven judges or deliverers whose stories are covered in detail. The first three judges—Othniel, Ehud and Deborah—receive positive evaluations. The three judges following Gideon—Abimelech, Jephthah and Samson—receive negative evaluations. Gideon gets a mixed, positive–negative review. His eventual fall into brutality, pride and idolatry sets the tone for the remaining cycles of deliverer stories. His story demonstrates that Israel is caught in a downward spiral towards destruction. With each cycle of deliverance, the people of Israel become more like their pagan neighbours.

PRAYER

Yahweh God, the only hope I have of escaping a downward spiral into sin is to stay faithful to you. Help me to trust and obey you.

A BRUTAL RISE to POWER

The consequences of Gideon's drift into brutality, pride and idolatry play out in the reign of his son Abimelech over the city-state of Shechem (9:1–57).

Abimelech's brutality and coronation

The story's first scene (vv. 1–21) opens with Abimelech going to Shechem, to his mother's house, to convince his relatives that he should rule over Shechem (vv. 1–2). Better to have one of their own to rule, he suggests, than to get caught in a miserable power struggle as the seventy sons of Jerubbaal (Gideon) fight for power.

Once the lords of Shechem agree (v. 3), the plot immediately turns ugly. The Shechemites give Abimelech seventy pieces of silver from the temple treasury of their pagan god, and he promptly hires 'worthless and reckless fellows' who accompany him on a killing spree to get rid of his brothers. His brothers would probably challenge his right to rule since he was the least prominent of the brothers—the son of their father's concubine.

The reference to Abimelech killing his brothers 'on one stone' reflects the later practice of King Saul, who slaughtered animals captured from the Philistines on a large stone rolled in for this purpose (see 1 Samuel 14:33–34).

Escaping the slaughter

One brother escapes, though. Jotham, the youngest son of Gideon, survives by hiding himself (v. 5). The name Jotham is a Hebrew expression meaning 'Yahweh is perfect'. This name is ironic in this story. Where is Yahweh's perfection? The only place where Yahweh's name appears in this story is in Jotham's name. So where is Yahweh? How can a God of integrity allow Abimelech to become the first king installed in Israel? In a sad turn of events, Abimelech's coronation takes place at the very site at Shechem where Joshua had placed the book of the law (Joshua 24:1, 26).

Jotham's fable

The plot gets complicated as Jotham emerges from hiding to denounce his brother Abimelech. Jotham's choice of Mount Gerazim as the site for his speech is significant (v. 7). It provided him with a safe location, good acoustics and historic precedent. At this very place, Israel had earlier reviewed the blessings and heard the cursings that Yahweh promised for their behaviour (see Deuteronomy 11:29; 27:11–13; Joshua 8:33–35).

Jotham's speech takes the form of a fable (vv. 8–15) and its interpretation (vv. 16–20). A fable is a brief story which uses plants and animals to represent people and which makes a moral point. Using a fable is a brilliant communication strategy. As a story, it can sneak the truth past the listeners' defences before they realize what has happened. In Jotham's fable of the trees, the details work together to make a single point. The initial three trees—the most valuable species in ancient Israel—selflessly decline the offer of kingship. Their service to society is too valuable to be traded for a position of honour over the other trees. So the trees offer kingship to a bramble, a tree that cannot offer shade, only thorns. The bramble reveals its self-serving interests when it promises destruction by fire for subjects who do not follow up their choice with allegiance. This tree also demonstrates a ridiculous sort of arrogance when it issues its threat against the cedars of Lebanon—trees much more powerful than a thornbush!

The point of Jotham's fable is clear: you will pay for crowning a worthless man who does not have your best interests in mind. In case his hearers have missed this, though, he offers a follow-up interpretation. After closing this interpretation with a curse on Abimelech and the lords of Shechem, he returns to hiding. The occurrences of 'Beth-millo' (Hebrew for 'house of fill') in verses 20–21 refer to a tower built on a huge base filled with earth and rocks.

By the end of the scene, the tension is high. What will happen to Jotham? Will Abimelech succeed, or will he experience Jotham's curse? Most importantly, will Yahweh remain in hiding, or will he live up to Jotham's name and emerge to demonstrate his perfection and integrity?

MEDITATION

What circumstances around you seem to cast doubt on God's perfection? How might he intervene to vindicate his perfection?

ABIMELECH DEFEATS SHECHEM

In the second scene of the Abimelech story (vv. 22–49), Jotham's curse upon the lords of Shechem comes true. The use of a rare Hebrew term in verse 22, translated 'ruled', portrays Abimelech's brief reign as different from the rules of other deliverers.

Sending an evil spirit

God intervenes by sending an evil spirit between Abimelech and the lords of Shechem (v. 23). The expression 'evil spirit' can refer either to a supernatural being, a demon, or simply to an evil attitude or disposition. Whatever the case, this evil spirit resulted in the lords of Shechem breaking their agreement (the meaning of 'dealt treacherously') with Abimelech. In verse 24, the narrator reveals the purpose of this turn of events. The rift that God causes between Abimelech and the lords of Shechem will accomplish vengeance on both parties for their violence against the seventy sons of Jerubbaal (Gideon). The conflict begins with the lords of Shechem robbing travellers (v. 25). Such terrorism would disrupt the economy as well as people's sense of security.

Gaal's challenge

The appearance of a new character in verse 26 complicates the plot. A man named Gaal moves into Shechem and wins the trust of the lords of Shechem. As the story unfolds, Gaal certainly lives up to the meaning of his name—'to despise, detest'—as he despises Abimelech.

A concentration of eight verbs in verse 27 highlights the intensity of the events that follow. Gaal and the lords of Shechem 'went... gathered... trod... celebrated... went... ate... drank... ridiculed'. At the height of their drunken celebration, perhaps a Canaanite harvest festival, they entered the temple of their god, Baal-Berith, to ridicule Abimelech. In verses 28–29, Gaal mocks Abimelech, noting that his father is Jerubbaal (Gideon)—an Israelite. Why should the Shechemites serve the son of a foreigner? Instead, Abimelech should serve them. Now, no one seems to remember that Abimelech's mother is a Shechemite, even though Abimelech had used this as a selling point to gain power.

Tension rises as the narrator reports that Zebul, Abimelech's officer or deputy, hears Gaal's speech (v. 30). Angry at what he hears, Zebul sends an urgent message to Abimelech, counselling him to ambush the city (vv. 31–33).

Vengeance upon the Shechemites

Abimelech follows Zebul's advice and sets an ambush against the city of Shechem (vv. 34–35). The circumstances behind the verbal exchange between Gaal and Zebul, Abimelech's commander, are not entirely clear (vv. 36–38). Is Zebul still inside the city? If so, he is trying to lure a reluctant Gaal into battle, suggesting by his 'shadows' comment that there are not as many enemy troops as Gaal fears. Or, is Zebul on the outside of the city, having led a group of Abimelech's warriors to the city gate? If so, his 'shadows' comment discounts Gaal's claim that the warriors pouring out of the mountains are coming to help Gaal and the Shechemites. Regardless, Zebul challenges Gaal to follow through with his previous boast about removing Abimelech (v. 28). Gaal accepts the challenge, but ends up being driven away from the city (vv. 39–41).

Abimelech then kills the remaining residents of Shechem in two brutal acts. First, two companies of his warriors kill the residents who come out the next morning to work in the fields, while Abimelech's company storms the city and kills the people inside (vv. 42–45). The act of spreading salt on the ruined city was probably a ritual, symbolic act which pronounced a curse on the city. Second, Abimelech sets fire to the Tower of Shechem (probably the stronghold in the city referred to as 'Beth-millo' in 9:20–21) and destroys the remaining lords of Shechem who had gone there to hide. Jotham's prophetic curse about fire from Abimelech destroying Shechem (9:20) has come true! But what about the fate of Abimelech? Will he get away with his brutal rise to power?

MEDITATION

The perverse get what their ways deserve, and the good, what their deeds deserve.

Proverbs 14:14

GOD REPAYS ABIMELECH

The final scene of the Abimelech story (vv. 50–57) describes the fate of Abimelech. God has made the lords of Shechem pay for their part in the brutal murders of Abimelech's brothers (see 9:22–49). But what about Abimelech? Will God repay him for slaughtering his brothers? Will the second part of Jotham's curse come true (see 9:20b)?

Abimelech's conquest of Thebez

The scene opens with Abimelech's conquest of Thebez—apparently a nearby city with ties to Shechem (v. 50). The narrator does not show an interest in the details. Rather, he quickly describes Abimelech's victory with three verbs: 'went', 'encamped', and 'took'.

However, there turns out to be a complication. For a moment, the narrator pauses the action to inform the reader that there was a strong tower in the city (v. 51a). This tower probably resembled the 'Tower of Shechem' in the previous scene (9:47). The action continues with all the citizens of Thebez, including the leaders, fleeing to the top of the tower and shutting themselves inside it (vv. 51b–d). Verse 52 then describes Abimelech's response. The narrator hurries the action along, using three verbs and minimal details to describe what happens next. Abimelech 'came' to the tower, 'fought' against it, and 'came near' the entrance in order to set fire to the tower. Nothing seems unusual. The reader expects Abimelech to burn the tower so that these citizens of Thebez will suffer the same fate as the leaders of Shechem.

A woman kills a warrior

However, the next event catches the reader by surprise. According to verse 53, 'a certain woman' (literally, 'one woman') throws an upper millstone at Abimelech's head and crushes his skull. In the ancient Near East, a woman would place grain on a stone base—a lower millstone. Then, she would crush this grain into flour with an 'upper millstone' that she operated with her hand.

There is double irony here. To begin with, the man who killed his brothers on a stone is himself killed by a stone. Furthermore, for the second time in the book of Judges, a woman has slain the leader of an army with a household utensil (see Jael's feat in 4:21). Abimelech's dying command to his armour-bearer reflects the disgrace that 'death by a housewife' would bring to a warrior. The report in verse 55 that the Israelites 'all went home' when they saw Abimelech die signals an end to the story. A significant reversal has occurred. At the beginning of the story, a nameless woman—Abimelech's mother—is responsible for Abimelech's life and rise to power. At the story's end, another nameless woman is responsible for Abimelech's fall from power, and death.

Although the story is finished, the narrator offers a denouement or conclusion which interprets the story's significance (vv. 56–57). The narrator simply elaborates on an earlier explanation (9:24), reaffirming that God repaid both Abimelech and the Shechemites for their violence against the seventy sons of Jerubbaal (Gideon), Abimelech's half-brothers. This story assures us that violence has a habit of rebounding on its perpetrators. While God delights in showing mercy, he will not leave evil unpunished (see Exodus 34:5–7). Vengeance may take time to play out. In this story, it took three years. But eventually God will bring judgment upon people who do evil.

At this point in the book of Judges, Israel is caught in a vicious downward spiral. The people of Israel resemble their Canaanite neighbours so closely that God has to deliver Israel by causing the death of an Israelite leader.

PRAYER

God of vengeance, I am appalled by the bloodshed, violence, and terrorist attacks that take place in the world. Help me to trust in your justice, your promise to repay people for their evil acts.

ISRAEL ABANDONS YAHWEH

Before exploring another cycle in Israel's downward spiral into evil, the narrator briefly mentions two 'minor' judges: Tola (vv. 1–2) and Jair (vv. 3–5). Both judges serve as foils. In literary terms, a 'foil' is a character who provides a contrast to a main character in order to highlight some feature of this main character.

Tola and Jair: character foils

In verses 1–2, Tola serves as a foil to Abimelech, the main character of the previous account. When we read that Tola 'rose to deliver Israel' (v. 1), we recall that such language was not used of Abimelech. Rather, he functioned more as a destroyer of Israel than as a deliverer.

In verses 3–5, Jair serves as a foil to Jephthah, the deliverer who will emerge in the following cycle. Jair was blessed with thirty sons (v. 3), while Jephthah's daughter was an only child (11:34). The detail that Jair's thirty sons rode thirty donkeys indicates wealth. These are riding animals, not pack animals. In modern terms, each son in the family drives a Porsche! Furthermore, each one of Jair's sons apparently presided over a town, indicating the scope of their father's political power. By contrast, Jephthah emerged to power from his position as a social outcast.

A return to evil and oppression

A new cycle begins with the report of the Israelites doing evil in the sight of Yahweh (v. 6). What follows is the most extensive description of Israel's idolatry in the entire book. The seven groups of false gods reflect the completeness of Israel's fall into idolatry.

The severity of Yahweh's response matches the severity of Israel's corruption. In his anger, mentioned for the first time since the initial cycle in Judges 3:8, Yahweh sells Israel into the hands of two enemies. The Philistines will oppress the Israelites from the west, while the Ammonites will oppress Israel from the east. The pair of verbs in verse 8, 'crushed' and 'oppressed', provide a vivid picture. In the Hebrew text, their back-to-back appearance at the beginning of the sentence and their similar sound (*wayyir'asu*, *wayyirsesu*) grab the reader's attention. The only other appearance of the first verb, 'crushed', is in

Exodus 15:6 (translated 'shattered'), where it describes Yahweh's defeat of the Egyptians. The second verb, 'oppressed', is the same verb used in Judges 9:53 when a woman dropped a millstone on Abimelech's head and 'crushed' his skull. The writer also pictures the severity of Yahweh's retribution on Israel through the verb 'distressed' at the end of verse 9. This verb pictures someone pressed into a narrow, tight spot—a circumstance caused by oppression from the west and from the east.

Israel's cry to Yahweh

As in other cycles, the Israelites responded to their oppression by crying out to Yahweh (v. 10). This cry is unique because, for the first time in the book of Judges, the people offer a confession of sin. This confession begins a dialogue between the Israelites and Yahweh. Yahweh's reply to their confession starts with a list of nations from which he had delivered the people (vv. 11–12). The list of nations numbers seven, so it serves as a counterpart to the seven categories of false gods that Israel worshipped (see v. 6). Yahweh's deliverance has been as outrageous as Israel's idolatry, but now he will deliver them no more (v. 13). At this point, Yahweh turns sarcastic, telling the people to cry for help to the gods they have chosen (v. 14).

Once again, the Israelites admit their sin and plead for Yahweh's deliverance (v. 15). Yahweh's response, as described by the narrator in verse 16, is interesting. The NRSV translation—'and he could no longer bear to see Israel suffer'—suggests a compassionate response. But the language of the clause suggests just the opposite. Literally, the Hebrew reads, 'And his soul became short because of the labouring (or 'suffering') of Israel'. The verb 'became short' is used elsewhere in the Old Testament to describe becoming impatient (see Numbers 21:4; Job 21:4; Zechariah 11:8).

Although Yahweh is rich in grace and forgiveness (see Exodus 34:5–7), he gets impatient with insincere confession. He detests people who cry out for deliverance but then abandon him as soon as the pain is gone and prosperity returns.

PRAYER

If you, O Lord, should mark iniquities, Lord, who could stand?
But there is forgiveness with you, so that you may be revered.

Psalm 130:3–4

An OUTCAST BECOMES RULER

Israel now faces an attack from the Ammonites. The Ammonites have set up camp in Gilead, a region east of the Jordan River (v. 17). Apparently, the Israelites in Gilead lack a military general, so they issue a call for a military leader and promise leadership over the entire region as a prize (v. 18). A reference to inquiring of Yahweh is strangely absent.

An outcast named Jephthah

In the opening clause of 11:1, the Hebrew grammar indicates a stop in the action. The narrator is now supplying background information which readers need to understand the story. In fact, verses 1–3 amount to a flashback. The narrator is describing a character who will emerge once the story continues.

The narrator introduces us to 'Jephthah the Gileadite'. The name 'Jephthah' is the Hebrew expression 'he opens'. Perhaps the name reflects his mother's gratefulness to whichever god she worshipped, for opening her womb. In verse 1, the NRSV reverses the order of the details given by the narrator. The first detail that appears in the Hebrew text is the designation 'mighty warrior'. Jephthah seems to be an ideal candidate for the position announced in 10:18. But the next detail complicates the situation. Jephthah's mother was a prostitute. As a result, Jephthah's half-brothers, the sons of his father's wife, drove him away when he got older (vv. 2–3). The irony is that Jephthah ended up in the 'land of Tob'. 'Tob' is the Hebrew word 'good', but Jephthah's life was anything but good. He ended up living as a bandit, surrounded by fellow outlaws.

Jephthah's rise to power

The opening words of verse 4, 'After a time', signal a return to the main plot, which was interrupted after 10:18. The war has begun, and the actions of the Israelite leaders in verse 5 suggest that no one has emerged to lead Israel into battle. They are so desperate for leadership that they go to the land of Tob—fifteen miles east of Ramoth-gilead—to find Jephthah.

Dialogue dominates the next scene in this episode (vv. 6–11).

Unlike their previous offer (10:18), the elders of Gilead offer Jephthah only a role as their military commander (v. 6). As we might expect, Jephthah questions their motives (v. 7). Why do the same people who drove him away now want him to return? In verse 8, the elders admit that they need him to lead them in battle against the Ammonites. This time, they include the incentive that Jephthah would become 'head' (the same term used in 10:18) over Gilead if he accepts their offer.

Jephthah accepts the offer, provided that the elders really make him their head (v. 9). The elders accept these terms with an appeal to Yahweh as their witness (v. 10). The narrator is careful to specify in verse 11 that the people of Gilead made him both 'head' (10:18; 11:7, 8) and 'commander' (11:6) over them.

While the parties making the agreement appeal to Yahweh, Yahweh does not appear to be directly involved. Rather, both Jephthah and the elders of Gilead appear to be opportunists who use each other to get what they need or want. Here, we need to recognize that Hebrew narrative resembles a child's dot-to-dot picture. The narrator provides us with the dots but, as readers, we must connect the lines to see the picture emerge. The narrator does not make his judgments plain, but he gives us enough detail to figure out what he is saying. In this scene, the narrator shows us that corruption in Israel extends to social morals. As a result of becoming more like their Canaanite neighbours, the people of Israel are losing their sense of community—their commitment to help and serve each other.

MEDITATION

As God's people in the 21st century, where do we face the temptation to sin by using each other only to get what we need instead of accepting each other as brothers and sisters in Christ?

JEPHTHAH'S SPEECH

After being installed as 'head and commander' over the people of Gilead (11:11), Jephthah takes the initiative to negotiate with the Ammonites. His initial message consists of a rhetorical question, which basically charges the Ammonites with unlawful entry into Israelite territory for the purpose of making war (v. 12).

The king of the Ammonites counters with an accusation and a challenge of his own (v. 13). He claims that the Israelites took away his land, and he commands them to return it. The land in question is east of the lower Jordan River and east of the northern half of the Dead Sea. The Arnon River, which runs into the Dead Sea, forms the region's southern border. The Jabbok River, which runs into the Jordan River, forms the region's northern border.

Jacob replies with a second message to the king of the Ammonites. This lengthy speech argues that the Ammonites are wrong to make war against Israel (vv. 14–27).

The appeal to 'history'

Jephthah begins his speech by appealing to history in verses 14–22. He reviews the events surrounding Israel's appearance in the region after leaving Egypt and wandering in the wilderness. Basically, the Israelites skirted the lands of Edom and Moab, ending up east of Moab on the other side of the Arnon River (vv. 17–18). Eventually, they requested permission from King Sihon of the Amorites to pass through the land into Canaan (v. 19). King Sihon, though, refused and fought against Israel (v. 20). Thus, concluded Jephthah, Yahweh the God of Israel gave Sihon and his people into the hand of Israel (v. 21a). Before leaving this line of argument, Jephthah presses home the point that 'Israel occupied all the land of the Amorites, who inhabited that country' (v. 21b).

So the Amorites, not the Ammonites, inhabited the land. Jephthah's claim certainly harmonizes with earlier accounts in Hebrew Scripture. Numbers 21:24 reports that the territory Israel conquered between the Arnon and the Jabbok belonged to the Amorites. In fact, this report mentions that Israel made it only as far as the Ammonite border—a boundary too strong to conquer. Moses confirmed this in his speech in Deuteronomy 2:16—3:17.

The appeal to 'religion'

Next, Jephthah makes a religious case for the Ammonites to abandon their efforts to seize this region. He argues that the Ammonites should recognize Yahweh's provision of this land for Israel and that they should be content with what their god, Chemosh, had provided for them (vv. 23–24). Chemosh is actually the national god of Moab, while Milkom (or Molech) is the national god of the Ammonites. This is either an intentional put-down or it simply reflects the common heritage of the Moabites and the Ammonites—people-groups who lived side by side. What does Jephthah's reference to Chemosh tell us about his own spiritual condition? We're not sure. Jephthah may have referred to Chemosh just for the sake of argument, or his perspective may have been corrupted by Canaanite culture.

The appeal to 'ability'

Jephthah pursues yet another line of reasoning when he questions the ability of the Ammonites. Does the king of the Ammonites think he is superior to Balak, the former king of Moab (v. 25)? The implication is that the Ammonite king should follow the precedent of Balak, who did not enter into conflict or go to war with Israel.

The appeal to 'opportunity'

Finally, Jephthah reasons that if the Ammonites had any claim on the land of Gilead, they should not have waited three hundred years to make a sudden play for it (v. 26).

Jephthah draws his conclusion in verse 27, accusing the Ammonites of wrongdoing and appealing to Yahweh as the judge who will render justice in this case. Despite Jephthah's rhetorical skill, the king of the Ammonites did not listen to him (v. 28). The reader is left wondering which nation Yahweh will vindicate.

MEDITATION

Lord, you are the supreme judge. Please let justice prevail in the ongoing dispute today over the land of Israel.

JEPHTHAH'S VOW

The episode about Jephthah's vow contains one of the most tragic, perplexing plots in the entire book. After rising from social outcast to head of his people, Jephthah's future holds so much promise. But by the end of the episode, Jephthah's future is all but gone.

Empowered by the Spirit of Yahweh

The episode begins by reporting that the Spirit of Yahweh came upon Jephthah (v. 29). The remainder of verse 29 describes the result: Jephthah tours the area east of the Jordan River, presumably to recruit troops, and then prepares to advance against the Ammonites.

Making a vow

Before attacking the Ammonites, however, Jephthah makes a vow to Yahweh (vv. 30–31). Is this a legitimate vow prompted by the Spirit of Yahweh? Or is it an attempt by Jephthah, a master-negotiator, to manipulate God? Jepthah's open-ended terms ('whoever comes out of the doors of my house…') make his vow appear foolish in light of the Mosaic Law's warning about making vows to Yahweh which are too difficult to keep (Deuteronomy 23:21–23).

Anyway, Jephthah fought the Ammonites, and Yahweh gave them into his hands (v. 32). The narrator labels it 'a massive defeat' (v. 33).

A tragic sight

When Jephthah arrived home, a shocking sight greeted him. Literally, the second clause of verse 34 reads, 'And look! His daughter was coming out to meet him with timbrels and with dancing.' At the end of verse 34, the narrator pauses the action to add a critical detail: this daughter was Jephthah's only child. Then, the narrator emphasizes it with negative terms: 'he had no son or daughter except her'.

Jephthah's daughter remains nameless throughout the episode. This is significant because a name provides a character with a measure of honour and identity. The narrator's decision not to reveal the name of Jephthah's daughter reflects her circumstances. She was dishonoured by her father and ended up without a lasting identity.

At the sight of his daughter, Jephthah tore his clothes—an expression of grief and mourning (v. 35). Then he offered a passionate lament which began with 'Alas', a cry of grief. His daughter's appearance from the house has brought him very low and has caused him great trouble. The next statement explains the cause of his grief. Jephthah, whose name means 'he opened', has 'opened' his mouth to Yahweh and made a vow he cannot rescind. Jephthah's daughter replies with a remarkable statement of resignation. She realizes that her father has 'opened' his mouth, and so she instructs him to act in accord with 'what has gone out of your mouth' (v. 36). Yahweh has fulfilled his part of the agreement. Now Jephthah must fulfil his. According to verse 37, she follows this statement with a request. She wants two months to spend mourning in the hills with her companions. She will die as a virgin, not as a mother. Sadly, she becomes what her father once was—an outcast with companions but no family. Her choice not to spend her final days with her father may reflect her attitude towards him and may serve as an act of judgment upon him.

No future for Jephthah

The most perplexing question of this episode is, of course, what exactly happened to Jephthah's daughter. Did Jephthah sacrifice her as a burnt offering? Or did he simply dedicate her to the lifelong service of Yahweh at Israel's central place of worship? We will explore this in the discussion on verses 39–40. But regardless of the circumstances, one detail is certain: Jephthah's line ended with his daughter. One way or the other, she died as a virgin. While Jephthah overcame his past, he ruined his future by treating Yahweh like a pagan god who can be manipulated. The presence of the Spirit of Yahweh at the outset of the episode guaranteed victory. His attempt to manipulate God, then, was both unnecessary and tragic.

MEDITATION

If you make a vow to the Lord your God, do not postpone fulfilling it; for the Lord your God will surely require it of you, and you would incur guilt.

Deuteronomy 23:21

JEPHTHAH'S DAUGHTER

The resolution to the episode about Jephthah and his daughter takes place in verse 39a. Then a conclusion in verses 39b–40 summarizes the impact of this resolution on the daughter's future. One of the most perplexing questions in the book of Judges—and even in the entire Old Testament—concerns the fate of Jephthah's daughter. In verse 39, the narrator simply reports that Jephthah 'did with her according to the vow he had made'.

Option 1—lifelong service as a virgin

Some Bible scholars think that Jephthah simply dedicated his daughter to remain a virgin the rest of her life while serving Yahweh at Israel's central place of worship. Several arguments seem to support this view. First, Jephthah would have dishonoured Yahweh by violating the clear commands in the Law of Moses which prohibit child sacrifice (see Deuteronomy 12:31; 18:10). Second, the wording of Jephthah's vow could be translated, 'And it shall be for Yahweh, *or* I will offer it as a burnt offering'. Thus, depending on what or who came out of the house, Jephthah could either devote it to Yahweh or offer it as a burnt offering. Third, the narrator never states that Jephthah offered his daughter as a burnt offering. Fourth, how could the writer of Hebrews cite Jephthah as a hero of the faith if he had engaged in child sacrifice? (See Hebrews 11:33–34.)

Option 2—offered as a burnt offering

However, the most natural reading of this episode suggests that Jephthah did, in fact, offer his daughter as a burnt offering. First, the people of Israel at this time resemble their Canaanite neighbours, so we should not overestimate Jephthah's spiritual sensitivity to the law of Moses.

Second, the two clauses at the end of verse 31 do not seem to reflect two alternatives. The last two clauses of verse 31 literally read, 'And it shall be for Yahweh, *and* I will offer it as a burnt offering'. As noted previously, some want to translate the term 'and' (the Hebrew conjunction *we*) which begins the second clause as 'or'. Such a translation is legitimate when the items it connects are obvious alternatives—for example, 'sons and daughters' in Exodus 21:4 is rightly translated as 'sons or daughters'. But it is not obvious that the last two clauses in verse 31 speak of different categories. Besides, Hebrew has another conjunction—*ow*—which is translated 'or' (or 'nor') and clearly distinguishes between two items. Our narrator even uses this conjunction in 11:34 ('no son or daughter').

Third, the narrator's reluctance to specify exactly what Jephthah did suggests that he actually offered her as a burnt offering. The statement in verse 39—'did with her according to the vow he had made'—reflects the narrator's hesitation to speak of such a horrible, detestable act.

Fourth, if Jephthah did sacrifice his daughter as a burnt offering, the problem of his appearance in the 'hall of faith' in Hebrews 11:33–34 is no greater than the problem of judges like Gideon or Samson appearing there.

Fifth, it is hard to imagine how the fate of Jephthah's daughter would lead to a four-day annual festival of lament if she had simply been dedicated to the lifelong service of Yahweh as a virgin. A response of this magnitude suggests a more tragic end.

In fact, some Bible scholars believe that Jephthah intended to offer a human sacrifice from the moment he made his vow. An animal sacrifice would not have expressed unusual devotion. However, he did not anticipate that his daughter would walk through the door first and thus become the victim.

Bargaining with God

As noted previously, we are not required to know the exact fate of Jephthah's daughter in order to understand the message of the story. In either case, she would have no children to continue Jephthah's family line. When God's people treat him like a pagan god and try to manipulate him to get his help, they will end up hurting themselves.

PRAYER

Father God, help me not to dishonour you by trying to manipulate you or bargain with you when I need help.

JEPHTHAH'S LEGACY

The Jephthah story draws to a close with an episode of internal conflict (vv. 1–6). Then, three brief accounts of 'minor' judges follow (vv. 7–15) and form a bridge to the Samson story (chs. 13—16).

Ephraim's threat

For the second time in the story line of Judges, the Ephraimites feel slighted about not being called to help fight a battle. Previously, they criticized Gideon for not calling them to help fight the Midianites (see 8:1). Now, they confront Jephthah because he had not called them to help fight the Ammonites (v. 1). Their threat to burn down Jeph-thah's house reveals the intensity of their anger.

Jephthah's reply

While Gideon had diffused their earlier anger with careful reasoning (8:1–3), Jephthah does not handle the present situation with the same degree of diplomacy. In his reply, Jephthah portrays himself as a contentious man (vv. 2–3). While the NRSV translates Jephthah's first statement as, 'My people and I were engaged in conflict with the Ammonites', the Hebrew text literally reads, 'I am a man of great contention, I, and my people, and the Ammonites.' Although the term 'contention' can refer to legal argumentation, its primary use in the Old Testament is to describe physical combat. The idea of being a fighter rather than a diplomat corresponds to the picture of Jephthah which has emerged in chapters 10—11. Furthermore, his words seem to contain a put-down, implying that he, his people, and the Ammonites are fierce fighters, while the men of Ephraim are not. According to Jephthah, he had called the Ephraimites to come and help, but they did not respond (v. 2). The contrast between Jeph-thah's words and Gideon's words is sharp. Earlier, Gideon had said: 'You have accomplished much more on the battlefield than we did.' Now, Jephthah says, 'You have accomplished nothing. We did it all by ourselves with help from Yahweh.'

Slaughtering the Ephraimites

Battle then breaks out, and the men of Gilead, led by Jephthah, defeat the men of Ephraim. The narrator offers a motive for this victory. The Ephraimites accused the men of Gilead of being fugitives from Ephraim (v. 5). The men of Gilead were so offended by this slur that they brutalized the men of Ephraim, who were now fugitives in the land of Gilead! When surviving Ephraimite soldiers tried to cross the fords of the Jordan River to return to their land, they apparently denied that they were from Ephraim. The men of Gilead devised a way to expose this lie. They simply asked the fugitives to say 'Shibboleth', a Hebrew word which means either 'ear of grain' or 'flowing stream'. Due to a regional difference in pronunciation, the Ephraimites pronounced the first letter in this word with a 's' sound rather than a 'sh' sound. Saying 'Sibboleth' instead of 'Shibboleth' identified them as Ephraimites and resulted in their execution.

Jephthah leaves a sad legacy at the end of his six years as a judge. Although he defeated the Ammonites, he contributed to Israel's self-destruction by foolishly sacrificing his own daughter and by leading his tribe in the slaughter of 42,000 men of Ephraim—fellow Israelites.

Three 'minor' judges

Before moving on to the Samson story, the narrator briefly mentions three more 'minor' judges in Israel: Ibzan (vv. 8–10), Elon (vv. 11–12), and Abdon (vv. 13–15). Their presence in the story of Judges accomplishes two things. First, it reminds the reader that the narrator has not intended to provide a detailed account of every judge in Israel. Rather, the narrator has selected the stories of several judges to make a prophetic statement. Second, these three judges, particularly Ibzan and Abdon, serve as foils to Jephthah and to Samson, the subject of the next story. Both Ibzan and Abdon possess large families —a sign of prosperity and prestige. In Abdon's case, the seventy donkeys that his offspring ride signal king-like wealth (v. 14). By contrast, Jephthah ends up with no offspring, and the narrator makes no mention of Samson having any offspring in the following account.

PRAYER

Father, I know that a house divided against itself cannot stand.
Help me to pursue unity and cooperation in the community
of faith to which I belong.

82 JUDGES 13:1-14

AN ASTOUNDING
BIRTH ANNOUNCEMENT

The final deliverance cycle in Judges centres on a deliverer named
Samson. As Israel's final judge, Samson epitomizes Israel as he leaves
his special calling and uses his privileges to satisfy his own desires.
The narrator's report in verse 1 about the Israelites again doing evil in
the sight of Yahweh indicates that another cycle has begun. Like the
cycles that precede it, this final cycle will lead Israel further downward on a spiral from health to decay. As the result of Israel's rebellion, Yahweh delivers them into the power of the Philistines for forty
years—the longest period of oppression mentioned in Judges (see
comment on Judges 3:3, pp. 128–129, for more on the Philistines).

Surprisingly, there is no report of Israel crying out to Yahweh for
help, nor any indication of repentance. This reflects the nation's sad
spiritual condition. However, Yahweh still graciously intervenes and
begins the process of raising up a deliverer.

The promise of a son

In verse 2, the narrator introduces us to a man named Manoah (a
Hebrew term meaning 'place of rest') and his unnamed wife. Here the
narrator shares a significant detail: Manoah's wife 'was barren, having
borne no children'. The inability to have children is saddening and
frustrating enough for couples today, but in ancient Israel, barrenness
amounted to a disgrace—even a tragedy. People considered barrenness a sign of God's disfavour. In fact, without children, a family had
no future.

The action begins with the angel of Yahweh appearing to Manoah's
wife and delivering the surprising announcement that she will con-
ceive and bear a son (v. 3).

Another surprise

Yet another surprise awaits Manoah's wife. After instructing her not to
drink alcoholic beverages and not to eat anything unclean (v. 4), the
angel tells her why. It turns out that her son will be a 'nazirite to God
from birth' and will deliver Israel from the Philistines (v. 5). The term

'nazirite'—from the Hebrew term *nazir*, 'set apart, dedicated'—refers to a person who volunteers to take the vow described in Numbers 6:1–8. This vow, taken to show dedication to Yahweh, required abstention from grapes and any grape-based products such as raisins or wine; refraining from cutting one's hair; and avoiding contact with a corpse. The nazirite vow described by the angel of Yahweh is unique, though, for two reasons: first, it will be lifelong, rather than for a limited period of time; and second, it is required rather than voluntary. The instruction not to eat anything unclean (v. 4) applied to all Israelites (see Leviticus 11), not just to those taking a nazirite vow. However, the angel of Yahweh probably cited it because of the general disregard for God's law in the period of the judges.

Sharing the good news

Verses 6–7 contain the woman's report to her husband, Manoah. Two details are striking. First, she accepted the divine origin of the message and did not ask for additional information or confirmation, as Gideon, for example, had done (6:17). Second, she added an extra detail in her report to her husband. The angel had indicated that the boy would be 'a nazirite to God from birth' (v. 5). However, the woman reports the angel's words as 'a nazirite to God from birth to the day of his death' (v. 7). The addition of 'to the day of his death' foreshadows the deliverer's demise.

The initial news is so full of hope. Yahweh is a God who delights in reversal. The woman's barren condition will be reversed, but through it, Yahweh will accomplish something even greater. He will begin reversing Israel's spiritual barren condition.

PRAYER

I praise you, Lord, for your efforts to reverse the terrible situations in my life and in the world. Rescue me, Lord, from evil and from the evil one.

83

JUDGES 13:8–25

YAHWEH'S WONDERFUL PROVISION

When Manoah finally enters the story, he complicates its plot.
Readers will need to wrestle with how to characterize him. Is Manoah
a model of faith, a man with a passion to know and obey Yahweh's
will, or do his actions betray a desire to control the situation? Is he
resentful or jealous, as the Jewish historian Josephus has suggested?

A quest for knowledge

Manoah's responds to his wife's report (13:6–7) by asking Yahweh
for a return visit from the 'man of God' (v. 8). Manoah wants to
learn what to do with the promised boy. On the surface, Manoah's
request seems to demonstrate a receptive heart to God's truth, but
subsequent plot develops cast doubt on this conclusion. Although
God answers Manoah's request, the angel comes to the woman. The
narrator pauses the action to inform us that Manoah was not with
her (v. 9). However, she hurries to tell her husband about the man's
appearance (v. 10).

The dialogue between Manoah and the man of God (vv. 11–14)
seems a bit curious. Manoah is eager to get information. Yet the man
of God replies only with brief or repetitive answers. When asked
about his identity, the man replies with only one word: 'I' (Hebrew,
ani)—as in 'I am the one'. Then, when asked for a sign of confirmation, the angel simply repeats his earlier instructions to Manoah's
wife. In fact, he frames his comments by beginning and ending them
with a directive for the woman to observe everything he had previously told her to do. In both places, the angel uses the same Hebrew
verb. However, the NRSV obscures this by translating it 'give heed' in
verse 13 and 'observe' in verse 14.

Yahweh who works wonders

As the scene continues, Manoah tries to detain the angel of Yahweh
by inviting him to stay for a meal (v. 15). Is Manoah simply showing
appropriate hospitality to this visitor, or is he trying to gain control
of the situation? Whatever the case, readers must remember that
Manoah does not yet understand that this is the angel of Yahweh
(v. 16). Readers must also be careful to avoid the kind of moralizing

184

that often skews the narrator's intent. The narrator does not seem interested in presenting Manoah as a good or bad example for believers to follow. Rather, Manoah serves as a character who will highlight the identity of this visitor.

The angel of Yahweh seems almost uncooperative. He refuses the offer of a meal (v. 16) and then refuses to divulge his name (v. 18). But in both cases, he is hinting at his identity. First, he suggests preparing a burnt offering to Yahweh rather than a meal. Second, he refuses to divulge his name because 'it is wonderful' (v. 18). The Hebrew term translated 'wonderful' refers almost exclusively in the Old Testament to God and his incredible acts (for example, 'Wonderful Counsellor' in Isaiah 9:6). The term is used of humans only when referring to situations or ideas which are too difficult for them to handle. The narrator draws attention to this term by working it into the description of events in verse 19.

What happens next is truly wonderful. As the flame of Manoah's burnt offering ascended, the angel of Yahweh ascended in it (v. 20). After this stunning event, Manoah finally knew that this was the angel of Yahweh (v. 21). Understandably, he expected death for seeing God (v. 22). But his wife correctly grasped Yahweh's intentions (v. 23).

A boy named Samson

At last, we learn that Manoah's wife bore a son as the angel of Yahweh had promised. This boy even has Yahweh's blessing and Spirit empowering him (vv. 24–25). The purpose of this entire birth narrative is to emphasize that Yahweh will do wonderful things to deliver his people. The name 'Samson'—Hebrew for 'little sun'—is intriguing. Perhaps it is a reference to sun-like strength. It may suggest that Samson's mother saw him as Yahweh's way of bringing light to the darkness in which the people lived. Whatever his mother's intention, the name borders on being pagan. Still, in light of the tone of verses 24–25, the name reminds us of Yahweh's wonderful acts for his people. In an era of darkness, Yahweh has raised up a 'sun' to deliver his people.

MEDITATION

Read Isaiah 9:1–7 and notice how God brought light into darkness through the gift of a child described as 'wonderful'.

A PHILISTINE WIFE & *a* LION

Following Samson's birth narrative (ch. 13), three episodes describe his victories over the Philistines (chs. 14, 15 and 16). But despite his victories, Samson is a tragic figure. In the opening scene of the first episode (vv. 1–9), Samson hardly appears to be a deliverer raised up by a wonder-working God. Rather, he reflects Israel's downward spiral into evil and destruction. Even the narrator's choice of verbs hints at this. Three times in this opening scene, we read that Samson 'went down' (vv. 1, 5, 7). Although the verb speaks of physical, geographical movement, it also reflects the downward spiritual movement in Samson's life.

In pursuit of a Philistine wife

The opening lines of chapter 14 catch the reader off guard. Samson wants to take a Philistine wife (vv. 1–2). Whether his parents realize it or not, their protest (v. 3) reflects Yahweh's perspective. Samson is about to take a wife from 'the uncircumcised Philistines'. Circumcision was the sign of Yahweh's covenant with Israel (Genesis 17). Samson's choice clearly violates Yahweh's command not to take a wife from among pagan neighbours (Deuteronomy 7:1–4). But Samson insists, 'Get her for me' (v. 3). Then, he offers a revealing reason. While the NRSV translates the words after Samson's command as 'because she pleases me', a more literal translation of the Hebrew is 'because she is right in my eyes'. The narrator will use this exact language later to describe Israel's moral deterioration (17:6; 21:25).

The Hebrew grammar of verse 4 indicates a pause in the action. The narrator stops the story to inform us that Yahweh is working through these events. Specifically, Yahweh was seeking a 'pretext' (opportunity) to act against the Philistines. Yahweh is so wise and powerful that he can use Samson's spiritually insensitive actions to accomplish his purpose!

Attacked by a lion

The action resumes in verse 5 with Samson and his parents going down to Timnah. Their attempt to persuade him not to marry a Philistine had obviously failed. A crisis occurs when a young lion suddenly comes roaring at him. But then the spirit of Yahweh 'rushed on him' so that he was able to tear apart the lion bare-handed as if it was a young goat (v. 6). The narrator pauses briefly to inform us that Samson did not tell his father or mother what he had done. This sets up events in the next scene. By the way, the setting of the event—the vineyards of Timnah—arouses the reader's curiosity. Why is Samson near a vineyard? Will he keep his nazirite vow which includes total abstention from grapes and grape-based products?

Doing what is right in his eyes

The plot keeps shifting back and forth between Samson's quest for a wife and his encounter with the lion. In verse 7, Samson 'goes down' again. He talks with the woman, and then the narrator reports that 'she pleased Samson'. Literally, the end of verse 7 reads, 'and she was right in the eyes of Samson'.

The action continues in verse 8 with Samson returning to marry this Philistine woman. But on the way, he turns aside, probably out of curiosity, to see the lion carcass. This should raise a red flag in the reader's mind. What is Samson doing near a carcass? Will he violate his nazirite vow? When Samson arrives at the carcass, he sees a surprising sight. The carcass housed a community of bees. Ordinarily, a carcass would be crawling with maggots.

As readers might expect, Samson violates his nazirite vow by touching the carcass (v. 9). He scrapes out honey into his hand, eats it as he goes, and even has the audacity to give some to his parents. Once again, Samson has done what is right in his own eyes. Still, Yahweh is accomplishing his purpose. As the plot moves forward, Samson's marriage and his encounter with the honey-filled carcass will create an opportunity (v. 4) for Yahweh to act against the Philistines.

PRAYER

Sovereign Lord, I praise you for your ability to take people's imperfect actions as opportunities for accomplishing your purpose. You are truly wonderful!

The FATEFUL RIDDLE

The episode that began in Judges 14:1 continues as Samson's father 'goes down' to the woman Samson plans to marry (v. 10). Apparently, Samson's father needs to complete the arrangements for the wedding. In this episode, the relationship between Samson and the Philistines begins to deteriorate, providing Yahweh with the pretext he sought to act against the Philistines.

A drinking feast and a riddle

For his part in the wedding preparations, Samson throws a feast (v. 10). But this is not just any feast. The Hebrew term translated 'feast' by the NRSV and most other English versions refers to a drinking party. Once again, Samson appears to violate a term of his nazirite vow. He has already touched a carcass, and now he probably drinks wine—a grape-based product. The only term of the vow he has kept so far is refraining from cutting his hair. The purpose of the 'thirty companions' in verse 11 is uncertain. Perhaps they were to function as friends of the bridegroom. However, they will turn out to be adversaries.

The conflict that Yahweh creates (in light of 14:4) starts out innocently. Samson proposes a riddle based on his contact with the honey-filled carcass (v. 12). He even challenges the Philistine to match wits with him. If they guess the answer, they win. If not, Samson wins. The losing side treats the winning side to expensive garments. The riddle consists of two balanced lines amounting to only six words in Hebrew:

1) From the eater	*2) comes out*	*3) something to eat*
4) and from the strong	*5) comes out*	*6) sweetness*

Threatening Samson's wife

Unable to guess the riddle after three days, the thirty companions threaten to burn Samson's wife and her family (v. 15). The term 'house' in verse 15 can refer to a man's family members as well as to the physical structure in which he lives. For the rest of the seven-day feast, she weeps and pleads with Samson to tell her the riddle. At first, he refuses (v. 16), but he finally gives in 'because she nagged him' (v. 17). Literally, the Hebrew text says, 'because she pressured him'.

The time reference—'on the seventh day before the sun went down' (v. 18)—indicates that time was running out. In the Hebrew way of reckoning, a new day started at sunset. So just in the nick of time, the men of the town provided the right answer: 'What is sweeter than honey? What is stronger than a lion?' Samson accuses them of cheating, with another six-word 'two-liner' in Hebrew:

1) If not	2) you ploughed	3) with my heifer
4) not	5) you find	6) my riddle

Referring to his wife as a 'heifer' was as derogatory then as it is today. Samson's strong words show contempt for these men.

Yahweh seizes the opportunity

The spirit of Yahweh now rushes on Samson (v. 19). The purpose for this is to give Samson the strength to carry out his mission of delivering the Israelites from the Philistines. So Samson 'goes down' once again, this time to Ashkelon, one of the five major Philistine cities. There he kills thirty men and takes their garments to pay the 'winners' who had solved his riddle. His return to his father's house (v. 19) signals the end of the scene. But he departs burning with anger. The plot gets complicated even further with the giving of Samson's wife to his best man after Samson's departure to his father's house (v. 20). Yahweh certainly has the pretext he was seeking.

MEDITATION

How does God overcome people's evil in today's world to accomplish his purpose? Think of actual examples, or at least identify possible ways in which God might choose to work.

SAMSON'S REVENGE

The time reference at the beginning of verse 1 signals a new episode. A significant amount of time has elapsed since Samson stormed out of his wedding feast in anger (14:19). Now, he returns to Timnah, obviously unaware that his wife has been given to his best man—a detail revealed to the reader in 14:20.

A disappearing bride

Samson arrives for the visit with his wife, bringing along a goat as a gift, in the same way that a man today might bring along a necklace or some earrings. The time of year is late May or early June, the time of the wheat harvest. However, when Samson announces his intention to visit his wife, his father-in-law does not allow him to go in to her (v. 1).

Instead, his father-in-law offers an emphatic, carefully reasoned explanation. A literal translation of the beginning of verse 2 brings out the force with which he spoke: 'And her father said, saying, "I say that hating, you hated her."' This explains why he gave his daughter to the best man. The father-in-law's offer of a younger daughter to Samson reflects the fact that Samson had paid a dowry or bride price. He even tries to convince Samson with the claim that his younger daughter is prettier (literally, 'better') than the older daughter whom Samson had married.

Torching Philistine crops

Samson reacts by blaming the Philistines for what had happened (v. 3). Then, he acts with purpose and intensity which is indicated by a flurry of eight verbs in verses 4–5. These verbs appear in rapid succession and all have Samson as their subject. Now the narrator's reason for locating this episode 'at the time of the wheat harvest' (v. 1) becomes clear. After all, there are no throwaway lines in Hebrew narrative. Samson's efforts to torch the fields will destroy the Philistines' harvest—both the standing grain and the shocks of grain, as well as the vineyards and olive groves.

The 'foxes' that Samson tied tail-to-tail and attached to torches were probably jackals. The same Hebrew word is used of both species. While foxes usually travelled alone, jackals travelled in packs.

Perhaps Samson tied the jackals in pairs, rather than sending them individually, in order to slow them down as they moved through the fields with torches attached to their tails. Also, this tactic probably forced the jackals to run back and forth instead of in a straight line, thus allowing the torches to ignite more fires.

Trading acts of revenge

The scene closes in verses 6–8 with Samson and the Philistines trading acts of revenge. Even though the Philistines identify Samson as the culprit who burned their fields, they take revenge on his father-in-law and wife. Their speech in verse 6 reveals their understanding of Samson's motive. They even refer to him as 'the son-in-law of the Timnite', and they also refer to 'Samson's wife' being given to his companion. In response, the Philistines burn out the woman and her father (v. 7).

But this only triggers another burst of outrage from Samson. To begin with, he promises revenge. What the NRSV obscures in verse 7 is that Samson makes his statement about revenge first and then follows it by saying, 'and afterwards I will stop'. This statement creates anticipation. Will this be Samson's last act of violence? Verse 8 records his act of revenge. The exact nuance of 'struck them down hip and thigh' is unknown. Obviously, a 'great slaughter' has occurred. Most likely, this expression, literally 'leg upon thigh', is proverbial for 'great slaughter'. It may picture the piling up of bodies —a tangle of legs and thighs—or it might reflect a wrestling image. The scene ends with Samson taking refuge from the Philistines in a narrow cut or crag in the rocks. The name 'Etam', Hebrew for 'place of birds of prey' adds an ominous note.

Yahweh's opportunity takes shape

The reader knows that Yahweh's plan is taking shape. By now, it is apparent that Samson is hardly living up to his calling. But ironically, Yahweh uses Samson's anger and his self-serving violence as his opportunity to act against the Philistines and bring deliverance to Israel.

PRAYER

Father God, we are truly like sheep who have gone astray. We praise you for overcoming our evil to bring us deliverance.

SLAUGHTER *at* JAWBONE HILL

Samson's personal conflict with the Philistines has now escalated to the point of war. In response to the field-torching incident, the Philistines take military action, as indicated by the verbs 'encamped' and 'made a raid' (literally 'spread out') in verse 9. The significance of this action taking place at Lehi, the Hebrew term for 'jawbone', will surface as the story continues.

Giving Samson to the Philistines

The resulting dialogue between the Philistines and the men of Judah reveals the reason for Philistine aggression: they want to take revenge on Samson (v. 10). But rather than standing up to the Philistines, the men of Judah send an army-sized group of men to get Samson (v. 11).

Irony abounds in the dialogue between Samson and the men of Judah. First, rather than being upset with Philistine rule, the Israelites are upset that Samson has threatened their 'peace'. Second, instead of asking Samson to lead them against the Philistines, the men of Judah announce their intention to bind Samson and give him over to the Philistines (v. 12). Oddly enough, Samson agrees to this as long as his fellow countrymen promise not to attack him. Third, in yet another twist of irony, both the Philistines and the Israelites have allied against the leader Yahweh has provided. Samson surrenders, though, allowing the men of Judah to bind him with two 'new ropes'. Being new, the ropes were strong. This creates tension and suspense. What will happen to Samson when he is delivered to the Philistines without any hope for escape?

Broken ropes and a donkey jawbone

When Samson arrived at Lehi, the Philistines came shouting a battle cry. But once again, the spirit of Yahweh rushed on Samson, enabling him to break the ropes as if they were charred fibres weakened by fire (v. 14). A quick succession of four verbs in verse 15 indicates the suddenness and intensity of what happened next. Samson 'found' a fresh jawbone of a donkey, 'reached down', 'took' it, and 'killed' a thousand men. The 'fresh' jawbone is significant. It provided a weapon that was moist and resilient instead of brittle. But even more significant to alert readers is the realization that Samson has once again broken his nazirite vow. He has taken this weapon from the corpse of a donkey. But Yahweh still accomplishes his purpose through Samson.

Samson celebrates his victory with another outburst of poetry, as indicated by the NRSV's arrangement of the text in verse 16. Samson's poem contains a clever play on words. In the Hebrew language, the terms 'donkey' and 'heap' are spelt identically. The most striking feature of Samson's poem, though, is the lack of any reference to Yahweh's help. After Samson completed his poem, he discarded the jawbone and named the place 'Ramath-lehi'—Hebrew for 'Hill of the Jawbone' (v. 17).

Dying of thirst

The episode is not over, though. A final scene describes a very thirsty Samson calling out to Yahweh to quench his thirst lest he fall exhausted into enemy hands. This final scene plays a key role in the story. It shows that while Samson was reluctant to give Yahweh any credit in his victory poem (v. 16), Samson had to admit his need for Yahweh's intervention to survive. Yahweh graciously responded by splitting open a hollow place or seam in a rock so that water gushed out from it (v. 19). After being revived by Yahweh's provision, Samson named the place 'En-hakkore'—a Hebrew expression meaning 'Spring of the Caller'. The summary note in verse 20 closes the episode.

Yahweh's grace

In this final deliverance cycle, Israel has sunk to a new low point. Samson, Yahweh's appointed deliverer, acts independently, and the people of Israel fail to rise to the occasion and join him against the Philistines. In fact, Israel takes its only military action against Samson himself. But Yahweh is still the main character in Judges. Once again, despite the selfishness and ungodliness of Samson, Yahweh graciously continues to work to deliver his people.

MEDITATION

I call upon the Lord, who is worthy to be praised,
so I shall be saved from my enemies.

Psalm 18:3

SAMSON'S TRAGIC IMPRISONMENT

While the summary in Judges 15:20 suggests an end to the Samson story, the narrator relates two final episodes which bring the story to its tragic conclusion.

A prostitute in Gaza

The first episode begins with Samson going to Gaza, one of the five major Philistine cities and, at 45 miles distant, the one furthest from Samson's home region. The Philistines are Israel's enemies, yet Samson continues to be drawn to them. At Gaza, Samson sees a prostitute. Once again, he acts from desire rather than calling.

When the Gazites found out about Samson's presence, they lay in wait for him all night at (literally 'in') the city gate. Ancient walled cities had elaborate gate systems, consisting of two or three gates. Guard rooms were located on both sides of the corridor created by the gate system. Although the Gazites expected Samson to leave at first light, he left the city at midnight. In a display of superhuman strength, he ripped off the heavy wooden doors and carried them up from the coastal region to the hill country. The 'top of the hill that is in front of Hebron' (v. 3) may have been almost forty miles away! By highlighting the contradiction between Samson's physical strength and spiritual weakness, this brief episode sets the stage for the final episode in Samson's life.

Delilah's deceit

In the second episode, Samson falls in love with a woman named Delilah. She is from the valley of Sorek (v. 4), which is located in the northern part of Philistine territory. Will Samson get involved with another Philistine woman? The plot thickens as the lords of the Philistines offer Delilah a considerable sum of money to betray Samson (v. 5). Specifically, they want to know the source of his strength so that they can capture him and subdue (or 'afflict') him.

Delilah's first attempt to find the source of Samson's strength fails (vv. 6–9). He claims that being bound with seven fresh 'bowstrings', made from animal intestines or tendons, would weaken him—but it did not. Again, Samson shows no regard for his nazirite vow, since contact with these items would amount to contact with a corpse.

Delilah's second attempt fails, too (vv. 10–12). The new ropes suggested by Samson prove to be as ineffective as the seven bow-strings.

Delilah's third attempt also fails (vv. 13–14). In response to her accusation and pleading, Samson tells her that she could deprive him of strength by weaving the seven locks of his hair into the fabric being woven on a loom and then securing them with a weaver's pin. While Samson is toying with her, however, he comes dangerously close to revealing the source of his strength. Refraining from cutting his hair is the one term of his nazirite vow that he has not yet violated.

Samson's capture

Finally, Delilah nagged Samson daily until he was tired to death (v. 16). Though physically strong, he could not resist her, especially when she made the disclosure of his secret a test of his love for her (v. 15). So he 'told her all that was in his heart' (the meaning of the Hebrew in verse 17a), including his status as a nazirite and the loss of strength that would come from shaving his head.

By letting Samson fall asleep on her lap, Delilah lulls Samson into a false sense of security (v. 19). But while he was sleeping, Delilah called for a man to shave Samson's head. When Samson woke up to Delilah's cry that the Philistines were upon him, he expected to free himself as before. Tragically, though, he did not know that Yahweh had left him. As a result, the Philistines captured him, gouged out his eyes, imprisoned him, and subjected him to grinding grain into flour—normally a woman's task (v. 21). Ironically, the man who lived according to what was right in his eyes (see 14:2–3) now loses his sight.

The scene closes with a note that raises tension and expectation. Samson's hair begins to grow again after it was shaved (v. 22). Does this deliverer have any future?

PRAYER

Oh Lord, help me not to sacrifice what is precious and sacred for what seems right in my own eyes.

Victory In Death

The setting of the final scene in the Samson story has shifted from the prison to the temple. Philistine leaders have gathered to praise their god, Dagon, for victory over Samson (v. 23). Dagon was the god of grain and the chief deity of the Philistines. The term 'praised' in verse 24 is the Hebrew term *halal*, used throughout the psalms in reference to the praise of Yahweh. However, the 'psalm of praise' sung here is offered to Dagon. The Philistines' praise was based on victory at last over one who had ravaged their country and killed many of their people.

The laugh of the party

At the height of their celebration, the Philistines called for Samson to be brought out of the prison to entertain them. The verbs 'entertain' (v. 25) and 'performed' (vv. 25, 27) are both variations of a Hebrew verb which means 'to laugh'. They brought out Samson, then, to poke fun at him and to laugh at him as he stood blind between the two temple pillars.

Samson is a pathetic sight, yet he has a plan. In verse 26, he speaks to the attendant (literally, 'young man') who has been assigned to help him. He asks the young man to help him feel the pillars between which he stood, so that he could lean on them. These pillars, probably cedar columns on stone bases, would have been located in the centre of the temple to provide the main support for the roof. At this point, the narrator pauses the action to provide some important background information (v. 27). The temple was packed with about 3000 people, including all the leaders of the Philistines.

Samson's prayer and final cry

Positioned now between the pillars, Samson calls out to Yahweh (v. 28). He begins by addressing him as 'Lord GOD'—in Hebrew, *Adonai Yahweh*. The title *Adonai* means 'lord' or 'master' and stresses God's sovereignty. The name *Yahweh*, as noted before in this commentary, is God's personal name by which his people knew him. It stresses his ongoing care and his willingness to act on his people's behalf. After the address, Samson asks Yahweh to 'remember' him and 'strengthen' him. The term 'remember' does not imply forgetfulness on the part of Yahweh. Rather, it emphasizes taking notice of or taking action on behalf of someone. Interestingly, the purpose of Samson's request seems to be personal vengeance—repaying the Philistines for gouging out his eyes.

But regardless of Samson's motives, Yahweh responds. With attention to detail, the narrator carefully describes how Samson grasped the two middle pillars and leaned his weight on them with the use of his hands (v. 29). Then, Samson spoke his final words: 'Let me die with the Philistines.' What a tragic reversal of events! The man set apart to Yahweh for the deliverance of Israel can hope only to die with the enemy. Verse 30 relates the action concisely. Samson pushed with all his might, and the house fell on the entire cast of Philistines. Here, the narrator adds a brilliant observation: Samson killed more Philistines in his death than he did in his entire life (v. 30).

The details in verse 31 indicate that his relatives honoured him in death by bringing his body home and burying it in the family tomb. The Samson story then closes with the note that 'he had judged Israel twenty years'.

The cost of unfaithfulness

The Samson story provides a sobering reminder that Yahweh will accomplish his purposes whether or not his people cooperate. Samson accomplishes more as a deliverer in his death than he did in his life. The truth is that unfaithfulness on the part of God's people does not hinder God, but it proves to be tragic for the people themselves. Samson resembles the nation of Israel by leaving his special calling and using his privileges to satisfy his own desires. When God's people fail to seek first his kingdom, they end up paying a tragic price. This story, then, confirms the message of the book: God's people disintegrate when they abandon God's standards to follow the values of the pagan culture around them.

PRAYER

Father, all that I have, all that I am, all that I hope to be,
I give to you. Help me not to waste what you have given me for
selfish purposes. Help me to use all you have given me to further
the advancement of your kingdom.

MICAH'S SHRINE

The narrator has finished the collection of 'deliverer stories' and now begins an epilogue which contains two stories. The first story, in chapters 17—18, reveals the extent of the religious decay in Israel. The second story, in chapters 19—21, demonstrates the depths of the moral decay in Israel.

A man named Micah

The first story in the epilogue concerns a man named Micah. The story consists of three episodes. Here in the first episode (vv. 1–6), the narrator introduces us to the main character. The name 'Micah' is the Hebrew expression 'Who is like Yahweh?' The story's opening scene consists of a dialogue between Micah and his mother. In Hebrew narratives, the authors tend to show us what characters are like rather than telling us. What the characters say often gives the reader insight into what they are like. At first glance, Micah's repentance reflects well on his character. He had stolen 1100 pieces of silver from his mother —the same amount that Delilah received for betraying Samson (see 16:5). When compared with the ten pieces of silver that Micah later offers a priest as an annual salary (17:10), he had robbed his mother of a sizable fortune! But now he confesses his sin and returns the money. However, Micah's speech betrays his real motive. He returned the money not so much out of remorse but out of the fear of a curse that his mother had pronounced on the criminal.

Corrupting the worship of Yahweh

Micah's mother pronounces a blessing on Micah in the name of Yahweh and dedicates the silver to Yahweh (vv. 2–3). But then the reader gets a shock. Micah's mother gives the dedicated money to her son for the purpose of making an idol. Curiously, she gives only two hundred pieces of the dedicated money for this project. Thus, she violates both the second commandment not to make an idol (Exodus 20:4–5) and the eighth commandment not to steal (Exodus 20:15). The idol ends up in Micah's house as part of his shrine.

Everything about this picture is wrong. First, Micah violates Deuteronomy 12:5 by maintaining a personal worship centre instead of respecting a centralized place of worship that Yahweh had chosen. Second, Micah violates the second commandment (Exodus 20:4–5) by worshipping idols. The teraphim (v. 5) were household idols often used for divination. Third, Micah violates the authority of Israel's priesthood (see Exodus 28) by making an ephod—a priestly garment —and sets up one of his own sons as priest. Micah certainly did not live up to his name! He and his mother provide an example of the religious corruption in Israel during the period of the judges. Basically, the people of Israel incorporated pagan practices and pagan gods into the worship of Yahweh. They did not live as if there was no one else who was like Yahweh.

Life without a king

The narrator summarizes the initial scene in the first episode of the Micah story with this ominous refrain: 'In those days there was no king in Israel; all the people did what was right in their own eyes' (v. 6). This refrain appears again in 21:25, and it also occurs without the second clause in 18:1 and 19:1. As noted previously, some scholars conclude from this refrain that the book of Judges defends the establishment of the monarchy. Supposedly, having a king would bring order to the chaos in Israel. Given the deteriorating moral conditions during the time of the monarchy, however, it's quite possible that the narrator's original audience longed for the 'good old days' when there was no king oppressing Israel. Thus, this refrain stresses to people living under the monarchy that the key to Israel's success is not the presence or absence of a monarchy. Life was just as rotten in the 'good old days' when there was no king. Rather, the success of God's people depends on whom they follow—Yahweh or the gods of their pagan neighbours. It's possible, too, that this refrain laments Israel's failure to follow Yahweh, who established himself as Israel's divine king when he gave them the law through Moses (see Exodus 19:3–6; Deuteronomy 33:5).

PRAYER

Yahweh God, I confess that only you are holy. Though the darkness hides you, there is none beside you. Even though sinful people do not recognize your holiness, you alone are perfect in power, love, and purity.

91 JUDGES 17:7-13

MICAH HIRES *a* PRIEST

Another episode in the Micah story begins in verse 7 with the introduction of a new character. Several important details emerge about
him: he is a youth; he comes from Bethlehem in Judah; he is a Levite
who has been residing or, literally, 'sojourning' in Bethlehem; and he
is looking for a new place to stay.

In this episode, the narrator shows a high level of sophistication as
a storytelling prophet. Rather than stating his judgments, he provides
enough detail to let the reader draw obvious conclusions. Readers
who know the Law of Moses will frequently respond, 'Oh no, that is
a violation of God's law!'

Wandering aimlessly

Several details add intrigue to the story. As a Levite, this man belongs
to a tribe set apart to oversee Israel's worship of Yahweh. As a young
man, he was probably too young to serve as a priest (see Numbers
4:3, 30). While Deuteronomy 18:6-9 allows Levites to serve as
'resident aliens' in other towns that Yahweh chooses, this young man
does not have such a definite purpose in mind. Twice we read that he
is simply looking to live wherever he can find a place (vv. 8, 9). The
final expression in verse 8—'to carry on his work'—is ambiguous.
Literally, the Hebrew reads, 'to make his way'. Does this mean that
he is looking for food? In the book of Ruth, an Israelite family living
in Bethlehem during the period of the Judges left for precisely this
reason. Or is this young man looking for other Levites or perhaps for
work? At this point in the story, we do not even know the young
man's name. The lack of specific information serves the narrator's
purpose. He portrays this young man as an aimless wanderer who is
looking for an opportunity to develop.

A job opportunity develops

An opportunity does develop for the young man. According to verse
10, Micah offers him a job as his personal priest. Priests were to provide the kind of spiritual authority, direction and care that a father
provides for his children. Ironically, Micah looks for a spiritual father
in a young man who is probably not old enough to serve as a priest!

200

The Levite agrees to Micah's terms, becomes like a son to him, and so Micah installs him as priest (vv. 11–12).

A careful reading of the text reveals a couple more irregularities. For instance, the young Levite does not appear to serve at a place chosen by Yahweh, but rather at a place chosen by a man. Furthermore, he receives a salary and benefits rather than the usual priestly share of the sacrifices that people offered to Yahweh (v. 10; Deuteronomy 18:1–8). In effect, then, this priest is serving Micah rather than Yahweh.

Earlier, Micah had installed his son as a priest (17:5). Now, he has installed another unauthorized priest. The term 'installed' in verse 12 (and previously in 17:5) is the Hebrew expression 'filled the hand'. This technical expression described the ordination of Aaron and his sons to the priesthood (see Exodus 28:41; 29:9, 29, 35, where it is translated in the NRSV as 'ordain'). The expression seems to reflect Moses' act of placing offering items in Aaron's hands. However, in our present story, Micah installs the young Levite by filling his hand with silver coins.

Micah's motive

What was Micah's motive for hiring himself a Levitical priest? In verse 18, the narrator reveals this motive by letting Micah speak for himself. Micah believes that Yahweh will prosper him because he now has a Levite for a priest. This conviction betrays Micah's view of Yahweh. He treats Yahweh as just another pagan god who can be manipulated. Since he has hired a man from the tribe from which Yahweh's priests are appointed, surely he has purchased Yahweh's favour. The narrator does not have to state the obvious here. The reader should be well aware that Yahweh will not honour a man who has the audacity to try to gain his favour even while disregarding the clear instructions given in Deuteronomy and elsewhere in the Law of Moses.

MEDITATION

Where do God's people today face the temptation to treat him
as a power source to be manipulated rather than as
a holy God to be honoured and obeyed?

The DANITES' SPY MISSION

In Judges 18, a third major character enters the Micah story—an entire Israelite tribe, the Danites. As readers we must keep in mind the narrator's strategy. He relates the events in chapters 17—18 to reveal the depth of Israel's religious decay. The establishment of a religious centre at Dan is a key event in this story. Once Israel is divided into two kingdoms after King Solomon's death, Dan becomes a major centre of idol worship in the northern kingdom of Israel (see 1 Kings 12:25–31). Eventually, it falls with the rest of the northern kingdom to Assyria. If the narrator of Judges is a prophet from the southern kingdom of Judah who composed the book after the northern kingdom had fallen (722BC), then his readers would have been quite familiar with the fate of the Danites. The story of how they set up a worship centre contains an even stronger prophetic warning about the bankruptcy of pagan religion.

Spying out a new land

The refrain in verse 1—'in those days there was no king in Israel'—marks the beginning of a new episode. Then, the remainder of verse 1 provides important background information. The Danites are looking for a new place to live. The problem is not that they failed to receive an allotted portion of land, as the NRSV's translation of verse 1 suggests. Rather, they had been unable to take full possession of their allotted land (see 1:34).

The action starts in verse 2 with the Danites sending out five mighty men to spy out the land for a new place to live. Their mission brings to mind two previous spy missions related in Numbers 13—14 and in Joshua 2. Unlike these two missions, this latest mission has no sanction from Yahweh. Rather than seeking Yahweh's help to conquer their allotted territory, the Danites pursue their own solution.

Meeting Micah and his priest

As the Danite spies head north and enter the hill country of Ephraim, they find lodging at Micah's house (v. 2). Their stop at Micah's house provides a surprise: 'they recognized the voice of the young Levite' (v. 3). While the spies may have had prior contact with Micah's priest, it is more likely that they simply recognized his southern accent, which he picked up in Bethlehem of Judah.

In the dialogue that follows (vv. 3–6), the responses of this priest betray his real spiritual condition. First, after being peppered with questions about how he ended up in Micah's house, the priest gives credit to Micah rather than to Yahweh. Second, when asked by the Danites to inquire of God about the success of their mission, the priest seems to offer a vague reply which the NRSV captures nicely (v. 6). Micah's priest does not really guarantee success, just that Yahweh has his eye on their mission. The narrator crafts the priest's reply as if it was given immediately, without much reflection. Thus, the priest's ministry shares much in common with the Danites' mission. Both efforts are a sham.

Reporting back

As the episode continues, the Danite spies arrive at Laish—about 100 miles from their land and much further north than any territory allotted to an Israelite tribe. After observing a people vulnerable to attack (v. 7), they return to offer a positive report. Their report recalls the report of the spies whom Moses sent to spy out the promised land. Ironically, Moses' spies who had Yahweh's blessing brought back a negative report. Yet these spies, operating without Yahweh's blessing, bring back a positive report. Then even have the audacity to attribute their discovery of a new promised land to God (v. 10).

PRAYER

Father in heaven, help me to face my problems with solutions
that reflect your instructions.

93   JUDGES 18:11–31

The DANITES STEAL MICAH'S PRIEST

Armed with a favourable report, six hundred Danite warriors head north to conquer a new land. After camping at 'Mahaneh-dan' (Hebrew for 'the camp of Dan'), they arrive again at Micah's house (vv. 12–13). This detail creates suspense. What will happen now?

The capture of shrine and priest

The spies inform their comrades that Micah's house contains all the elements needed to set up a religious shrine. The speech closes with a challenge: 'Now therefore consider what you will do' (v. 15). When the five spies seize the religious objects that comprise Micah's shrine, the priest protests against their actions (v. 18). However, his attitude quickly changes when he receives an offer for a better opportunity—presiding as priest over an entire tribe rather than over a single household. Unfortunately, the NRSV does not capture this attitude change when it reports that 'the priest accepted the offer' (v. 20). Literally, the first line of Hebrew text in verse 20 reads: 'And the heart of the priest was glad.' Thus the priest's opportunity for career advancement trumps any feelings of loyalty to Micah or any feelings of resentment to the Danites for stealing Micah's shrine.

Ending up with nothing

The act of placing their little children, livestock and goods in front of them shows that the Danites expected Micah to pursue them (v. 21). Micah does overtake them with a band of neighbours that he has called together. The dialogue that follows is interesting. The Danites speak first and seem to mock Micah for pursuing them. While the NRSV offers a good translation of their speech, the Hebrew text of verse 23 literally reads, 'What is the matter with you that you cried out?' Although the verb 'cried out' certainly refers to a call for help or even a battle cry, it is the same verb used throughout the deliverance stories earlier in Judges to describe the Israelites' cries of oppression. Here, the oppressors are not foreigners but fellow Israelites.

Micah offers a passionate reply (v. 24). In the Hebrew text, the words 'my gods that I made' appear first in his reply. This draws the readers' attention to the absurdity of Micah's situation. Micah made gods to protect himself, but in the end he has to attempt a mission to try to protect them. Anyway, Micah chides the Danites for implying that he is over-reacting. From his perspective, he has nothing left. The Danites end the conversation with a threat (v. 25). Micah can shut up or risk a fierce attack which will cost him his life and the lives of his family members. At the end of the scene, Micah is a pathetic figure. He is powerless before the Danites, so he returns home empty-handed.

Ending up in bondage

What about the Danites? The final scene in verses 27–31 indicates initial success. They overtake the city of Laish and rename it Dan. There, they set up a religious shrine. Verse 30 provides a bit of a shock to the reader. The young Levite who served first as Micah's priest and now serves as priest of Dan turns out to be a descendant of Moses (v. 30). Readers should not miss the irony here. Instead of obeying the Law of Moses, the Danites set up one of Moses' descendants to lead them further into idol worship.

Despite initial success, the Danites end up in bondage. The mention of 'the time the land went into captivity' in verse 30 refers to the fall of the northern kingdom of Israel to Assyria in 722BC. Verse 31 provides a stark contrast. Throughout the period of the judges, false worship continued at Dan while true worship took place at the house of God at Shiloh.

Message for today

Although the narrator presents his message subtly, he offers a clear prophetic word which is relevant for God's people today. When God's people pursue religion without a relationship with him, their religion will not work for them. Man-made religion will attract Yahweh's judgment, not his favour.

MEDITATION

How do God's people today fall prey to pursuing religion devoid of a true relationship with God? Where do you face this temptation in your own life?

From HOSPITALITY to INHOSPITALITY

Beginning in chapter 19, the epilogue of Judges moves from a focus on Israel's religious decline to Israel's moral decline. After using the Micah story to expose Israel's utter failure to love God (chs. 17—18), the narrator relates a second and final story to reveal the people's complete failure to love each other as neighbours (chs. 19—21). The story in Judges 19—21 breaks down into three episodes which track Israel's nose-dive to destruction.

Nameless characters

The narrator marks the opening of the first episode in Judges 19 with a familiar refrain: 'In those days, when there was no king in Israel…' He then introduces two of the major characters in this story: a Levite and his concubine. Neither character is named throughout the episode. In fact, none of the characters in chapters 19—21 are named except for one (Phinehas in 20:28). Perhaps the narrator has left them nameless in order to reflect their dishonourable states. Naming a character provides a measure of dignity and honour which the narrator did not wish to give. It is possible, too, that the anonymity of these characters allows them to represent all members of the same class. Thus, the Levite represents all other Levites at this time in Israel, the concubine represents all other women and wives in Israel, and so on.

The Levite somewhat resembles the Levite in the previous story. The Hebrew term translated 'residing' by the NRSV in verse 1 indicates that he was a temporary resident in the hill country of Ephraim. Like the Levite in the previous story, this Levite has some connection with Bethlehem in Judah, but instead of travelling from it (see 17:7), he travels to it and takes a concubine.

Unending hospitality

A crisis occurs when the concubine becomes angry with her husband and returns to her father's house in Bethlehem (v. 2). A textual issue arises here. The NRSV follows some ancient versions and translates the first verb in verse 2 as 'became angry'. However, most other major English versions follow the translation of the verb as 'played the harlot'. Whatever the case, this is the only place in the story where the concubine takes action. In the remainder of the story, she is only acted upon. Four months later, her husband arrives to persuade her to return. The expression translated 'speak tenderly' is literally 'speak upon her heart' (v. 3). The narrator then tells us that the concubine's father received him with joy—although the narrator does not explain why.

What follows is intriguing. The Levite respects the ancient Near Eastern custom of hospitality by staying three days at a feast thrown by his father-in-law. But the plot gets bogged down as the narrator gives a detailed report of the father-in-law's attempts to detain his son-in-law. The Levite finally leaves late in the afternoon of the fifth day after three prior unsuccessful attempts—early morning on the fourth day, later on the fourth day, and early morning on the fifth day. The narrator gives us no details that reflect negatively on the father-in-law. He appears in this story as a model of generous hospitality.

Hospitality denied

In the next scene, the Levite arrives with his servant and concubine near Jebus, or Jerusalem. The narrator makes a point of informing us that 'the day was far spent' (v. 11). But when the servant suggests spending the night there, the Levite refuses, identifying the place as 'a city of foreigners, who do not belong to the people of Israel' (v. 12). This explains the reference to Jerusalem as Jebus, thus highlighting the foreigners who occupied it. Presumably, the issue is one of safety. The Levite suggests going on to Gibeah.

Gibeah, however, does not turn out to be the safe haven that the Levite expected. The lack of an invitation to spend the night in someone's home (v. 15) is shocking. In the ancient Near East, refusal to provide lodging to a travelling stranger was a serious breach of hospitality. But as the next scene will show, inhospitality is only the tip of the corruption in Israel's social relationships.

MEDITATION

How can God's people today express hospitality?

From INHOSPITALITY *to* SEXUAL VIOLENCE

The 'Levite–concubine' episode continues in verse 16 with the introduction of a new character, an old man who is returning to the city after a day's work in the field. The narrator calls attention to this old man with an attention-grabbing Hebrew particle translated by the NRSV as 'then'. Like the Levite, the old man hailed from the hill country of Ephraim and was a temporary resident of Gibeah.

An old man's hospitality

Oddly enough, this outsider provides the hospitality that the city's citizens were unwilling to offer. When the old man sees the Levite—described in verse 17 as a 'wayfarer', that is, a traveller—a dialogue begins. This dialogue confirms the reader's already negative impression of Gibeah. When asked about his destination and place of origin, the Levite offers a lengthy reply (vv. 18–19). He makes it clear that he and his contingent will not create undue hardship for anyone who would show them hospitality. They have food and drink for themselves, as well as food and bedding materials for their animals. Yet nobody has offered to provide lodging. The old man, though, graciously invites them to spend the night at his house. In his invitation, he hints at the city's social and moral decay when he warns them not to spend the night in the square (v. 20).

Sodom revisited

The group's enjoyment of hospitality (v. 21) comes to an abrupt halt, however, when a gang of 'perverse' men start pounding on the door (v. 22). Hospitality gives way to horror. In fact, the narrator relates the sickening events of verses 22–26 in a way that causes the reader to recall the story of Sodom and Gomorrah's destruction (Genesis 19). The two stories share several parallels in their overall flow of events as well as in their choice of terms.

Like the Genesis 19 story, the evil men in the present story demand access to the visitor in order to have sexual intercourse with him (v. 22). The narrator uses the old man's reply to provide the proper perspective on this demand. The old man urges them not to do this, describing their intention with the Hebrew verb *ra'a* ('act so wickedly') and the Hebrew noun *nebalah* ('vile thing') (v. 23). The verb *ra'a* appears in its noun form throughout Judges in the oft-repeated observation that the Israelites 'did what was evil [*ra*] in the sight of the Lord' (Judges 2:11; 3:7, 12; 4:1; 6:1; 10:6; 13:1). The noun *nebalah* refers to a disgraceful act. The gang's intention is wicked and vile because it amounts to an act of homosexuality, a definite violation of the law of Moses (see Leviticus 18:22; 20:13); and it amounts to an act of violence against a non-consenting person.

A horrible alternative

Until this point in the story, the old man appears to uphold the social and moral requirements of the law of Moses. But the alternative he suggests to the gang pounding at his door demonstrates that he, too, has been corrupted by the Canaanite culture around him. His alternative is to offer his virgin daughter and the Levite's concubine to the men (v. 24). The Hebrew term *anah* ('ravish') in verse 24 is a technical term for rape. The expression 'do whatever you want to them' is literally 'do whatever is good in your eyes'. Sadly, the old man takes seriously the customs of showing hospitality, but totally disregards the sexual ethics of the law of Moses—not to mention the disregard for his precious daughter. Verse 25 seems to picture a scene of desperation. The old man grabs the concubine and pushes her out of the door in a panicked attempt to get rid of the gang.

Unlike the story in Genesis 19, no angel intervened. After being repeatedly raped and sexually abused all night, the concubine was released at dawn. As the sun rose, she was lying at the door of the old man's house where her master was staying (v. 26).

The reader cannot avoid the conclusion that Israel has become thoroughly Canaanized. God's people resemble wicked pagans, not a chosen race nor a holy nation.

PRAYER

Loving Father, I pray for victims of rape and violence. Heal them and give them peace in place of despair.

From SEXUAL VIOLENCE *to* DISMEMBERMENT

The final scene in Judges 19 ranks as one of the most sickening, grotesque scenes in the Bible. Still, the narrator displays his skill as a master storyteller who can craft his story carefully to proclaim his prophetic message. The scene takes place the morning after the Levite's concubine has been gang-raped and has somehow ended up at the door of the old man's house where she and her husband were staying.

The Levite's discovery

The narrator paints a vivid picture in verses 27–28. First, he calls the Levite 'her master' rather than 'her husband'. This impersonal title probably depicts the Levite's utter failure as a husband. Second, the narrator's description of the Levite's action portrays him as a cold, dispassionate man who seems unconcerned with the fate of his concubine. He opens the doors not to look for her, but to continue his journey. Third, he paints a compelling picture of the woman which elicits sympathy from the reader. She is 'lying at the door of the house, with her hands on the threshold' (v. 27). Apparently too weak to knock or open the door, protection and security elude her grasp. Fourth, in verse 28, the narrator's account of the Levite's speech to the woman pictures him as a heartless, callous man. The Levite simply issues two commands: 'Arise; let's go.' But there is no answer. Finally, the narrator confirms the picture of the Levite as cold and callous by his description at the end of verse 28. The Levite simply puts her on his donkey and sets out for his home.

A revolting message

Nothing prepares the reader for what the narrator shares next in verse 29. When the Levite arrived at his house, he carried out a grotesque, shocking act. He dismembered his concubine. The four steps he took portray this as a calculated, deliberate act. He took a knife, seized his concubine, cut her into twelve pieces, and sent the pieces throughout the territory of Israel.

What is the point of such a hideous, repulsive act? Basically, its purpose was to promote a unified response by creating a sense of shock and then fear. The question posed by the delivery-men in verse 30 certainly implies that nothing this horrible had ever happened before in Israel from the time of the exodus to the present time. Even the nature of the question betrays a rather Canaanite perspective of the exodus event. Yahweh is not even mentioned as the one who brought the people of Israel out of Egypt.

In the next episode in chapter 20, the people of Israel will assemble as 'one body' (20:1) to go to battle, so the unified response anticipated by the Levite seems to involve war. Other evidence seems to confirm that this act functioned as a call to war. In 1 Samuel 11:7, King Saul issued a call to arms by cutting up a team of oxen into pieces and sending them with a message throughout Israel. This created dread. Furthermore, a document discovered in the ancient city of Mari in northern Mesopotamia contains a message to a king Zimrri-Lim, a contemporary of Hammurabi. This message suggests dismembering a prisoner and sending out pieces in order to create a sense of fear. This would cause people to come together quickly to carry out a military campaign.

How to respond

The NRSV follows the Septuagint in expanding verse 30 so that it reads as the message the Levite wanted his messengers to deliver to Israel. Most English translations present it as the response of the people to the piece of corpse they received. Regardless of who spoke the words, the concluding clause offers a prophetic challenge: 'Consider it [literally, 'hear']; take counsel; and speak out.' The implication is that God's people cannot ignore such a cruel, violent act, which resulted from the breakdown of relationships in the family, the community and the nation.

PRAYER

Father God, give me the courage to speak against and work against the cruelty and violence I see in my culture. Help me to reflect your righteousness in the way I treat people around me—family members, neighbours, strangers and co-workers.

From DISMEMBERMENT to CIVIL WAR

The gruesome call to arms (19:29–30) achieved the Levite's desired effect. Israelites came out from every region—from Dan in the north to Beersheba in the south and even to Gilead to the east of the Jordan River—and assembled as 'one body before the Lord at Mizpah' (v. 1). The statement in verse 3 about the Benjaminites hearing about this gathering implies that they did not have representatives present. In verses 1–3, the language identifies this as an assembly of warriors prepared to engage in holy war. Sadly, the holy war will be carried out against an internal rather than an external enemy.

The Levite's testimony

At last, the Levite has the opportunity to explain why he dismembered his concubine and sent pieces of her corpse to the various Israelite tribes. As readers, we are not sure whether the question in verse 3—'Tell us, how did this criminal act come about?'—refers to his actions or to the events that precipitated his actions. At any rate, he provides a straightforward account of what took place (vv. 4–7). Near the end of his testimony, he calls their act 'lewd' and 'disgraceful'. The term 'lewd' is the Hebrew term *zimmah*, which refers to evil schemes such as incest, adultery and idolatry. The term 'disgraceful' is the Hebrew term *nebalah*—the same term used by the Levite's host, the old man, in 19:23, where it is translated 'vile thing' and refers to a disgraceful act. The Levite concludes his testimony with a call for the Israelites to give their advice and counsel (v. 7).

A unified response

According to verses 8–11, the people offered a united response. The expressions 'as one' in verse 8 and 'united as one' in verse 11 are identical in Hebrew (along with the expression 'one body' in verse 1). Thus, verses 8 and 11 frame the paragraph. The united decision consists of going up to the Benjaminite city of Gibeah to repay them for the 'disgrace' [Hebrew *nebalah*] they have committed (v. 10).

The tribes of Israel show restraint, though, and pursue a course of action with the potential to avoid war. They call the Benjaminites to account for the crime (v. 12) and to hand over the 'scoundrels' who committed the crime. Sadly, the Benjaminites side with the scoundrels in Gibeah and prepare for war (vv. 14–16).

Brother against brother

Since war is inevitable, the Israelites head to Bethel to inquire of God as to who should go first. Yahweh provides an answer: 'Judah shall go up first' (v. 18). The language of verse 18 recalls the scene in Judges 1:1–2. But the comparison is disheartening. In Judges 1:1–2, the Israelites were preparing to battle the Canaanites. Here, they prepare to battle one of their own tribes!

The story now takes a bizarre turn. The numbers are heavily against Benjamin. While the Benjaminites muster 26,000 men (v. 15), the Israelites muster 400,000 warriors (v. 17). But even with Yahweh's commission, 22,000 Israelite warriors are struck down by the Benjaminites (v. 21). However, the Israelites take courage and prepare to launch another attack (v. 22). Prior to this second attack, they engage in weeping before Yahweh and inquiring of him about attacking their kinsfolk, the Benjaminites. Yahweh's commission is clear: 'Go up against them' (v. 23), but for a second time, Israel tastes a bitter defeat. This time, the Benjaminites strike down 18,000 Israelite warriors (v. 25).

What are we to make of this bizarre turn of events? Apparently, Yahweh is, for now, releasing the fury of his judgment on the whole nation. The Israelites are fighting brother against brother with the same force that they should have mustered against the Canaanites. Now, they all look like Canaanites! Who wins and who loses in a battle like this? As readers, we wait to see if and how this mess will be untangled.

PRAYER

God of righteousness, what a mess we make when we abandon your plans for us and pursue evil plans. Our only hope is your mercy. Though our sins are like scarlet, may they be as white as snow.

From CIVIL WAR *to* DISASTER

After two crushing defeats, what can the Israelites do? They had over-whelmingly outnumbered the Benjaminites (20:15, 17), and had even received a clear commission from Yahweh each time (20:18, 23). Once again, the defeated Israelites return to Bethel to mourn, sit, fast, sacrifice, and inquire before Yahweh (vv. 26–27).

Promise of victory

The priest before whom Israel inquires of Yawheh is Phinehas son of Eleazer, son of Aaron (v. 28). He is the only character named in Judges 19—21. This is the same Phinehas whose zealous actions stopped an earlier plague that Yahweh brought upon the Israelites for their gross immorality and idol worship (Numbers 25:1–13). By naming Phinehas, the narrator may intend to show how quickly Israel became like the Canaanites after entering the promised land. Further-more, Phinehas deserves to be named because he is one of the few characters in Judges who is completely committed to Yahweh.

The only mention in Judges of the ark of the covenant occurs here in verse 27. This object served as the vehicle through which Yahweh related to his people (see Exodus 25:10–22). The ark consisted of a gold-plated box, about 110cm long by 66cm wide and 66cm high. On the lid of the ark were two figurines—angels with spread wings, facing each other. In between those angels, Yahweh revealed his pres-ence. The absence of any other mention of the ark in Judges reflects the people's disregard of the presence of Yahweh.

Phinehas' question in verse 28 indicates that the Israelites were prepared to give up the fight. But once again, Yahweh commands them, 'Go up'. This time, however, he promises victory.

Ambush and slaughter

The remainder of the chapter describes the Israelites' defeat of the Benjaminites. At first reading, the account seems confusing. By verses 35–36, the Benjaminites have faced defeat, but then the narrator starts describing the battle again. Basically, Judges 20:29–48 contains three panels: verses 29–34, verses 35–41, and verses 42–48. The first two panels serve as two descriptions of the same event, much as

Genesis 1:1—2:3 and 2:4–25 look at the creation event from two different perspectives. While the first panel looks at the big picture, the second panel focuses on the details of the ambush. Both panels close with a similar refrain: 'disaster was close upon them'. The third panel describes the aftermath of the defeat.

A couple of details deserve a closer look. First, the Israelites use an ambush to defeat the Benjaminites. This strategy and its outcome resembles the ambush that had worked for Joshua at Ai (Joshua 8:1–29). Basically, one group of Israelite troops lured the Benjaminites away from the city (vv. 30–32a). Because the Israelites lost about thirty men, the Benjaminites expected victory (vv. 31b–32a, 39). However, a second group of Israelite warriors rushed the city once the Benjaminites were drawn away from the city (vv. 32b–33, 36b–39a). Here, the reader should note a second detail. The Israelites set the city of Gibeah on fire to signal to the first group of Israelite troops to stop their pretended retreat (vv. 38–39a). When the Benjaminites looked behind them, they saw a startling sight. The narrator uses the Hebrew particle *hinneh* in verse 40 to introduce the surprising sight. While the NRSV does not directly translate this particle, it expresses surprise by using an exclamation mark at the end of the sentence. What the Benjaminites see is the whole city going up in smoke. The language here in verse 40 pictures the town as a burnt offering (see Deuteronomy 13:16). As the third panel shows, the Benjaminites fled, only to be overtaken and slaughtered by the Israelites (vv. 42–48).

A surviving remnant

At the end of the slaughter and burning of towns in the region, only six hundred Benjaminite warriors survived (v. 47). The narrator's comment about the slaughtered Benjaminites being 'courageous fighters' (v. 46) seems to reflect his sympathy and sadness for them. The people of Israel have become so corrupt that they have to wage holy war on themselves.

PRAYER

Spirit of the living God, keep us from evil so that we do not destroy ourselves. Protect us from ourselves!

From DISASTER *to* NEAR EXTINCTION

The prologue's second story—the story of Israel's moral decay—draws to a close with a final episode in Judges 21. This rather strange episode puts an exclamation point on the message of Judges: God's people in pre-monarchy days disintegrated when they became like their Canaanite neighbours. This final episode focuses on preserving the tribe of Benjamin. In the aftermath of dealing out retribution to the Benjaminites, the people of Israel express grief over the plight of these kinfolk and the possible loss of one of their tribes (vv. 6, 15).

A tribe in jeopardy

Verses 1–7 describe Israel's concern about the prospect of losing one of their tribes. Verse 1 supplies background that the reader must understand once the action begins in verse 2. At the previous assembly at Mizpah (see 20:1), the Israelites had taken an oath not to give their daughters in marriage to the Benjaminites. After this information, the action begins in verse 2 with the people assembling again at Bethel and weeping. Instead of celebrating their victory, they were mourning the possibility of losing an entire tribe. The question posed to Yahweh in verse 3 is at least an expression of lament, and possibly an accusation against Yahweh. But the reader knows the answer: the loss of a tribe stems from God's people becoming like their Canaanite neighbours.

In an effort to seek Yahweh's input and help, the people build an altar and offer sacrifices (v. 4). At this point, the people also raise a question about which tribes of Israel did not participate in the previous 'assembly to the Lord' at Mizpah (v. 5). The narrator explains why the people raised this question: they had taken an oath to put to death any tribe that did not attend. Before seeking an answer to their question, however, the Israelites express their grief over the apparent loss of an entire tribe (v. 6). The expression 'had compassion' in verse 6 translates the Hebrew verb *naham*, which means 'have sorrow or regret over'. The people's speech in verse 7 contains a hint of what they have in mind. They need to find Israelite wives for the surviving Benjaminites without violating their earlier pledge not to give their daughters as wives to the men of Benjamin.

Devising a solution

In verse 8, the Israelites return to their former question about which, if any, tribes 'did not come up to Yahweh to Mizpah'. They realize that no one from Jabesh-gilead showed up. The surprising nature of this discovery is indicated by the NRSV with the words 'it turned out'. The town of Jabesh-gilead, located east of the Jordan River, belonged to the tribe of Manasseh.

Sadly, the Israelites once again send warriors to wipe out one of their own towns for showing rebellion (vv. 10–11). In the process, they spare four hundred young virgins, perhaps finding a precedent in Numbers 31:17–18, and bring them to Shiloh.

Four months later (see 20:47), after the virgins had had time to mourn the loss of their families, and after Israel's anger against the Benjaminites had perhaps subsided, the Israelites made contact with the Benjaminites. The Benjaminites were still in hiding, but the leaders of Israel offered them peace (v. 13). The Benjaminites responded to the offer, returning and receiving the young virgins from Jabesh-Gilead who had been saved alive (v. 14a).

At the end of verse 14, however, a new crisis appears. There were not enough women of Jabesh-Gilead for the surviving Benjaminite warriors. A reader can only say, 'What a mess this has turned out to be!' Israel's scheming has still not solved the problem. What will the people of Israel do now?

Message for today

The first scene in this episode shows the damage that communities of God's people suffer when they resemble their culture instead of their God. The consequences of sin create complex problems that are difficult to solve.

MEDITATION

What are some difficulties you have seen or experienced
in the church which emerged because people followed
popular cultural values rather than God's standards?
Read Romans 12:1–2 and turn it into a prayer.

100 JUDGES 21:15-25

From NEAR EXTINCTION to an IMMORAL SOLUTION

In verse 15, the narrator continues the previous episode with wording borrowed from verse 6. He notes that Israel 'had compassion' on Benjamin. A second clause explains the cause of this compassion: Yahweh 'had made a breach in the tribes of Israel'. To the Israelites, the destruction of the tribe of Benjamin represented a break in their strength as a nation. Now, even after the creative plan to provide the surviving Benjaminites with wives from Jabesh-Gilead, two hundred of the men still did not have wives.

Solving the dilemma: another ambush

In verses 16–18, the elders of Israel wrestle with their dilemma. How will the nation of Israel provide the rest of the surviving Benjaminites with wives? After all, they cannot violate their oath not to give any of their daughters as wives to the Benjaminites.

They realize that a yearly festival of Yahweh—perhaps Passover, Weeks, Tabernacles (see Deuteronomy 16:1–17) or a paganized version of one of them—is taking place at Shiloh.

Verses 20–22 contain the solution presented to the Benjaminites. The Benjaminites should hide in the nearby vineyards. Then, when the young women of Shiloh come out to dance, each Benjaminite can 'carry off'—that is, 'catch' or 'seize'—a wife. Ironically, the Benjaminites who found themselves in this predicament because of an ambush by the Israelites are now instructed to remedy the situation by setting up an ambush against Israelite girls. Presumably, the proximity of Shiloh to a major highway (see v. 19) would make their escape possible.

At an all-time low

The reader cannot fail to notice how severely Israelite morals and social structures have eroded. Essentially, the elders of Israel are sanctioning violence against their own daughters. Interestingly enough, they suggest this kidnapping scheme because it seems to provide a loophole which will keep them from violating their prior oath. While the Benjaminites will get Israelite girls for wives, the parents of these girls will not be guilty of breaking the oath and giving them as wives to the Benjaminites (v. 22). In effect, the Israelite leaders operate from a skewed picture of Yahweh. How can they think he will honour them for taking their oath seriously when they do not take seriously the protection of their daughters? How can Yahweh honour an obedience made possible by kidnapping? Such faulty reasoning demonstrates that the Israelites have sunk to the moral and social level of their Canaanite neighbours. They have oppressed one group of 'innocent' people to help another group to solve the consequences of their own wickedness. Thus, it is quite fitting for the narrator to end the book with the now familiar refrain: 'In those days there was no king in Israel; all the people did what was right in their own eyes' (v. 25).

God's sovereign grace

The sad ending to Judges underscores the narrator's prophetic message: God's people will come to ruin when they live like their pagan neighbours instead of living for God. However, it is quite apparent that God's people are unable to live for him. This realization prepares the reader for the later promise of a new covenant which will provide the increased spiritual resources needed for obeying God's commands (Jeremiah 31:31–34; see also Ezekiel 36; Joel 2). Amazingly, in God's sovereign grace, a key minister of this new covenant will be the apostle Paul (2 Corinthians 3:6)—a descendant of the very Benjaminites who salvaged their future by gaining wives through bloodshed and kidnapping (see Romans 11:1; Philippians 3:5).

PRAYER

*Father, like the ancient Israelites, I tend to wander from you
and to make a mess of my life. Restore me by your grace,
and help me to follow you.*

Suggestions *for* Further Reading

If you wish to do further study or reading in the books of Joshua and Judges, here are some suggestions. None of the books I recommend require a knowledge of the Hebrew language. They are challenging, yet they are also 'entry-level'. You can find full details for these resources in the bibliography that follows this section.

Books on Old Testament narrative

To learn more about how Old Testament stories work, start with *The Art of Biblical Narrative* by Robert Alter, a professor at the University of California at Berkeley in the United States. Alter writes in a narrative style, and his book has become a classic. Shimon Bar-Efrat, the head of Biblical Studies at the Hebrew University Secondary School in Jerusalem, provides more of a catalogue of literary techniques and devices in his book, *Narrative Art in the Bible*. These two books work well together. They may be the most user-friendly books available on Old Testament narrative.

Four additional books will help readers to understand Old Testament narratives. Some may find these volumes slightly more challenging than the books by Alter or Bar-Efrat, yet they are still quite readable. Jean Louis Ska, a scholar at the Pontifical Bible Institute in Rome, has produced a slim volume entitled *'Our Fathers Have Told Us': Introduction to the Analysis of Hebrew Narratives*. Ska's work helps beginners through the forest of new terms used by specialists who study Old Testament narratives. J.P. Fokkelman, who teaches at the University of Leiden in the Netherlands, has written *Reading Biblical Narrative: An Introductory Guide*. This book uses twelve stories from the Old Testament to teach narrative reading skills. Also, a volume in the *Oxford Bible* series, entitled *Narrative Art in the Bible*, combines a discussion of method with the application of this method to several Old Testament narratives. The authors are David M. Gunn and Danna Nolan Fewell, professors respectively at the Columbia Theological Seminary, Atlanta, Georgia, and at the Perkins School of Theology at Southern Methodist University, Dallas, Texas.

Finally, Yairah Amit, Professor of Biblical Studies at Tel Aviv University in Israel, has written a helpful book entitled *Reading Biblical Narratives*. Her book is loaded with insights and concise explanations for readers of Old Testament stories.

Commentaries on Joshua

The best entry-level commentary by far on the book of Joshua comes from Richard S. Hess in the *Tyndale Old Testament Commentaries* series. Hess, formerly a reader in Old Testament at the Roehampton Institute in London, now teaches in the United States at the Denver Seminary in Colorado. His work is meaty, yet concise and quite readable. He is familiar with the most recent archaeological and linguistic research on the book. Another recent volume in the *New American Commentary* series contains about twice as much material as Hess's commentary, yet it is still quite readable. The author is David M. Howard, Jr., a professor at New Orleans Baptist Theological Seminary in Louisiana. His scholarship is likewise up to date.

Commentaries on Judges

Some of the best commentaries on Judges are more technical in nature. As far as entry-level commentaries go, readers might consult the volume on Judges and Ruth in the *Tyndale Old Testament Commentaries* series. The author of the Judges section is Arthur E. Cundall, Principal of the Bible College of Victoria in Australia. Probably the best all-round commentary on Judges is the recent volume on Judges and Ruth by Daniel I. Block in the *New American Commentary* series. However, while it is quite readable, it probably provides more information than entry-level readers desire.

Additional thoughts

As a general rule, older commentaries on Old Testament narrative books, including Joshua and Judges, are less helpful. They tend to focus more on historical and cultural issues than on the literary strategy of the narratives they discuss.

You might watch for the publication of volumes on Joshua by Robert Hubbard and on Judges/Ruth by K. Lawson Younger Jr. in the *NIV Application Commentary* series published by Zondervan. If the already-published New Testament volumes give any indication, these volumes should provide concise discussions of what the text means, as well as useful leads for applying the text to one's life.

Many of the recommended books may be found at www.amazon.co.uk. Alternatively, try www.amazon.com.

BIBLIOGRAPHY

General works on the Old Testament and its background

Roland de Vaux, *Ancient Israel*, 2 volumes, McGraw-Hill, 1965

Yohanan Aharoni and Michael Avi-Yonah, *The Macmillan Bible Atlas*, 3rd revised edition, Macmillan, 1993

Albert H. Baylis, *From Creation to the Cross*, Zondervan, 1996

Brevard S. Childs, *Introduction to the Old Testament as Scripture*, Fortress, 1979

David A. Dorsey, *The Literary Structure of the Old Testament*, Baker, 1999

Barry J. Beitzel, *The Moody Atlas of Bible Lands*, Moody Press, 1985

Works on Old Testament narrative literature

Robert Alter, *The Art of Biblical Narrative*, Basic, 1981

Yairah Amit, *Reading Biblical Narratives*, Fortress, 2001

Shimon Bar-Efrat, *Narrative Art in the Bible*, Almond, 1989

Adele Berlin, *Poetics and Interpretation of Biblical Narrative*, Almond, 1983

Robert Bergen, ed., *Biblical Hebrew and Discourse Linguistics*, Eisenbrauns, 1994

J.P. Fokkelman, *Reading Biblical Narrative: An Introductory Guide*, Westminster John Knox, 1991

David M. Gunn and Danna Nolan Fewell, *Narrative in the Hebrew Bible*, Oxford University Press, 1993

Steven D. Mathewson, *The Art of Preaching Old Testament Narrative*, Baker, 2002

Robert Polzin, *Moses and the Deuteronomist*, Indiana University, 1980

Jean Louis Ska, *'Our Fathers Have Told Us': Introduction to the Analysis of Hebrew Narratives*, Editrice Pontificio, 1990

Meir Sternberg, *The Poetics of Biblical Narrative*, Indiana University, 1985

Commentaries on Joshua

Robert G. Boling and G. Ernest Wright, *Joshua*, The Anchor Bible, Doubleday, 1982

Trent C. Butler, *Joshua*, Word Biblical Commentary, Word, 1983

Richard S. Hess, *Joshua: An Introduction and Commentary*, Tyndale Old Testament Commentaries, IVP, 1996

David M. Howard Jr., *Joshua*, The New American Commentary, Broadman and Holman, 1988

Martin H. Woudstra, *The Book of Joshua*, The New International Commentary on the Old Testament, Eerdmans, 1981

Commentaries on Judges

Daniel I. Block, *Judges, Ruth*, The New American Commentary, Broadman and Holman, 1999

Robert G. Boling, *Judges*, The Anchor Bible, Doubleday, 1975

Arthur E. Cundall and Leon Morris, *Judges & Ruth*, Tyndale Old Testament Commentaries, IVP, 1968

Barnabas Lindars, *Judges 1—5*, T&T Clark, 1995

Herbert Wolf, 'Judges' in *The Expositor's Bible Commentary* (vol. 3), Zondervan, 1992

NOTES

NOTES

NOTES

NOTES

NOTES

NOTES

NOTES